A Great Big Girl Like Me

WOMEN AND FILM HISTORY INTERNATIONAL

Series Editors
Kay Armatage, Jane M. Gaines, and Christine Gledhill

A new generation of motion picture historians is rediscovering the vital and diverse contributions of women to world film history whether as producers, actors, or spectators. Taking advantage of new print material and moving picture archival discoveries as well as the benefits of digital access and storage, this series investigates the significance of gender in the cinema.

A Great Big Girl Like Me

The Films of Marie Dressler

Victoria Sturtevant

University of Illinois Press
Urbana and Chicago

∞ This book is printed on acid-free paper.

Library of Congress Cataloging-in-Publication Data
Sturtevant, Victoria
A great big girl like me : the films of Marie Dressler / Victoria Sturtevant.
p. cm.
Includes bibliographical references and index.
ISBN 978-0-252-03428-2 (cloth : alk. paper)
ISBN 978-0-252-07622-0 (pbk. : alk. paper)
1. Dressler, Marie, 1869–1934—Criticism and interpretation.
I. Title.
PN2287.D55S78 2009
792.0'28092—dc22 2008034986

To Jim

Contents

Acknowledgments

I thank Joan Catapano, Rebecca McNulty Schreiber, and everyone at the University of Illinois Press for their faith in my manuscript and their extraordinary efforts on its behalf. Thanks also to Kay Armatage, Jane M. Gaines, and Christine Gledhill for putting together the Women and Film History International book series, in which I am proud to have this work included.

I owe a tremendous debt to the staffs of many archives whose patience, knowledge, and generosity have been nothing short of amazing: Jenny Romero and Barbara Hall of the Margaret Herrick Library of the Academy of Motion Picture Arts and Sciences, Jared Case at the George Eastman House, and Ned Comstock at the University of Southern California Cinema/Television Library. This book is also far richer for the efforts of the wonderful members of the Marie Dressler Foundation of Cobourg, Ontario, and especially Barbara Garrick.

Thanks, too, to the many scholars who have given me feedback and made this work immeasurably stronger for their insight and wit, especially Matthew Bernstein, David Cook, David Desser, Jennifer Bean, and Martine Watson Brownley. Thank you to all my colleagues at the University of Oklahoma who have pitched in to help with this project: Sam Huskey, Ben Alpers, Ben Keppel, and Andy Horton. Boundless thanks, also, to the administrative staffs, whose kindness and skills I shamelessly exploited in trying to get this done: Jane Dye, Valoree Biggs, Debbie Rush, Sarah Denton, and Annie Hall.

I am so grateful to Matthew Kennedy and Roberta Raider Sloan, scholars who have already done tremendous research on Marie Dressler and who were generous enough to share some of their resources with me.

Two people in particular have been heroic in their aid; I could not have gotten started on this project without their exceptional help. Thank you to Ross Lipman of the UCLA Film and Television Archive for giving me access to his restored print of *Tillie's Punctured Romance* and for talking to me about the process of restoration. I am equally indebted to Scott McGee for helping me acquire a trove of Dressler's still-obscure movies so I could begin this book.

My family has put up with a lot in order to see me through the long process of writing this book. Loving thanks to my parents, whom I wish I could see more often, and to my husband, Jim Zeigler, who spent the month after our wedding locked in an apartment with no cable TV and very little air conditioning so I could finish writing. Thanks, honey.

Finally, I would be lost without the kindness of my colleague, the formidable Joanna Rapf, who loves Marie Dressler as much as I do. No new scholar has ever benefited from smarter advice, more unwavering support, or warmer friendship.

A Great Big Girl Like Me

1

Tillie's Punctured Romance

Genre and the Body

> A great big girl like very truly yours
> Has very little cause for glee.
> They always make a pet
> Of some stingy-faced soubrette;
> Not a great big girl like me.
>
> —"A Great Big Girl Like Me," sung by Marie Dressler in *Higgledy-Piggledy,* 1904

Marie Dressler was never a delicate beauty. In her earliest films, she played ugly ducklings and old maids, and in her later career she played doting mothers and imperious dowagers. Though this sounds like the career trajectory of a supporting actress, Dressler was definitely a star, the central protagonist of most of her films, and the woman you can't take your eyes off, even in the films that tried in vain to push her to the background (figure 1). Many of her extraordinary early sound pictures, such as *Min and Bill* (MGM, 1930), *Politics* (MGM, 1931), *Emma* (MGM, 1932), and *Tugboat Annie* and *Christopher Bean* (both MGM, 1933), stand up with the best work that the studio system produced, and Dressler herself was one of the most important studio-era movie stars. Yet only now is her work receiving serious attention from scholars of film comedy and the history of the star system in Hollywood.[1]

Dressler achieved film stardom in the heart of the Great Depression,

FIGURE 1. MGM publicity photo of Marie Dressler (c. 1932).

when film comedies spoke to an audience looking for escape, for an intensive experience of comfort and fantasy. But her films are not palliatives; her expressive performances explode the business-as-usual rules of classical Hollywood film genre. Business was indeed not operating as usual in the early 1930s, when talkies were new, the economy was in the basement, and Hollywood was grasping for stable narrative formulas to build from the hodgepodge of vaudeville, radio, and theatrical traditions they now borrowed. Marie Dressler's body, hijacking the camera's gaze from her costars, refocuses the generic frame of her films. The shallow problems of the young and beautiful and rich and healthy are sidelined. Her films instead dignify the marginalized: older folks, women, and the poor. They build Depression-era fantasies not from an excess of material goods, or sexual license, but from the exuberance of Marie Dressler's own body.

At five foot seven and around two hundred pounds, Dressler's body is the site of considerable emphasis in her films. Her trademark slapstick comedy is based on an athletic and fearless physicality that foregrounds her size and flouts rules of feminine comportment, emphasizing pratfalls on the rear end, hair caught in the machinery, celery stuck in the cleavage, a skirt blown up by a gust of wind. In scenes where she is not called upon to perform physical comedy, Dressler is still in constant motion, using her expressive face, her fidgety hands and feet, and nearly constant physical contact with other performers to hold the camera's gaze. This insistent movement centralizes Dressler and invests her characters with a subjectivity and an agency that often exceeds the written boundaries of the narrative. As her star rose and roles were developed specifically for her, Dressler's film vehicles necessarily and increasingly combined, transformed, and simply broke generic molds in order to create coherent frames for Dressler's insistent presence. Because she was too famous for supporting roles, too maternal for slapstick comedy, too funny for maternal melodrama, and too old for sentimental romance, Dressler's films are often hybrids of all these genres, making broad and sudden shifts in tone, situation, and theme from one moment to the next. A close analysis of those films provides a new perspective on the social, generic, and industrial contexts that permitted Marie Dressler's rapid and explosive rise to stardom in the early 1930s.

Dressler's robust performances tended to exert a kind of gravity on the narrative around her, breaking the rules of genre and reshaping the film's social world in ways that insist on her subjectivity, agency, and sexuality. An analysis of her career requires, among other adjustments, a singular rethinking of the workings of spectatorial *fantasy* in American commercial film of the early sound era. She is, for instance, probably the least effective representative of commercial desire ever to appear in American film. Her hairstyles, makeup, clothes, and hats are nondescript at best, in many cases crossing the boundary to the outlandishly unfashionable. And yet, it is unquestionable that Marie Dressler's films occupied a prominent place in the collective fantasy life of a Depression-era public, a fact verified by her spectacular popularity. She was bigger than Mae West, bigger than the Marx Brothers, bigger, for a while, than Chaplin.

Dressler's stardom must be understood instead in terms of a maternal fantasy, one that centralizes the excessive body as a sign of plenty, amplitude, and generosity, framed against a Depression-era landscape of encroaching want. It is a maternal fantasy that also figures the mother as a child, falling on her bum and tripping over her clothes, in slapstick style. This rich combination of maternal and infantile characteristics creates a space for the spectator to regress to a more childlike relation to the screen—Dressler's maternal persona acts as a comfort to the regressive spectator, while her childlike antics validate infantile responses and defy the seriousness of poverty and despair. The films of her later career constantly vacillate between maternal melodrama and anarchic slapstick in ways that provide rich challenges to our understanding of the logic of film genre. Her performances tend to reject the ethereal light-and-shadow femininity of the conventional star, insisting instead on the mass, the texture, the volume, the velocity, and the dignity of her body. She occupies the space of both mother and child, authority and transgressor, sentimental fantasy and chaotic destroyer. Marie Dressler's film performances, then, alter the ideological and generic frameworks of many of her film vehicles by centralizing a physicalized, insistent female subjectivity that slips the bonds of conventional categories.

This book is an examination of the extraordinary films that emerged.

Biography

> Any time Marie Dressler will stand in front of the camera and make faces I'll go to see her. And if she does any more than that—well, a team of army mules couldn't keep me out of the theater.
>
> —Dan Thomas, *Los Angeles Post-Record,* 1933

Born in Cobourg, Ontario, in 1868, Marie Dressler left home at the tender age of fourteen to join a small-time road company. She became a Broadway star by the turn of the twentieth century, starring in her first hit, *The Lady Slavey*, in 1896.[2] She eventually became known for her work in raucous musical comedies from the noted theatrical producers Joe Weber and Lew Fields, who specialized in nearly plotless romps with doggerel titles like *Higgledy-Piggledy* and *Topsy-Turvy*. These shows were characterized by a loosely causal narrative structure punctuated with vaudeville-like episodes of comic performance in the form of songs, dances, acrobatic routines, and bantering dialogue.

Dressler's greatest success on Broadway was a 1910 musical takeoff on *Cinderella* called *Tillie's Nightmare*, in which she played Tillie Blobbs, the overworked daughter of a boardinghouse matron (figure 2). Tillie is left home to clean while her mother and her pretty sister have an evening out. She falls asleep, and the show segues into a bizarre dream about her marrying a millionaire, moving to Paris, riding in an airship, and other fantasies. The dream sequence was a vehicle for the loose narrative structure of the Weber and Fields comedy. The play transformed the lightness and whimsy of broad comedy into a working girl's fantasy of freedom, punctuating Tillie's life of drudgery with dreams of escape.

In this way, despite the loosey-goosey narrative, *Tillie's Nightmare* was a fantasy of liberation for the socially marginalized. The most popular song in the show, and Dressler's calling card for years afterward, was "Heaven Will Protect the Working Girl," which championed New York's most vulnerable workers:

> A village maid was leaving home, with tears her eyes was set,
> Her mother dear was standing near the spot;
> She says to her: Neuralgia Dear, I hope you won't forget
> That I'm the only mother you have got.
>
> The city is a wicked place, as anyone can see,
> And cruel dangers round your path may hurl;
> So ev'ry week you'd better send your wages back to me,
> For Heaven will protect the working girl.

One of the city's "cruel dangers" turns out to be a suave gentleman whose advances Tillie valiantly refuses: "You may tempt the upper classes / With your villainous demi-tasses / But Heaven will protect the working girl."[3] The joke is predicated on the girl's naïveté; lacking the sophistication to know what a demitasse might be, she suspects her suitor of illicit intent. But the song's blithe humor displaces the real threats to working women in the cities of 1910s America—poor factory conditions, low wages, crime, sexual harassment, and prostitution—with the absurdly exaggerated figure of the villainous suitor. The fire in the Triangle Shirtwaist factory in 1911, the year after *Tillie's Nightmare* opened, claimed 148 lives and brought into relief how very vulnerable the working girl could be.

FIGURE 2. Newspaper caricature of Marie Dressler in *Tillie's Nightmare* (1910).

Quickly and permanently, this tune became linked with Dressler, and her comedy always held this populist note and associated her with the working classes, the marginalized people of the city. Dressler personally led Broadway's chorus girls in an Actors' Equity strike of 1919, becoming the first president of the Chorus Equity Association, which demanded that Broadway's lowest-ranked women performers should share in the benefits of unionization. Off-stage, she did what she could to protect the working girl.

During her stage years, Dressler married twice, the first time very briefly and the second time to the man who became her manager, "Sunny" Jim Dalton. Dalton was something of a shady dealer, and his business practices helped alienate Dressler from many theatrical producers. So when the film producer Mack Sennett approached her in 1914 to star in *Tillie's Punctured Romance* (Keystone), the American cinema's first feature-length comedy, she accepted the job in part because she needed the shot of publicity. Based on the Tillie persona from Dressler's stage success, but bearing an entirely different narrative about a wealthy country girl, Tillie Banks, duped by a slick city boy (Charles Chaplin), the comedy was an enormous hit. But Dressler had no more luck with film producers than she did with theater producers. Following a legal dispute with Sennett, Dressler tried her hand in a few more "Tillie" films with lesser production teams at the Lubin Film Company and the World Film Corporation, none of which achieved the same popularity as her first. She then produced four shorts under the Marie Dressler Motion Picture Company, but she was unable to make the venture a success.

Professionally ostracized because of her manager husband, her litigious tendencies, and her union activities, Dressler struggled to remain in show business. Still a star of the first magnitude, she threw her energy into the World War I Liberty Bond drives, working with Chaplin, Mary Pickford, and Douglas Fairbanks on nationwide tours to sell the bonds. Following the bond drives, a brief stint on vaudeville, and the death of Jim Dalton in 1921, Dressler was unable to restart her career on stage or screen. She was embarrassed by newspaper coverage of Dalton's death, which revealed he had never ended his first marriage, despite being known as Dressler's husband for many years.[4] Saddled with debts and lacking a recent success, Dressler spent the 1920s largely unemployed, a has-been in a world of flaming youth, prosperity and consumerism, and changing comic sensibilities.

She returned to the spotlight in 1927, at the age of sixty, when her friend Frances Marion, an MGM screenwriter, convinced the producer Irving Thalberg to help bring her out of obscurity to star opposite Polly Moran in *The Callahans and the Murphys* (MGM). Dressler and Marion had become friends years before, when Marion, then a cub reporter for a Hearst paper, had been sent on a fool's errand to interview the Broadway star at a time when Dressler was involved in a very public feud with William Randolph Hearst. Dressler felt sorry for the young journalist and granted her an exclusive interview. The two women had stayed friends through the years, and in 1927, hearing that Dressler was in financial and emotional trouble, Marion returned the favor by creating the *Callahans* screenplay for her and convincing her boss, Irving Thalberg, to put Dressler under contract for the role. Famously, this film was pulled from release under pressure from Catholic organizations, which opposed MGM's stereotyped characterization of the Irish.[5] Passing her sixtieth birthday, Dressler toughed out this setback, stayed in Hollywood, and distinguished herself in a series of small supporting parts and two-reel comedies with Polly Moran.

After the *Callahans* debacle, Dressler's emergence on American screens was a gradual one. She was first cast in the sorts of supporting roles that were the bread and butter of older Hollywood actresses—queens, society ladies, mothers, and grand old broads. In supporting roles, Dressler nearly always used old vaudeville tricks to steal scenes from the younger stars she supported. Twitching, striding, mugging, and fussing through other actors' lines, Dressler resisted the invisibility endured by other actresses her age. Rather than be put out to pasture, she subtly centered herself in the image, claiming her right to be seen and heard. In the chaotic industrial environment of the first talkies, Dressler's vivid performances attracted positive attention from reviewers and audiences, which eventually placed her in a position to anchor narratives herself, no longer in support of younger stars. Though her reemergence as a star was partly a result of Frances Marion's writing vehicles that showcased Dressler's talents, Dressler claimed the privilege through her three years of riveting supporting work at MGM.

In 1930, Marion helped Dressler land the role of Marthy, the old wharf drunk in Greta Garbo's first talkie, *Anna Christie* (MGM), based on the Eugene O'Neill play of the same title. Dressler's excellent performance in a dramatic role surprised nearly everyone, and she received considerable publicity, bringing the comedienne more prominently into the public eye. *Anna Christie* was followed by her first feature-length costarring vehicle with Polly Moran since the *Callahans* fiasco, *Caught Short* (MGM, 1930)—a financial success, despite the critics' lack of enthusiasm for the film's lowbrow humor. The two sides of Dressler's Depression-era persona—affecting character actress and raucous comic harridan—were established in these two

1930 releases. Her tremendous success in the next four years would result from the imaginative combination of these two sides of her character.

The first film to combine these two elements of Dressler's persona into a compelling, powerful character was MGM's runaway 1930 hit *Min and Bill*, based on another Frances Marion script. Teaming her with Wallace Beery as Bill, the film won Dressler an Academy Award for her role as the owner of a wharfside boardinghouse who commits murder to protect her surrogate daughter. The popular comedy/melodrama hybrid was the model for a new sentimental era in Dressler comedy. It cast her as an earthy, funny, protective, motherly woman, combining physical comedy and wisecracks with sentimental narrative forms. As this new star persona caught on, Dressler spent the next three years enjoying a string of successes, including three more immensely

FIGURE 3. Dressler's late career was characterized by more sentimental and prestigious roles: with Wallace Beery in *Tugboat Annie* (1933).

popular films with Polly Moran, the legendary *Tugboat Annie* (figure 3), and perhaps her best-remembered film, the prestigious *Dinner at Eight* (MGM, 1933), which teamed her with Jean Harlow and two Barrymores.

Between 1930 and her death in 1934, Dressler won an Academy Award, was nominated for another, topped the exhibitors' charts two years in a row, was the first actor to appear on the cover of *Time* magazine, counted President Roosevelt as a close friend, and enjoyed uninterrupted adoration from the press.[6] She was beatified in both fan magazines and mainstream publications as a woman of boundless generosity, humor, and wisdom. One interviewer describes the star weeping over a desk full of fan mail because so many Depression-stricken families had written to ask her for money that she couldn't fulfill all their needs.[7] Another journalist emphasizes her folksy humor in an anecdote about Vice President Charles Curtis's visit to Hollywood. The politician reputedly gushed to the star, "I admire you so greatly, Miss Dressler, do you mind if I call you Marie?" The unflappable Dressler is said to have replied, "Charlie, you can call me anything you like."[8] Dressler's homespun advice to parents and her philosophies on life appeared in *Photoplay* with striking regularity, offering high-flown optimistic perspectives on the country's ability to survive the Depression. Behind the giddy press reports, Dressler maintained a quiet but unapologetic domestic partnership with another actress, Claire DuBrey, in the 1930s and was an important part of the support network of gay performers in 1930s Hollywood.

Sadly, Dressler's career was cut short when she died of cancer in 1934 at age sixty-five. The *New York Times* and *Los Angeles Times* had offered nearly daily accounts from her deathbed, reporting, "Marie Dressler Rallies from Coma" and then "Dressler's End Near."[9] The gushing obituaries and posthumous tributes upped the ante on the sentimental rhetoric that had surrounded Dressler in the press since her big comeback. At the time of her death, Marie Dressler was at the top of her game, one of the most well known, accomplished, complicated, and beloved actresses in America. Buster Keaton called her "the greatest comedienne I ever saw."[10] But the brevity of Dressler's starring years in films, the low-brow humor and moralistic narratives of her films, her unorthodox star persona, and the fact that her most prominent work happened during the dark ages of early sound contributed to her being quickly forgotten in the history of American film comedy.

Authorship and the Studio System

> All they wanted in those days was—just give us beauty, and—you know—give us plenty of beauty—and they couldn't come too young or too dumb. And she's the first one to come out and kind of do away with that whole theory. She started the whole new thing: that you didn't have to be so beautiful, and that you didn't have to be so young.
>
> —Will Rogers radio tribute to Marie Dressler, July 28, 1934

As is perhaps profoundly obvious, Marie Dressler is the only woman in her sixties ever to achieve the status of top-grossing star in America.[11] Her career, inevitably, raises the question, how did this happen? When Hollywood formula filmmaking so predictably favors the young, beautiful, and virile in narratives that follow them on the road to heterosexual closure, how did a queer, grandmotherly, slapstick comic reach the top? There are two answers to this question. The first is that Dressler was simply riveting to watch. Few people have ever shown such perfect aptitude for film comedy—the charisma, the comic timing, the minutely expressive face, and the sentimental rapport with the camera were all capably exploited by the actress herself. The second answer is that she achieved her comeback by taking canny advantage of what was clearly a perfect storm of technological change (the arrival of sound) and catastrophic social and economic change (the onset of the Great Depression) that threw Hollywood's formula-driven star system into disarray. Both these answers require some investigation into how Dressler functioned as an industrial and ideological agent.

It is a truism of star scholarship that most movie stars of the studio era had very little control over the terms of their own representation. In 1972, the Italian sociologist Francisco Alberoni coined the phrase "powerless elite" to describe the paradox of the star's function in twentieth-century popular culture as a "sign" or symbol, rather than as a political agent.[12] Many subsequent scholars have taken up the point that while stars may not have direct political power, their ideological function can be profound.[13] But a consistency of theme among roles, or even a consistency between the star's offscreen life (if she can even be said to have such a thing) and her roles, is grossly insufficient to establish that the star is actually the agent or author of her cultural impact. While Richard Dyer concludes his influential book *Stars* with a chapter called "A Note on Authorship," he clearly doubts the value of investigating how stars contribute to the process of creating their personas:

> The major problem that all concepts of authorship present us with—in, be it said, all the arts—is the relationship between the semiotic or aesthetic text and the author. Traditionally this has been thought of as "expression": the text expresses the ideas, feelings and/or "personality" of the author. . . . The problem, however, with any version of the expression theory is that it supposes a transparency between an author and her/his text. Yet it is a feature of all human expression that it "escapes" those who use it, precisely because expression is only possible through languages and codes that are more general, because shared, than an individual person or even group.[14]

So the first problem with trying to decode film authorship is simply the fact that the whole notion of authorship is based on an assumption that the author has some inner truth that exists prior to her ability to articulate it. This idea presupposes a rather romantic and dubious notion of individual identity.

The second problem with trying to decode film authorship is the sheer number of "codes" of cinematic representation that come between the author's intention and the final evidence of that intention available to the scholar. If the actions of the woman Marie Dressler could have ever given evidence of her "inner self," that self would have to be liberated from a mountain of codes in order to be intelligible: the grammar of film shots and editing, the rules of genre, the subtle inflections of voice and gesture, the industrial machine of the studio system, the hyperbolic language and patent falsehood of fan profiles, the self-constructing conventions of autobiography, the imperfect record of studio transactions, the narrativizing tendency of history, and the nostalgia with which Old Hollywood is now invested. It is not that theorists of stardom doubt that film actors played a hand in constructing their offscreen and on-screen star texts, but rather that it is essentially impossible to establish firmly what that role is.

While it is necessary to have some theory of authorship in order to analyze the work of a director, to find some reason for isolating these particular films together when the director herself is not visible in the text, it is not necessary, and it is also decidedly inconvenient, to bother with authorship when dealing with stars. To treat the star as pure sign is methodologically pristine—the scholar simply must read the codes as they are presented. But to treat the star as both sign and partial author of that sign is methodologically messy—the scholar must read the codes and also make sometimes problematic and always incomplete reference to the ways those codes came to be. And there is no clear-cut method for doing that, particularly when the director is often given de facto credit for being the true mastermind of the film. Dyer finally concludes that while the actor herself is clearly one of the "voices" participating in the construction of the star image, "each example has to be argued on the basis of the evidence."[15] This is hardly the detailed roadmap one would wish for in undertaking a study of this size.

But there are compelling reasons to retain a critical focus on authorship, particularly when the authors in question, like Marie Dressler, are underrepresented in the current histories of Hollywood. In recent years, a whole raft of female writers, directors, and producers of early cinema have come to light, and historians are scrambling to rewrite the history of early Hollywood. But to talk about the work of Alice Guy Blaché, Lois Weber, June Mathis, Frances Marion, Dorothy Arzner, or Nell Shipman, feminist scholars of early cinema have had to revisit fraught debates around cinematic authorship in order to parse out how exactly the gender of these authors matters to the films they have produced.[16] The word "auteur" has often been used to suppress the communal, mechanical, and industrial complexity of the filmmaking process, subsuming the whole text within a romantic cult of the (usually male, usually white) director. Clearly, basing film history and criticism on the celebration of a set of genius filmmakers who show an uncanny and individualistic ability to rise above the crass financial or generic limits of the form is an outmoded and unproductive form of analysis. But it would be shortsighted to discard the whole question of authorship. Janet Staiger has argued that "forgetting authorship and individuals takes away a history necessary for social activism and utopic imaginings."[17] In particular, the history of Hollywood does not yet account for the contributions of actors, choreographers, costumers, production designers, women, gays, minorities, and other "outsiders" working in the studio hierarchy.

One of the most productive recent alternatives to the more romantic and masculinist impulses of the auteur theory is the model of multiple, collaborative, and contested authorship under the studio system. Jane Gaines has suggested that scholars can productively investigate the role of women in early film production, without the excesses of auteurist criticism, by considering the "range of contributors and alternative authors," including not only the many production personnel, but even the mechanical and industrial basis of the image.[18] Indeed, paying attention to the contributions of actors, rather than those of the directors or producers who have traditionally been regarded as the authors of their films, already provides a more inclusive and accurate understanding of how agency is exercised in an industrial context than does the classic auteur theory.

The notion of multiple authorship is particularly useful to a feminist study of Marie Dressler's career because a quarter of the screenwriters at MGM in the early 1930s were women.[19] Nearly all of Dressler's films boast at least one female screenwriter: Zelda Sears, Sylvia Thalberg, Sarah Y. Mason, Beatrice Banyard, Eve Green, Marion Jackson, Bess Meredyth, or, of course, Frances Marion. The story executive Samuel Marx testifies that Irving Thalberg sought out women writers to ensure that the studio's films attracted female audiences. "'Wives and shop girls can always get their men to the movies they want to see, but a man can't get a woman to one that doesn't interest her,' he said."[20] So while the presence of the women screenwriters was partly a conscious tactic to earn the ticket money of women consumers, there is reason to believe that it also led to an atmosphere of cooperation and creativity in the development of MGM's films. Cari Beauchamp describes Marion and her women colleagues as existing always a bit apart from the male writers at MGM and working together to help each other succeed.[21] Beauchamp quotes Marion, "I owe my greatest success to women. Contrary to the assertion that women do all in their power to hinder one another's progress, I have found that it has always been one of my own sex who has given me a helping hand when I needed it."[22] This cooperative model of women's participation in studio-era filmmaking suggests a methodology for understanding Dressler's improvisational performance style as one part of a nexus of female authorship at work in her extraordinary films.

Finding a way to describe how Marie Dressler and her allies behind the scenes influenced the production of her star image, then, could shed light on how the studio system accommodated and failed to accommodate the individual voices of production personnel, and it could also help model the multiple authorship of studio-era film texts. It is my hope that by embracing the messiness of an eclectic, empirical methodology, it will be possible to find evidence of Dressler's agency in a variety of ways. There is not ample evidence of her expressed intentions for her career, and the expressed intentions of those who wrote for and directed her pictures is likewise sparse (although I have tried to take those into account where information has been available). More broadly, this study accounts for Dressler's authorship by looking at how the studio shaped its practices in order to contain the work that Dressler was doing within an industrially and ideologically coherent structure. Norms of genre, promotion, and performance could bend somewhat when faced with the pressure of Dressler's stardom, as well as pressure from her allies behind the scenes. Because Dressler was an entirely new "type" of star—a woman in her mid-sixties who was suddenly the most popular actress in Hollywood—the narratives that were developed for her had to deviate from the models of melodrama, romantic comedy, musical comedy, and "comedian comedy" (usually starring a male comedian) that dominated Hollywood's output of this time. A new set of narrative conventions had to be created to accommodate her, a set created mostly by Dressler's friends. Her work could not be encompassed under any type that already existed—and her films never ended with a heterosexual clinch. These narratives—an exciting and unique patchwork of generic, performative, and narrative conventions—owe as much to Dressler and the screenwriters as they do to formula. And Dressler herself came to Hollywood in the late 1920s well trained in the art of reworking scripts to suit her own purposes.

Improvisation and Parody

> One did not direct Marie Dressler at all. . . . One simply gave her the script, time to formulate her character and learn the lines, and then sit, inspired at a magnificent, spontaneous performance. I think Marie Dressler was the greatest dramatic figure on the screen in the character field.
>
> —George Hill, director of *Min and Bill*

Marie Dressler's contract gave her no more than the usual control over her roles, but the singularity of her body and performance style influenced the narrative and generic qualities of her films from the writing stage through the editing of retakes.[23] It was much more common for comic stars of the studio system, like Charles Chaplin, Buster Keaton, or Mae West, to take on an authorial function relative to their films, because they understood better than anyone else how to showcase their particular comic skills. The same logic that permitted Fred Astaire to choreograph his own dances permitted Marie Dressler to design her own outlandish costumes and improvise her physical comedy, as well as some lines. She understood the comic potential of her own face and body, and she came to that understanding through her training on Broadway and vaudeville stages.

Dressler's work in Broadway comedies often emphasized the skill of improvisation, permitting her to develop her own part or to expand the part she was given. Because she never fit the conventional lead role, and usually her skills and fame exceeded the supporting parts to which she was more physically suited, canny producers applied some ingenuity to creating parts that made sense for her. A 1914 article entitled "Marie Dressler Is Her Own Stage Manager" makes this point by describing how a stage director pushed the young actress so hard to play a part the way he envisioned it, she broke down and cried. The crisis was eventually resolved in Dressler's favor.

> The manager, George Lederer, was out in front of the house and cried out to the stage director:
>
> "Oh, let her do it her own way; she's funny!"
>
> So I was permitted to have my own way in playing this role and I created a lot of new business and put in some funny ideas which the stage manager would never have thought of. After that . . . it was an unwritten law with all stage producers that Marie Dressler was to have the privilege of interpreting her own part as she saw fit, and putting in any new business that she wished to create.[24]

Though surely the fan press exaggerates, from the beginning of her public life Dressler's persona and her strengths as a performer were patently unique. This meant that after about 1910, roles were always tailored to her skills, either by herself or by a perceptive writer or stage director. Dressler later claimed that when *Tillie's Nightmare* bombed at its tryout in Albany, she revised the whole play herself, much to the chagrin of the original playwrights. The play went on to a sensational premiere in New York.[25]

Of her stage success *Higgledy-Piggledy*, a reviewer commented on the obvious disjunction between the limp writing and Dressler's vigorous performance: "Marie Dressler, with a part which it is easy to divine she has built out of faggots and lichen, made one of the greatest indisputable hits which can be credited to a comedienne this year."[26]

Another article from 1914 picks up the same theme:

> When she was a youngster managers realized that audiences loved her and they quickly boosted her to an eminent place among actresses, but they scratched their heads when it came to providing an adequate vehicle for her. She has run through the gamut of comic opera of the older school and she has done a little of about everything else that an actress could be expected to do; and yet as one glances back and makes a reckoning it becomes pretty plain that she has not frequently played a part as it was written or as anyone else would play it.[27]

Dressler's charisma and her skill at improvisation gradually expanded her authorial influence over her stage productions. In 1913, she launched her own variety show at the West End Theater, titled *Tid Bits*. The program listed the company as the "Dressler Players" and included these credits: "The entertainment staged by Miss Dressler, curtains and decorations designed by Miss Dressler, costumes designed by Miss Dressler."[28] She was clearly a star who took part in many aspects of the production process.

Marie Dressler's improvisational skills were most often put to the service of parody. Dressler was particularly skilled at using the contrast between her body and the bodies of those around her (short men, thin women, children) to reverse generic norms, particularly the ideological conventions of sentimental melodrama. Often paired with the diminutive Joe Weber, Dressler perfected a comedy style based on her ability to tower over the smaller man. In a number called "Without the Law" (a reference to the popular melodrama *Within the Law*, about a shop girl who goes to prison), Dressler made an entrance as a criminal handcuffed to a policeman, played by Weber. Protesting the injustice of her imprisonment, Dressler gestured broadly, lifting Weber off the ground by the handcuff that linked them.[29] In *The Lady Slavey*, she danced with the British star Dan Daly. She recalled, "As we started off stage, I whispered, 'Jump on my hip and I'll carry you off!' He hesitated a second, then did as I told him and we went off in a whirlwind of applause."[30] A critic described Dressler's performance in a parody of *Camille* in this way: "The dying coughs of the rotund Marie are very destructive to the furniture and when she finally collapses into 'Almond's' arms, 'Almond' collapses too."[31] Dressler's comedy in this era was based on constructing clever parodies of feminine helplessness by showcasing her strength, stature, and energy, while making her face and body as unglamorous, unconstrained, and ludicrous as possible. Her performances, therefore, commented scathingly on the absurdity of diminutive Victorian stage heroines, forever dying of consumption or fainting at the sight of danger.

When she made the move to films in 1914, Dressler was well suited to Mack Sennett's breakneck physical comedies, which relied on a similar aesthetic of parodic reversals and a similar methodology of improvisation. Sennett originally intended to star Roscoe "Fatty" Arbuckle with Dressler in *Tillie's Punctured Romance*, but she turned him down in favor of the smaller Chaplin because she knew their bodies would create a more humorous contrast.[32] Describing her success in motion pictures to a trade paper in 1917, Dressler boasted, "I find that this game of nip-and-tuck with which I had the pleasure of having a hand in the old days [in Weber and Fields's highly improvisational stage shows], helps me beyond measure in my motion picture work. Directors have complained that I don't follow their scenarios, but they've been obliged to agree when I finish a picture that there were some funny situations they hadn't thought of."[33] Silent film comedy lent itself to improvisation beautifully, and Dressler thrived in the new medium. She thereby created the conditions for translating the style of self-directed genre parody she had developed on stage to the screen. Like her plays, her silent films used the sheer size of her body to critique melodrama's fetishization of feminine weakness as virtue.

Melodrama and *Tillie's Punctured Romance*

> I have a great deal of soul, and I ought to know, for I pay the penalty for it. I am never in the middle of emotions; I am either sad or happy, sore or glad. If I weren't an emotional extremist, I wouldn't act in burlesque, for burlesque consists in speaking a serious line in precisely the manner that it ought to be spoken and then suddenly wrenching yourself away from it and adding the unexpected touch that produces laughter.
>
> —Marie Dressler, 1906

The term "melodrama" usually refers to a "mode" of film, rather than a true genre.[34] According to Linda Williams, "In cinema the mode of melodrama defines a broad category of moving pictures that move us to pathos for protagonists beset by forces more powerful than they and who are perceived as victims."[35] Women's pictures, or "weepies," action films, "social problem" films, soap operas, family dramas, courtroom dramas, romantic dramas, and many other American film genres can all use melodrama to achieve their effects. Although it is obvious that these different narrative forms operate by different rules, they share the goal of pushing the viewer to an emotionally excessive engagement with the protagonist (pathos) in pursuit of a narrative resolution that is structured around the moral and physical well-being of the characters. In many ways, melodrama is a formal opposite of comedy, which requires that the spectator retain a kind of critical *distance* from the characters in order to laugh at their antics.

Because melodrama is such a broad category, it is useful to read the parody *Tillie's Punctured Romance* against the historically specific background of "sensational" or "blood-and-thunder" melodramas, popular in the 1910s. Like any genre, sensational melodramas were given to recognizable clichés, like the mustachioed villain, the heroine tied to the railroad tracks, and the last-minute rescue. On the high end of respectability, D. W. Griffith was a master of sensational melodrama and pioneered the use of parallel editing to give drama to the just-in-time rescue. On the low end of respectability, adventure serials with sensational titles like *The Perils of Pauline* (1914), *The Yellow Menace* (1916), or *Terror of the Range* (1919) were intensely popular. Ben Singer argues that sensational melodrama relied on five key features to produce its emotional effects.[36]

Pathos is the process by which the audience identifies with the suffering of the virtuous character, usually a woman. The audience members' experience of pathos moves them to confront the agents of injustice: for example, white slavery dealers, avaricious landlords, or crooked politicians.

Overwrought emotion is the heightened emotional content of the melodrama's intense situational confrontations. It is our anxiety about the lady tied to the railroad tracks or the man rushing to save his family from bandits.

Moral polarization is the process by which melodrama draws its dramatic conflict from clear-cut distinctions between good and evil.

Nonclassical narrative structure is the emphasis on "outrageous coincidence, implausibility, convoluted plotting, deus ex machina resolutions, and episodic strings of action."[37] In extreme form, this tendency leads the sensational melodrama to develop into the action serial, which strings the action along through several false closures.

Sensationalism is the process by which melodrama subjects the audience to extreme shocks and thrills. This often takes the form of stunting: characters leaping from trains onto moving cars, sword-fighting, or swinging across canyons on flimsy ropes.

Mack Sennett, a parodist, and D. W. Griffith, a melodramtist, both started their careers at Biograph, so Sennett could lay claim to an across-the-lot familiarity with the logic of Victorian melodrama that fueled early narrative cinema. Sennett's films nearly always feel like jabs at his former colleague and hold the conventions of sensational melodrama up to ridicule. Made just after the 1914 appearance of sentimental epics like the Italian *Cabiria* (Giovanni Pastrone, 181 minutes) and *The Birth of a Nation* (D. W. Griffith, 187 minutes) on the American film market, *Tillie's Punctured Romance*'s six-reel length was already a joke about bloated melodramatic films—one review calls it "the *Cabiria* of comedy."[38] The genre parody begins with the very running time of the film, before moving to the narrative and performance style of the film.

Charlie Chaplin's iconic status has proved very good and also very bad for *Tillie's Punctured Romance*. As Chaplin's star rose, the film was frequently reissued, rented, and shown in tribute to the silent comic. Unfortunately, it was also recut and recut and recut, mostly to favor Chaplin, until key pieces of Dressler's performance had gone missing. A recent restoration at the University of California at Los Angeles has given the film a new life, and the energy all comes from Dressler. In the restored version, the film begins with a quick prologue, showing Dressler stepping out from behind a curtain, beautifully dressed and coiffed, and spreading her arms, acknowledging an audience as though from the stage. She places her left hand on her hip, her right on the stage curtain. A clever dissolve replaces the star Dressler with the character Tillie, left hand on her hip, right hand on a garden hoe. The poised and gracious woman is gone, and in her stead stands a hunched, surly woman with her hair plastered down, an ill-fitting cotton dress exaggerating her awkwardness. This opening flourish not only pays homage to the star who is able to bury herself beneath this characterization, but it also points to Dressler's ownership of the Tillie character, which had been her most famous theatrical success. The opening title card reads "Marie Dressler in 'Tillie's Punctured Romance'" and this credit is repeated in small scroll across the top of every intertitle of the film. In its restored version, Dressler's stardom is written all over this film (figure 4).

American cinema's first feature-length slapstick comedy specifically lampoons popular melodramas about the exploitation of poor country girls: white slavery films, romantic tragedies of cross-class entanglements, stories of girls who lost their sweethearts to heartless vamps, and so on. The narrative benefits from the way that both slapstick comedy and sensational melodrama rely on episodic structures of situation and coincidence. But this fact also makes it difficult to summarize the narrative with any sort of brevity.

Marie Dressler plays the naïve country bumpkin Tillie Banks, who lives alone with her father. The film begins with Tillie throwing wooden blocks for her dog to fetch and accidentally wounding a passing stranger, Charlie (Chaplin). She brings the stranger into her home and lavishes unwanted attention on him. Charlie soon notices Farmer Banks's ample savings stashed in a cookie jar, and he feigns interest in Tillie in order to convince her to steal her father's money and run away with him. She complies eagerly, and the two make a dash for the city. There Tillie takes her first alcoholic drink at a small café and Charlie runs off with the stolen money and his old girl-

FIGURE 4. Dressler's stardom dominated the publicity materials for *Tillie's Punctured Romance* (1914).

friend, the petite, sophisticated Mabel (Normand). When Tillie cannot pay the bill, she is hauled off to jail. The thieves spend the loot on fancy new duds and a picture show, but when Charlie notices in the newspaper that Tillie's rich uncle has fallen off a mountain during a ski trip, bequeathing all his money to his niece, he leaves Mabel flat. He finds Tillie working as a waitress at the same café where he left her and marries her before she learns of her good fortune. When the inheritance arrives, the couple move into the uncle's mansion and throw a lavish party, which Mabel crashes in the guise of a maid. She and Charlie reunite at the party, which enrages Tillie, who pulls a gun, chasing and shooting at the pair. The uncle who had been presumed dead returns and throws the whole party out into the street.

The final scene of the film is an extended chase sequence: the Keystone Cops pursue Tillie; Tillie, gun blazing, pursues Charlie and Mabel. The chase ends when Tillie falls off the end of a pier, and the Cops, after several incompetent tries, finally pull her out of the ocean. Tillie gives her wedding ring back to Charlie. Charlie turns to Mabel, but she rejects him as well. Tillie and Mabel embrace each other, and the police drag Charlie away. A curtain suddenly closes over the scene, signaling the end of the narrative. A damp Dressler steps out from behind the curtain, summons her two costars, all three bow, and then Normand and Chaplin disappear. Dressler takes her final bows alone.

The film takes apart each of the five key features of melodrama, using Dressler's body to counteract the emotional register of each element of Singer's list.

Pathos is undermined by the essential impermeability of the human body in this film. The characters do not suffer, so the audience cannot experience outrage on their behalf. When Charlie lures Tillie away from her father, she is leaving not a loving home but a man who insults and kicks his daughter at every opportunity. When Tillie is abandoned at the café, she dances drunkenly off to jail. She enjoys her time there so much that when the matron comes to release her, Tillie cries to think she has to leave, and she bids a very fond goodbye to the crooks with whom she shared a cell. She takes her leave of one police officer by planting a kiss on the top of his bald head before she literally dances out of the station. Although she has been victimized, she does not behave in a way that suggests the pathos of victimhood.

The pathos of melodrama is the occasion for the comedy's most self-referential moment of genre criticism. Halfway through the film, Mabel and Charlie go to the picture show and see a crime melodrama titled *A Thief's Fate*, about a young couple robbing a poor, innocent country girl and eventually being caught and punished for this transgression. The film's victim is a young woman who is thinner, weaker, and more terrified than Dressler's Tillie. Mabel points out to Charlie that this is a facsimile of themselves upon the screen, and she experiences terrible guilt in being confronted with the narrative of their own transgressions. It is a remarkably self-conscious moment in the film, a projection of the cinematic conventions being parodied in this comedy. The crooks' intense experience of anxiety upon watching this film-within-a-film toys with the way melodrama works by inducing pathos in the viewer. They are outraged at themselves and deeply uneasy. Their anxiety exceeds the film frame when Mabel notices that the man sitting next to them at the picture show wears a detective's badge. She grabs Charlie's hand just as she sees the villain and villainess of the piece being handcuffed. The crooks make a hasty retreat from the theater, where the emotional energy of the audience is building into outrage at their crime.

But for audiences of the comedy, the presence of the wilting ingénue in *A Thief's Fate* highlights the extent to which Tillie's powerful body and force of character inspire astonishment, rather than pathos. She freely steals her father's money, enjoys her time on the town, gets a job when she needs to, figures out Charlie's game as soon as she has all the information, and gamely, if unsuccessfully, attempts to shoot him. The sheer robustness of Dressler's Tillie renders absurd the neurotic and hysterical femininity that forms the emotional center of crime melodrama. The weak female body as a vehicle for the audience's pathos is utterly destroyed by her physical dominance of the frame.

Overwrought emotion is suggested by Tillie's volatility; she is subject to extremes of passion, joy, and rage. But the long-shot structure of the film and Dressler's exaggerated performance of these emotions encourages the audience not to identify with the emotion being expressed, but to laugh at it. The whole film is built on big gestures that mock the histrionic excesses of melodramatic action: double-takes to express shock, kicks in the pants to express anger, and arms thrown wide to express joy. Dressler was particularly skillful in using gestures that suggest an overwrought ingénue caught in the grip of first love. The robust Dressler reveals the neurotic physicality of the Griffith-style young heroine as the center of an infantile and ludicrous charade. When flirting with Charlie, she doesn't just finger the hem of her skirt shyly but puts the hem of her skirt into her mouth, an outrageously excessive bit of business. When she throws a flower at her suitor as a teasing gesture, she does so with such force that he responds as though he has been hit with a brick. And when Tillie clasps her hands together and throws up one foot in a spontaneous act of modest romantic joy, she inadvertently but quite forcefully kicks her admirer in the hind end. Dressler's physicality insistently mocks the excessive emotional register of the melodrama.

Moral polarization is overturned in the constant oscillation between victim and villain that structures the film. The film begins with Tillie knocking Charlie on the head with a heavy wooden block; he is the first victim of violence. But when he decides to take her money, he turns to the camera and gestures his evil intent in the hackneyed style of the melodramatic villain, plucking at his bow tie and twiddling his fingers greedily. Thereafter he spends much of the film dodging blows from his intended victim. Sennett's original title for the film, "She Was More Sinned Against Than Necessary," suggests an exuberant play with the morally weighted language of melodrama.[39] Although this title was cast aside, the film still revels in the hackneyed vocabulary of sentimentality in its intertitles, which speak and then undercut the moral polarity of villains and victims. Charlie wins Tillie's misplaced trust when he stops her father from yelling at her, heroically ordering the man, "STOP! YOU CANNOT ABUSE THAT POOR GIRL IN MY PRESENCE." It is an utterly incorrect description of what is happening in his presence, but Tillie is charmed by the implied moral logic that labels her a "poor girl." Mabel is similarly rendered a mock-melodramatic character when she is introduced with the melancholy title "The Girl He Left behind Him," as though she is a hometown primrose rather than his partner in crime. And Tillie's adventures at the café are framed by the generically conventional intertitle "The Effect of Tillie's First Drink," which suggests the many sensationalistic films at the time about the negative effects of alcohol on moral virtue and family life. This title is followed by a comic shot of Tillie spitting her first drink in Charlie's face. Indeed, the alcohol here and at the final party does not signify the corrosive effects of city life on the moral lives of the characters. It signifies only the pleasures of physical freedom.

The film's most insistent imagery casts Tillie as the hunter and Charlie as the hunted. She begins the film by throwing a block of wood for her very large dog, a game that retrieves a man instead of a toy. The home she inherits from her uncle (the outdoors enthusiast) is strewn with bear-skin rugs and decorated as a lodge, placing the married couple in a setting that celebrates conquest. When Tillie picks up a gun from the cluttered mise-en-scène of her uncle's house and starts shooting at her errant husband, she is simply occupying the position of hunter that places her in the family business. Charlie may have nefarious plans, but his moral relationship with his intended victim is thrown into chaos by her huntress persona.

Nonclassical narrative structure is present in the film's many sudden reversals and the episodic nature of the plot. The hasty appearance, disappearance, and reappearance of Tillie's uncle gives the plot a core instability to reverse the course of the characters' actions. Dressler's performance style emphasizes the suddenness of these reversals by playing against the obvious emotional content of each scene. When she is taken off to jail, she is joyful instead of ashamed. When Charlie returns to marry her, she is dubious rather than ecstatic, even mouthing "no" when the minister asks for her vows, before Charlie bullies her into compliance. When her uncle returns from the dead, she is angry instead of relieved. Perhaps the most extraordinary departure from conventional narrative structure is the film's ending, in which Tillie embraces her rival, Mabel, and sends her husband packing. The film ends in an un-marriage, resisting the rush toward the heterosexual clinch that defines both Victorian melodrama and conventional comedy. The two women set aside their rivalry and their opposing moral positions of innocent country girl and sophisticated city girl; their embrace is the utterly nongeneric final image of the film.

Sensationalism is referenced in the film's many thrills and spills. The physicality of the gags builds slowly throughout the film, from little knocks on the head and kicks in the rear, through some recurring swinging-door knockdowns in the restaurant, to a drunken dance between Tillie and Charlie that allows Dressler to throw her diminutive partner around like a bag of feathers. The gags finally explode into the all-out chaos of the party at the mansion and the final chase to the pier. This structure of slowly escalating stunts mimics the melodrama's inflationary sensational aesthetic.

The sensationalism of melodrama is often based on the daredevil physicality of the star—Wallace Reid's stunt driving, Pearl White's leaping on and off of moving trains, or Tom Mix's breakneck horsemanship. Dressler's reckless physicality in *Tillie's Punctured Romance* reproduces some of these same "wow" moments of the blood-and-thunder melodrama in ways that force the viewer to recognize the flexibility and power of her body, as well as its resilience. The *Moving Picture World*'s review of the film marvels at the star's bodily energy. "Marie Dressler breaks into the story at the first jump. She is in the scene every minute right to the finish. . . . She kicks and is kicked, she falls and gets up or is laboriously picked up: sober or unsober she is inimitable. Trouble follows in her ample wake; if at any moment there seems an insufficiency of disturbance she beats a strategic retreat and takes a fresh strangle hold on everything and everybody and starts something new."[40] Jennifer Bean has documented how the stunt heroines of the 1910s, such as Pearl White, enacted a form of physical daring that rallied a host of extratextual sources emphasizing the authenticity and danger of the women's feats. Both Dressler and her costar Mabel Normand are included in Bean's list of stars whose bodies thus articulated "a particular synthesis of femininity, athletic virility, and effortless mobility."[41] Certainly Normand's lithe comic antics fit this description, but the greatest demonstration of Dressler's athleticism was not her "effortless mobility" but rather her virtuoso clumsiness. Pearl White leapt; Marie Dressler fell.

Dressler's catastrophic plunge into the Pacific Ocean references this heroic mode of female physicality on screen, but it reads like a stunt gone wrong. The empty police car falls off the pier after her, and for a moment it appears that Tillie is about to be crushed, a stunt that suggests real danger. But Tillie is unharmed, and the problem of getting her out of the water prompts the next series of athletic gags. Dressler's flexible, active body is set expertly to the purpose of appearing to lose control—of expending energy in every direction and finding no solution to her physical peril. She reaches out to grab some support and closes her hand around a fish, pulling it from the water in astonishment. Tillie is so frustrated by this discovery that she slaps the poor fish. This moment suggests both Dressler's athleticism, in performing physical comedy while treading water, and Tillie's energetic incompetence, in being unable to rescue herself, despite her brave efforts. The contrast between the two bodies—Dressler's and Tillie's—suggests the heroism of the serial queen while it mocks the helplessness of the melodramatic victim.

The physical shock of danger is thereby transformed into the physical shock of laughter. The reviewer for the *New York Daily Mail* was unsure whether audiences could tolerate the film's sustained comic onslaught for the full six-reel running time (about eighty minutes). "It is difficult to keep an audience in continuous laughter through six reels of film; facial muscles rebel and demand a rest. If they did not, if it were natural for people to maintain the same mirthful pitch for an hour and a half at a stretch, *Tillie's Punctured Romance* would provide sufficient provocation. The picture is an experiment that must show whether rapid, farcical action is wanted in large doses."[42] If sensationalism is the film's ability to produce a shock in the body of the audience, this slapstick comedy channels that shock into comic violence, with a similarly depleting physical effect on its spectators. This landmark film turned the emotional register of sensational melodrama on its head by means of Dressler's extraordinary body in motion.

The assault on genre central to *Tillie's Punctured Romance* is rendered subtler in her work of the late 1920s and early 1930s, and never again would Marie Dressler star in a straightforward genre parody on screen. But her training in physical comedy, improvisation, mimicry, and parody deeply informed Dressler's later roles, when she became the most popular female star in the country, playing characters designed around her particular skills. Dressler's core set of gestures and expressions tended to work in opposition to the ideological drive of film narratives throughout her career, and her melodramas were always transformed by the destabilizing effects of her exuberant performance style. Her later films could all be aptly characterized as "punctured romances": films that undermine a sentimental narrative progression with Dressler's outbursts of comic bodily spectacle.

Evolutions of Melodrama

> In the woman's film, the woman has to choose, always choose. She is not supposed to have two of anything. She can't have both a career and a home. She can't love two men. She shouldn't have two personalities, and frequently she can't even have two children, because one has to die for her sins. What these movies tell an audience is that women have to make choices, and once the choice is made, they must live with the consequences. The way the plots shape up, the movies are frequently defining a no-win situation in which the choice is, in some fundamental way, always wrong.
>
> —Jeanine Basinger, *A Woman's View*

Dressler's 1930s star vehicles targeted a new generation of generic conventions.[43] Instead of sensational melodramas, Dressler's talkies trafficked in the conventions of sentimental melodramas or "woman's films" like *Stella Dallas* (Samuel Goldwyn Company, 1925), *East Lynne* (Fox, 1931), *The Sin of Madelon Claudet* (MGM, 1931), and *Madame X* (MGM, 1929). There is a significant scholarly debate about whether it is appropriate to link these two very different genres of film under the critical concept of melodrama.[44] It is hard to trace an evolutionary relationship between the sensational form, defined by action and often set in the outdoors, and the sentimental form, defined by suffering and often set inside the home. For the purposes of this study, however, I will treat the two types of melodrama as complementary and related. As Linda Williams has argued persuasively, "Action-centered melodrama is never without pathos, and pathos-centered melodrama is never without at least some action."[45] Ben Singer's list of five characteristics of sensational melodrama, for instance, can readily be adjusted to describe the genre's sentimental form.

Pathos is present in the audience's identification with the suffering heroine, usually expressed as the audience's tears. Women's pictures were regularly called "weepies" or "weepers" in the early sound years and were specifically crafted to move audiences to tears.

Overwrought emotion is produced by the highly contrived situation the heroine must face. Indeed, the narratives of sentimental melodramas are designed to create intense emotional situations for the heroine: she becomes a wealthy man's mistress to secure the money to pay for her husband's radiation-poisoning treatments (*Blonde Venus*, Paramount, 1932). Thinking her beloved is dead, she joins a convent, only to discover he is alive. Alas! She cannot bring herself to break her vows (*The White Sister*, MGM, 1933). Or she kills herself in a spectacular airplane crash in order not to burden her married lover with her illegitimate unborn child (*Christopher Strong*, RKO, 1933). An impossible choice or terribly necessary (if terribly contrived) sacrifice ratchets up the emotional register of the film.

Moral polarization is present in the way characters suffer for their wrongdoings. Singer points out that many sentimental melodramas have far more nuanced moral schemes than the hero/villain dichotomies of sensational melodramas.[46]

In the iconic *Stella Dallas* (1937), for instance, both Stella and Stephen love their daughter and do their best to raise her well, but their difference in class status creates an unbearable fracture in Laurel's identity that can be resolved only through Stella's sacrifice of her maternal position. There is no villain. Yet, working-class Stella's ambitious pursuit of the upper-class Stephen can certainly be read as the "original sin" of this film, which sets the fragmented identity of the child in motion. Indeed, most of classical Hollywood's best weepies have such finely tuned moral compasses that the slightest infraction will incur an overwhelming punishment. Melodramatic heroines who indulge in extramarital sexuality (*Madelon Claudet*), who give up their children (*Torch Singer*, Paramount, 1933) or smother them with overprotection (*So Big!* Warner Bros., 1932), who drink (*Madame X*) or who put career ahead of love (*Dr. Monica*, Warner Bros., 1934) undergo agonies of loss, and the narrative demands that they make a profound sacrifice in order to right the ship. Williams argues, "In a postsacred world, melodrama represents one of the most significant, and deeply symptomatic, ways we negotiate moral feeling."[47] The sentimental melodrama has as powerful, and as righteous, an interest in moral polarities as does the sensational melodrama. But its negative examples and its positive examples of moral behavior tend to be embodied in the same flawed but utterly sympathetic heroine.

Nonclassical narrative structure is still the combination of "outrageous coincidence, implausibility, convoluted plotting, deus ex machina resolutions, and episodic strings of action." Like sensational melodrama, sentimental melodrama is often criticized for its lack of adherence to a moderate or "realistic" narrative logic: characters presumed dead suddenly reappear (*Today We Live*, MGM, 1933), a bump on the head induces extreme amnesia (*As You Desire Me*, MGM, 1932), and women are forever reencountering the men who did them wrong, no matter how far away they might move (*The Purchase Price*, Warner Bros., 1932). In extreme form, this tendency of sentimental melodrama is channeled into the serial format of soap opera, which refuses closure altogether and strings a series of narrative coincidences along for generations.

Sensationalism is often used to underscore the emotional effects of sentimental melodrama. The shock of the new in 1930s melodrama can be represented by urban social problems linked to prostitution (*Waterloo Bridge*, Universal, 1931), women's prisons (*Ladies They Talk About*, Warner Bros., 1933), alcoholism (*A Free Soul*, MGM, 1931), organized crime (*Paid*, Warner Bros., 1930), the stock market (*Skyscraper Souls*, MGM, 1932), or a woman's entry into business (*Female*, Warner Bros., 1933). The physical "shock" of early sound technology further rendered these melodramas "new," and the hiss sometimes heard on the soundtracks of these early talkies served as a constant reminder that the cinema was entering a new and still-raw technological realm. The sentimental women's films of the early talkie years used the moral polarities of melodrama to anchor sensational narratives of modern life, not yet burdened by the censorious oversight of 1934's Production Code Administration.

Each of the following chapters deals with ways Dressler's performances retooled the generic logic of her films, using several different forms of melodrama as a basis for the analysis. Chapter 2, "Breaking Boundaries: The Unruly Body," investigates how the star's expansive use of her body upset boundaries of gender, ethnicity, and class during the transitional years of the early sound era, paving the way for her later stardom. Here Dressler's posture and style of movement are used as a basis for discussing how melodramatic and comic narrative modes are dynamically combined in her performances. Chapter 3, "*Politics* and *Prosperity:* The Body Politic," uses the conventions of the maternal melodrama to argue that Dressler's ample body collapsed the public sphere/private sphere binary in her comedies, allowing her characters to figure as the maternal/matriarchal center of imagined utopian communities. Chapter 4, "*Min and Bill* and *Tugboat Annie:* The Mythic Body," uses the models of the trickster and the frontier hero to demonstrate how Dressler's films can be read as folkloric media texts that ennoble suffering and sacrifice while they argue for the essential heroism of women. Using Peter Brooks's analysis of "moral melodrama," this chapter describes the ways that melodrama does the cultural work of defining morality in a "postsacral" age. Chapter 5, "*Emma* and *Christopher Bean:* The Sexual Body," argues that Dressler's romantic melodramas mimic her public life by concealing a lover in plain sight. By removing her characters' lover and refocusing their energies on children, the romances effect an incomplete containment of the middle-aged sexuality so little recognized in other films of the era.

Stubbornly perhaps, I have left Dressler's most famous film, *Dinner at Eight*, for the conclusion. Coming at the end of her career, and casting Dressler as an actress whose glory days are behind her, this film nicely captures the duality central to Dressler's film career: she is lavishly dressed but broke, motherly but imperious, widely scorned but still magnetic, a scintillating dinner guest but not a polite one. The grand dame's disruptive influence on the party suggests the ways Dressler's function as star contained but did not erase her identity as unruly outsider. Dressler's artful vacillations between melodrama and comedy puncture the romance of narrative coherence and closure, finishing the film with a joke rather than a clinch.

This book aims to use Dressler's extraordinary career to engage a question from two different directions—not only how an active and transgressive star can stretch the boundaries of genre, but also just how far a genre can stretch in order to contain or absorb the ideological challenges posed by an active and transgressive star. Each of these chapters ultimately points to the limits of Dressler's influence on the generic trajectory of the films: they locate the point where the generic form snaps back into place to restore a more conventional order. In this sense, the career of a highly exceptional star—too large, too old, too active, too queer, too sick for stardom's normal rules—throws into sharper relief the boundaries of generic and ideological flexibility in the chaotic space of early sound filmmaking.

2

Breaking Boundaries

The Unruly Body

> Her secret was simple but effective—inject some humility into regal characters and some majesty into the downtrodden.
>
> —Matthew Kennedy, *Marie Dressler*

From 1927 to 1930, Marie Dressler played queens or slatterns and very few other types in between. A publicity still juxtaposing two very different characters from her films of 1930 illustrates some of the extraordinary paradoxes of her supporting roles (figure 5).[1] Dressed in cotton and wool, the shadow of her rumpled hat falling across her face, the Dressler on the right is in character as the degraded wharf-front prostitute Marthy from *Anna Christie*. Her face is wrinkled and soft, the lines of her mouth turned gently downward with good humor and the slackness of a drinker. She leans tentatively into the frame, half-hiding behind a tavern door while peeking toward a painting of another Dressler, this one in royal regalia as the haughty Princess Beatrice in *One Romantic Night* (United Artists, 1930). The Dressler on the left is virtually wrinkle-free, her smooth face turned up toward the light, framed by the diamonds on her necklace, earrings, tiara, and brooch. Her spine is straight, her shoulders back, and her gaze is directed commandingly down her nose and into the middle distance. Both Dresslers look like they might burst out laughing at any moment.

This photo neatly sums up the duality of Dressler's persona, which in

FIGURE 5. Supporting roles placed Dressler on the margins of the narrative—lofty characters or outcasts. MGM publicity photo, 1930.

the early years was separated into very high and very low characters, but in her starring years merged into one figure. In Dressler's transition to talking films the actress played a variety of roles the were either very high or very low in social station—queens, society ladies, broken-down drunks, wicked stepmothers—the usual hodgepodge of roles assigned to an aging character actress with a flair for comedy. While the young leads in the film are usually still working out what their final class status will be—fighting their way into and out of the bourgeoisie, marrying up or down, achieving success or failure at business—Dressler's characters have already achieved a stable station in life. She suggests the future that young women could expect to reach, depending on their choices, and so her characters are usually caricatures—very high, very low, very happy, or very miserable. The audience could not fail to miss the point.

Dressler's remarkable skills as a performer, though, allow her to overturn the secondary status and simplistic character traits assigned to those roles. Rather than accepting the marginality of age, Dressler developed a repertoire of facial expressions, gestures, and postures she used to steal the scene from the rightful star. In comic genres defined by manic motion, she moves and speaks with infuriating slowness. In contemplative films, she flutters constantly. By using her body in ways that contrast with the conventions of character, she also makes class visible, and ridiculous, in her performances. When playing powerful characters, she behaves ridiculously. When playing the downtrodden, she holds herself like a queen. Though this is the least-known era of Dressler's career, the period 1927–30 is among the most important for the ways it shows Dressler's active body slowly refocusing the narrative trajectory of her MGM films. The romantic entanglements of young characters are reframed, displaced, and overshadowed by Dressler's powerful reminders that life does not end at the altar. The progress of these roles shows the degree to which Dressler's use of her body helped reshape the films in which she appeared. Through her incorrigible and rebellious scene-stealing, Dressler forced herself back into public awareness and created the conditions for her reemergence in starring roles. Dressler actively resisted the process of her erasure, and the ideological richness of the films of her starring years can be partly attributed to the ways she demanded centrality by disrupting any film that tried to push her to the background.

The Unruly Woman

> Everyone is fair game for humor in comedies, but in twenties films—which set the precedent for those of subsequent decades—older and dowdy women were a little less fair and more game than others.
>
> —Marjorie Rosen, *Popcorn Venus*

Kathleen Rowe's book *The Unruly Woman* draws upon Mikhail Bakhtin's notion of the "carnivalesque" to argue that women's comedy can be transformative, liberating, and transgressive of repressive codes of female normativity. Bakhtin claims that the carnivalesque is an aesthetic that emphasizes the body, particularly what he delicately labels the "lower bodily stratum," as a class equalizer. Birth, death, defecation, sex, all act as the basis of an ambivalent humor that mocks artificiality, social mores, and the pretensions of the upper classes and renders a culture temporarily chaotic or inverted until the carnival ends and the class system is imposed again. During the chaos of the carnivalesque moment, inversions of social roles create a world where women, constrained perhaps most of all by the social labors of propriety, can become "unruly": angry, sexually aggressive, physically exuberant, or socially rebellious, all behaviors outside the boundaries of feminine compliance. These inversions thereby show the artificiality of those rules by easily dismissing them. Comic narrative, though not as intense a cultural ritual as the carnival, participates in the carnivalesque through its interest in inversion, anarchic behavior, bodily freedom, the physical and the grotesque, and the transgression of social norms.[2]

Christopher Beach argues that although it was an industrialized medium, early sound film relates to Bakhtin's populist carnival in many ways, "as part of its own history as a form of popular entertainment (vaudeville, the nickelodeon, the peep-show); as a setting or locale within the film (the fairground, the sideshow, the circus, the amusement park, the red-light district); through a number of metonymic references (laughter, clowns, masks, the use of stock comic characters); or, more generally, through a spirit of hyperbole, excess, anarchy, or manic behavior."[3] This list should make clear how strongly Marie Dressler's performances evoked the context of the carnival. Her history in vaudeville, her uses of song and dance, her stock comic bits, her drunk routine, her energy, and her rotund body all fit quite well into the Bakhtinian model of carnivalesque excess.

Ironically, the very attention to the bodily that Bakhtin celebrates for its ability to strip class distinctions from a population can also reinforce gender difference. Women's bodies are the site of social anxiety and contempt, fetishization and voyeurism. A comedy based on the corporeality of the body holds as much social danger for women as it does the potential for liberation. So Bakhtin's sage use of the term "ambivalent" for the carnivalesque moment is important. It is not all liberation and proletarian revolt. The carnival is an institution that exists fully within a bourgeois capitalist structure. It permits these moments of transgression only in marked and limited ways. For example, Henry Jenkins, in his study of early sound comedy, shows how female comics of the thirties, especially the former vaudevillians Charlotte Greenwood ("the only woman in the world who could kick a giraffe in the eye") and Winnie Lightner ("tomboy of the talkies"), were coded as masculine, undesirable, and aggressive in their exuberant performance of physical comedy. He argues that although these women were contained within narratives dedicated to domesticating the "wild woman" (as Greenwood is called in *So Long Letty* [Warner Bros., 1929]), these performers rupture the generic frame with liberating experiences of physical performance that offer pleasures in defiance of the censure of narrative closure.[4]

Often the unruly body of the female comic is mocked because it does not comply with cultural codes of female beauty, even while women in the audience may pleasurably identify with her unconventional appearance and behavior. The historian Peter Stearns argues that the American propensity toward thinness that emerged at the end of the nineteenth century was linked to other regimes of bodily control: "emotion, sexuality, posture and dress, propriety of language, cleanliness."[5] The female body that was excessive, fat, or too energetic violated the fundamental virtues of self-control associated with early twentieth-century American life. Hence the female comic's ambivalence: she is both an appealing model of feminine energy and transgression and a warning for women that such unseemly behavior threatens their social status under patriarchal systems in which women rely on men for economic and familial security. Even the structure of the narrative, the closure of the "happy" ending (especially under Production Code prescriptions for narrative morality that privileged the ending as a site of moral fixity), unplugs the current of the woman's anger, her energy, and her transgressions, often implicitly punishing her for the chaos that her actions have wrought.

Dressler's comedy is all about the body, and her body is excessive—too old, too large, and too active for feminine propriety. Because Dressler was large, her voice and gestures expansive, the way she occupied space was often read as masculine, transgressing the boundaries of feminine containment. In her very early years on stage, she was sometimes called upon to play male roles. She recalled, "As a general thing, I played the Queen, if there was one. But if the King had spent too much time propped against a local bar, I was given his beard and his lines."[6] In the play *1492*, she took over the role of Queen Isabella from Richard Harlowe, a female impersonator who had originated the role.[7] A review of her stage work described the androgyny of her stage presence: "Marie Dressler has a certain virility in her humor. Feminine enough by the natural limitations, her grip of the comic is masculine in its strength."[8] Rebecca Bell-Metereau observes that at least one reviewer made a point of referring to Dressler as an "actor" rather than an "actress" in a way that suggested "the attributing of masculine traits to a woman was a compliment."[9] A common way of approaching Dressler's ruptures of feminine containment was simply to label them masculine.

But just as important as the gender boundaries she crosses, Dressler's body also crosses boundaries of class. The first shot of her in *Prosperity* (MGM, 1932) is typical. A man enters a bank asking for the president. The teller invites him to go on in, and the man passes through an office door to catch sight of Dressler's rear end, bouncing right and left. The bank president is hanging out her office window shouting to the ice cream man below that she wants raspberry and not tutti-frutti for her son's wedding later that day. A baby urinates on Dressler in *Emma;* her weight tears a sink from the wall in *Chasing Rainbows* (MGM, 1930); and in *Reducing* (MGM, 1931) she performs a kind of hopping shimmy to retrieve money she has tucked into her bosom and that has slipped beyond her reach. Her body, her ample, flexible, and mobile body, causes chaos in the controlled systems of social propriety.

Dressler specialized in performing a very specific social transgression: she frequently played drunk. From the drunken dance in *Tillie's Punctured Romance*, her first film, to the drunken dance in *Tugboat Annie*, filmed the year before her death, few of her movies bypassed the opportunity to showcase this specialty. Dressler's performance of intoxication is always a spectacle of the body in ecstasy: face muscles slackening, balance lost, powerful big body reduced to lurching around, giggling, hiccupping, and pratfalls—the whole bag of comedian's tricks. It is a demonstration of perfect physical control (Dressler's) communicating the loss of control (the character's). In the Prohibition world of Dressler's comeback years, her drinking is also profoundly transgressive: of the law, of conventions of feminine propriety, of moderation. And her urge to dance, the physical freedom and exuberance of drunkenness, as Bakhtin celebrates it, shows the enormity of her flesh and emphasizes unassailably the life of the body. Her drunk routine is precisely an expression of carnival excess, a body temporarily, dangerously, and pleasurably out of control. Although many male comic stars were known for their drunk specialties, most obviously Chaplin and W. C. Fields, it would seem to be a measure of exactly how dangerous the whole prospect of a drunk woman could be that I can find no other female comedienne who did a regular drunken "bit."

Dressler's comeback years traced a progression from a drunken scene in the comedy *The Callahans and the Murphys*, which audiences read as scandalous, crude, and lowbrow, to a drunken scene in the heavy drama *Anna Christie*, which audiences read as sensitive, heartwarming, and sophisticated. Dressler's use of her body in these years shifted slightly, and the vehicles in which she appeared shifted tremendously. While her parodic slapstick comedy had always relied on a judicious combination of slapstick and sentiment, these were the years when Dressler's unruly body found a new outlet in the service of melodrama. Her *Tillie* films of the 1910s and her comic shorts were shot primarily in long shot, so her broad gestures and mugging had to be readable from a great distance. The last few silent films and early talkies put the camera much closer to Dressler's face, allowing her to develop the riveting rapport with the camera that would become a hallmark of her late stardom. The journey from one drunk scene to the other demonstrates Dressler's contrarian approach to gender and class, her canny manipulation of the uncertainties of early sound filmmaking, and her developing sentimental star persona. The thread that binds these three processes is Dressler's unruly body, exploding generic and narrative boundaries.

The Callahans and the Murphys

> By a combination of offense to the Irish race, affront to the Catholic Church, and violation of the common decencies of life the Metro-Goldwyn-Mayer Company has stirred indignation and resentment against their vulgar photoplay "The Callahans and the Murphys." This distortion of Kathleen Norris' novel is without excuse either as art or amusement; its only explanation seems to be a deliberate purpose to travesty the Irish people and to discredit the Catholic Faith.
>
> —Press Release, National Catholic Welfare Conference News Service, July 25, 1927

Kathleen Norris's short-story collection *The Callahans* is a sentimental, often mournful remembrance of two Irish families facing triumph and loss over the years. Not so the film. When Frances Marion used these vignettes as only a loose foundation for her slapstick comedy of warring Irish matriarchs, it was quickly stripped of its fond sentimentality and set in a fictional neighborhood called Goat Alley, which, as an intertitle explained, was a part of town "where a courteous gentleman always takes off his hat before striking a lady."[10] Dressler was shocked and baffled by the outrage that greeted the picture's release. She recalled, "But there was a joker in the deck. One that none of us had dreamed could be there. The picture was about the Irish, and the Irish didn't like it. No sooner was it shown in a few test theaters than an avalanche of protest came in. Loyal sons of Erin rose up in their might. They said we were poking fun at them. It did no good to explain that we weren't. The Irish didn't like it and we couldn't afford to alienate the Irish."[11]

MGM made several attempts to edit the film to remove the offending material, but studio executives quickly discovered that it was not just a matter of a few scenes. At the root of the controversy was the whole premise of feuding Irish characters and the appearance of Dressler and Moran as rowdy Irish mothers. The film was pulled from release and destroyed. Because no copies of the film are currently believed to exist, I base my discussion on production correspondence and screenplay records from the Academy of Motion Picture Arts and Sciences' Margaret Herrick Library, and also on archival resources at the University of Southern California.

It is precisely the fact that this kind of caricature of stock Irish characters had nearly disappeared in 1927 that fanned the controversy around the film's regression to the bad old days. In her work on Colleen Moore's Irish-themed stardom of the 1920s, Diane Negra has argued that the generation of young Irish Americans in this decade were already being held up as a highly assimilated "model minority" before *The Callahans* appeared.[12] Moore's most obvious Irish-assimilation film, *Irene*, was released in 1926, just a year ahead of *The Callahans and the Murphys.* This film cast Moore as a spunky and virtuous daughter of Irish immigrants who first achieves success as a fashion model (model minority, indeed) and then marries her wealthy boss. Negra argues, "Moore's Irishness established a connection to purified, virginal sexuality at a historical moment when American female sexuality was suddenly (and to some Americans, shockingly) unbounded."[13] At the very moment that Irish femininity had become the model of Old World sexual restraint, Marion's script for her rowdy Irish Dressler comedy threatened to dredge up a host of old prejudices, specifically by challenging the sanctity and containment of Irish women's bodies.

In the original script, Frances Marion had centered the conflict around the sexual transgressions of young Ellen Callahan, in love with the young bootlegger Danny Murphy. In this early version, Ellen becomes pregnant but finds that Dan Murphy has suddenly left town; there is no possibility that he can marry her before the baby's birth. In desperation, Ellen goes out to the country to give birth to her out-of-wedlock child while most of her family think she is recovering from a grave illness. Because his sister cannot raise the child alone, Jim Callahan, Ellen's only confidant, places the baby at their own mother's doorstep, knowing that Ma will take him in and raise him, in her beneficent, motherly way. When Dan Murphy returns to town, marries Ellen, and discovers what has happened to their child, the couple offers to raise the "orphan" baby, since they are young and strong and Ma Callahan needs a rest. Ma Callahan refuses to give them the foundling, insisting that he is a great happiness to her, and they would be selfish to take him away. Though Ellen wants to tell Ma the truth so she will give them back their child, Dan talks her out of it by insisting that they will have many more children in the future. From the original script:

Just then Dan's eye wanders and he sees:
PORTRAIT SEMI CLOSEUP IRISH FAMILY
A typical Irish family, father, mother, and about seven kids. This is only a flash.

BACK TO ELLEN AND DAN . . . And there is a twinkle in Dan's eye as he says quite pointedly to Ellen:
"One baby's no great loss—
Thank heavens we're Irish!"
"Oh, Dan," says Ellen, suddenly embarrassed, bringing her head against his shoulder . . . as we
FADE OUT.[14]

This portrait of the sexually undisciplined Irish family never made it to the screen at all. Revisions of the script dictated that Ellen and Dan were secretly married the day the child was conceived, and that by revealing this fact to Ma Callahan and Ma Murphy in the final scene, they easily reclaim the orphan baby as their own. And although this first ending was wisely cut, Marion's vision of her Dressler comedy as a celebration of the bodily excesses of a caricatured Irish family deeply informed the film that was eventually made.

Frances Marion later claimed that if the film had just been called "The Browns and the Joneses" everything would have been all right, but this is disingenuous.[15] It is a script that is in fact obsessed with ethnicity and its relationship to the physicality of the body.[16] Ma Callahan puts a flower in her mouth and does a dance, noting, "I feel Spanish." A Jewish family across the street is evicted and comes over to the Callahans' to share a big meal: "Give me some of that fish, Issy." "But it's *ham*, Mama." "Did I ask you what it was?" The Irish kids play cruel pranks on a black child at the St. Patrick's Day picnic—indeed, early drafts of the screenplay included half a dozen racist jokes about the tension between Irish and black city-dwellers, ranging from a group of black waiters refusing to serve at the picnic to a baseball-throwing carnival concession called "dip-the-nigger."[17] Dan's boss in the bootlegging enterprise is called "Tony the wop" (though he was renamed "Jack the Bootlegger" in the final draft). And perhaps most strikingly, when Ma Callahan finds the baby on the doorstep, the family gathers around the table:

MA: "Maybe it's a black Protestant."
GRANDPA: "And it might be a Jew baby."
Jim offers to take the infant to the orphanage.

MA: "I'll be changin' him before you take him. Get me a dish towel."
JIM: "Maybe it really is a Jew baby."
Close-up on Ma Callahan: "It ain't a Jew baby!"

This, too, was cut from the release print. *The Callahans and the Murphys* is a study in ethnic body stereotypes, an exploration of how marginalized ethnicities work and play and fight with each other. And ethnic bodies, in this film, are the vehicles of excess and pollution.

The largest target of this reading of ethnic bodies was of course the Irish. Nearly all the film's gags were predicated on the notion that Irish bodies were coarse, excessive, undisciplined, drunken, dirty, and hypersexual. The original opening showed Ma Callahan pulling fleas off herself because she and her young sons all share a bed with the family dog. This vision of insects invading the family home, a potent image of pollution and impurity, is repeated several more times in the film: Ma Callahan later swats flies as she's making dinner; Mrs. Murphy nearly eats an inchworm when she takes a bite of salad. References to Jim Callahan's job as a "sewer-digger" were also singled out for criticism.[18] The Los Angeles archdiocese argued in its newsletter that the film vilified "one of the cleanest races in America," again locating the offensive material in the realm of pollution or dirt.[19]

Although Dressler and Marion both insisted that preview audiences loved the film, there is some evidence that its slapstick comedy was a touch too "carnivalesque" for bourgeois and urban audiences. *Life*'s Robert Sherwood gave the film a scathing review:

> There are plenty of words with which to describe "The Callahans and the Murphys." Most of them, however, are unprintable. The adjective that comes quickest to mind is "loathsome," and that may be permitted to stand in lieu of more expressive but more discreet epithets. I had imagined that the depths of vulgarity had previously been plumbed on the screen, but now I know that the slimy surface had hardly been penetrated before Metro-Goldwyn-Mayer dived down and fished up this monstrous mass of bad taste from the bottom.[20]

It is not coincidental that the words Sherwood associates with "bad taste" all imply physical excess: the nausea of "loathsome," the viscosity of "slimy," the permeability of "penetrated," the cancerousness of "monstrous mass."

And there is no question that the outrage over the film was particularly virulent because the film's excessive comic bodies were female. Taking their cues from the outraged letters being circulated by major Irish and Catholic organizations, state censor boards targeted images of the film's women for critical attention. The studio collected data on the deletions ordered by individual state censor boards. Ohio's requests centered exclusively on female bodily excess: "Ohio, June 18, 1927: ... All scenes of 'Mrs. Callahan' and 'Mrs. Murphy' pouring beer down inside front of their dresses. ... Scenes where masseuse lifts 'Mrs. Murphy's' legs high in the air as she is giving her treatment. Closeup scene of 'Sally' in negligee as she is going through doorway. ... Reel 7: Scenes of 'Mrs. Murphy' on floor with her legs up in the air after she has fallen on roller skate."[21]

The scene that raised the most controversy shows the matriarchs of the Callahan and Murphy clans drinking beer at the annual St. Patrick's Day picnic. Eddie Mannix received a telegram requesting the elimination of this scene and warning that images of "mothers drinking and drunk at Irish picnic proved absolutely objectionable to Father Kelly and of course this entire sequence has been the butt of most of the Irish societies' complaints because it shows Irish mothers drunk."[22] The *New York Times* reported that a member of the audience at Loews Orpheum stood up in the middle of the drunken picnic scene and shouted, "My mother never acted like that."[23] The Ancient Order of Hibernians issued a statement condemning the film for "representing Irish home life as degraded and reflecting upon Irish womanhood."[24] Later, *Irish World* laced its defense of Irish women with anti-Semitic comments directed toward the Jewish film moguls, railing, "Let them confine their talents to the Rebeccas and Marthas of their own families. If they want filth and stupidity and indecency, they needn't go out of the Ghetto to find it. ... But they are not going to put their filthy hands on Irishwomen any more."[25]

Irish World was particularly aggressive in locating the offensive caricature specifically in Marie Dressler's body, which was singled out for negative comment: "Marie Dressler, who appears as Mrs. Callahan, has successfully impersonated a gorilla. Miss Dressler, as she appears in this film, might take the beauty prize as an ape in the jungles. That Miss Dressler chooses to look like this is her own business—or misfortune. That she should pretend to be an Irish woman is an insult to every woman of the race."[26] This article mentions monkeys twice: "a gorilla" and "an ape in the jungle." This language echoes the painful history of discrimination against the Irish in the late nineteenth century, when they were often caricatured using "simian or Africanoid" facial features.[27] In the racist logic of a post-Darwinian nineteenth century, Anglo-Saxon Protestants were the most "evolved" race, while other ethnicities were closer to humanity's simian ancestors. By lumping the Irish together with African Americans, and both races with monkeys, the dominant WASP culture excluded them from complete access to political and economic equality. Political cartoons like Thomas Nast's famous image "The Ignorant Vote—Honors Are Easy" represented Irish faces by giving them upturned noses and a short upper lip, a simian caricature (figure 6). The comparison of the Irish man and the African American man, in similar

FIGURE 6. African American and Irish stereotypes balance the scales in Thomas Nast's "The Ignorant Vote—Honors Are Easy." Originally published in *Harper's Weekly*, December 9, 1876. (Image courtesy of the Library of Congress, Prints and Photographs Division.)

poses and weighed equally on the scale, is typical of the devices employed to exclude Irish immigrants from the category "white."

Although it is no longer possible to see *The Callahans and the Murphys*, the publicity stills that survive suggest that the film uses Marie Dressler's body in ways that recalled this previous generation of ethnic stereotypes. Figure 7, for instance, shows Dressler, dressed in bloomers and rag curls, her shoulders shockingly bare, scolding her young son, who appears to be wearing a dressing gown several sizes too large. Dressler's slightly hunched posture, the broad expanse of her back, and the forward tilt of her neck all suggest that she is earthy, fleshy, and animal. She lacks the straight backbone, not to mention the constricting clothing, that expressed the bourgeois ideal. Her bloomers make her backside and legs look too large for her body and obscure her waist, making her proportions comically out of balance—and they turn her figure into a kind of cartoon ape's. Finally, the rag curls in her hair suggest the stereotyped image of the black pickaninny. Dressler's history on the stage, where she was a celebrated interpreter of so-called coon songs like "Rastus Take Me Back" (1909), also contributed to the audience's ability to read her as nonwhite.[28] By reverting to this previous generation of comic conventions, with its broad interpretation of ethnic bodily excess, Dressler's performance in *The Callahans and the Murphys* pushed her well outside the bourgeois mainstream of the late silent picture.

Marie Dressler's body was thereby branded vulgar and polluted; she was an unruly woman. And because she had been such a visible part of this financial and public relations disaster, Dressler's stock at MGM plummeted as well. Frances Marion's description of her friend's ill-fortune replicates the imagery of pollution from the film: "Let a picture fail, and everyone in it, regardless of how good his or her performance, is relegated to the ash heap. And that is where Marie Dressler landed, kerplunk!"[29] Reduced to bit parts, supporting roles, and long periods of unemployment, Dressler spent two years trying to escape Goat Alley and the ash heap. To cleanse herself of this pollution, Dressler the performer had to modify her gender, class, and racial status through a series of roles that gave her the opportunity to demonstrate the fluidity of these categories. She achieved her greatest successes by merging high and low class status in her characters, playing dignified peasants and ludicrous queens and avoiding roles that spotlighted ethnic difference. By spending the next few years playing small roles in unexpected ways, against the grain of the narrative, Dressler slowly reclaimed the bourgeois middle ground that would inform her sentimental later pictures. But in doing so, she

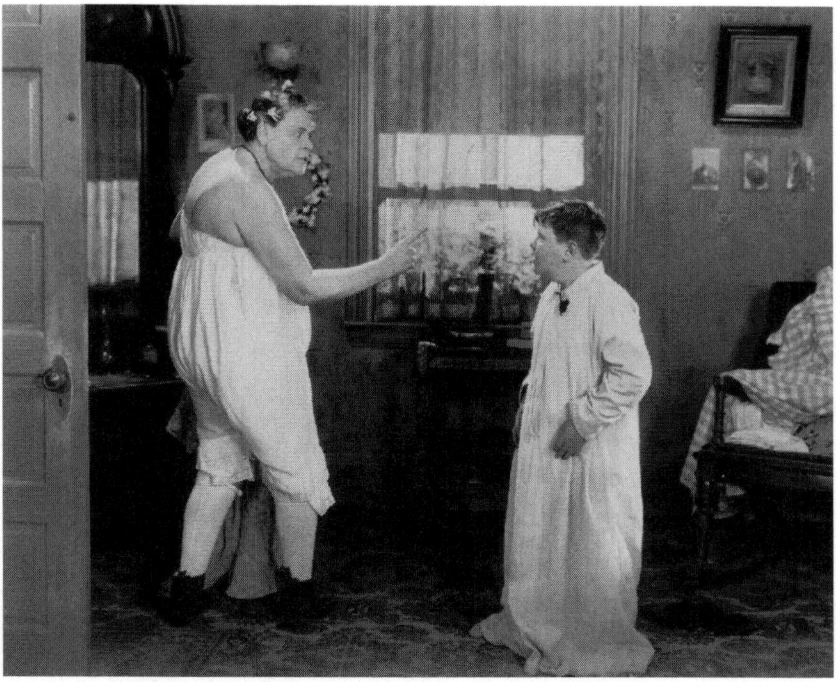

FIGURE 7. Publicity still from the lost film *The Callahans and the Murphys* (1927).

resorted to a different kind of unruliness: a rejection of the studio hierarchy that marginalizes the supporting actor.

Scene-Stealing

> Stars today yell "Foul!" when they're made to work with babies or dogs. Making a picture with Marie Dressler in camera range was more rugged than working with quintuplets or all of Lassie's clan.
>
> —Hedda Hopper, *From Under My Hat*

The phrase "scene-stealing" is often misused. When a character actor is particularly memorable, even when she outshines the lead actor, it is not necessarily a case of theft. Most often it is just a case of superior training and talent, for which no one can reasonably blame the supporting actor. The true *theft* of a scene happens when one actor intentionally distracts the audience from another person's performance, usually by moving conspicuously in the midst of a big speech or emotional moment. An anecdote from the screenwriter/director Garson Kanin's memoir illustrates the issue.

Kanin recalls an incident during the filming of *The Great Man Votes* (RKO, 1939) in which John Barrymore was performing an emotional speech to his granddaughter, played by ten-year-old Virginia Weidler.

> Take one. Barrymore began. All of us watching knew he was reaching deep down into himself. He was playing beautifully. Virginia, on his lap, was listening carefully and I found myself admiring the marvelously childish thing she was doing—twisting Barrymore's necktie around her finger, letting it go, twisting it again.
>
> I watched, enthralled. My reverie was broken abruptly, brutally, by a scream from Barrymore.
>
> "God damn it! What the hell do you think you're doing, you hammy little bitch!"[30]

Real theft of a scene is an intentional—and aggressive—act. It runs counter to the studio hierarchy of stars and supporting actors and to the narrative hierarchy of protagonists and ancillaries. A habitual scene-stealer runs the risk of alienating directors, other actors, and others in the industry, because the effect usually benefits only the thief, and not the narrative as a whole. The film suffers from the breaking of its intended emotional effects.

Marie Dressler was an inveterate scene-stealer. She described her ambitions in a kind of rambling monologue to a *New York Times* reporter in 1930: "I was patient. I said to myself, 'All these stars and prima donnas around here think they're mighty important, but you've been a star and a prima donna, Marie, and now you've only got one ambition. And that is to go into every picture you can and upset the plot at least twice. That's all you want, Marie.'"[31] This remarkably frank admission that she went into pictures not to serve but to "upset" the plot is an extremely apt description of how Dressler's scene-stealing operated. If she had been cast in very good films, this effort may have been a problem, and her coworkers may have come to resent her. But in the first years of the talkies, Hollywood was not in the business of making very good films.

In the early sound world of long shots and interminable dialogue, Dressler's mugging, her gestural range, and the richness of her deep voice added movement, dimension, and immediacy to films that were grasping for just these qualities to enliven a stilted visual style and low-range soundscapes. In an industrial context that was reinventing some of the fundamental structuring devices of the cinema—narrative, genre, and technical transparency—there was a great deal of room for Dressler's antics and her improvisational style.

Movie actors were often uncomfortable with the microphone, while the imported stage actors were often uncomfortable with the camera. Revue musicals, musical shorts, and the incorporation of vaudeville "acts" like Ukulele Ike or baby-voiced Helen Kane undermined the primacy of narrative in Hollywood formula filmmaking in favor of novelty "attractions." Among the first sound films were a number of shorts and revue musicals that treated sound as a novelty, experimenting with and showcasing the new technology in ways that emphasized sensation over narrative. Also, the awkward multicamera setups that characterize the early talkies, particularly the lower-quality movies that Dressler inherited at the outset of her comeback, privileged the master shot and often gave equal space to the lead and the supporting actor. Dressler was rarely cut out of the shot through closeups or a moving camera, so she could haunt the edges of the frame, drawing the audience's eyes away from the young lead.

An image from 1930's *Chasing Rainbows* illustrates the point (figure 8). The film is a backstage melodrama in which Marie Dressler and Polly Moran play a supporting actress and costume supervisor, respectively, who are always fighting with one another backstage. One day, sharing a flask in a dressing room, they get falling-down drunk and renew their friendship in a sentimental alcoholic haze, while accidentally destroying some of the company's props with their antics. This image from the film shows this pair standing backstage, singing, while the show goes on. Another cast member, Charles King, gestures for them to "shhhh!" as their noise threatens to disrupt the proper play they are putting on. Dressler was often in this very position in her transitional films; she is treated as though she is interrupting the show, when in fact the audience understands that she *is* the show. Her unruly antics created a real tension between the forward trajectory of the narrative, with its values of youthful coupling and career success, and the spectacle of her performance, with its emphasis on bodily excess and affective pleasure. Because the narrative could rarely stand up to the pleasures of Dressler's comedy, bodily excess usually won.

These ruptures of narrative coherence, and Dressler's history in Broadway and vaudeville stage comedy, suggest Henry Jenkins's paradigm of the "vaudeville aesthetic" in early talkies.[32] Jenkins analyzes how Hollywood's adoption of vaudeville players and writers in the early sound era prompted the adoption of new narrative rules in early comedies. The anarchic performance styles of skit-based vaudeville performers emphasized virtuosic spectacle over narrative coherence. This vaudeville aesthetic created an un-

FIGURE 8. Charles King goes backstage to quiet Dressler and Polly Moran in *Chasing Rainbows* (1930), because they are disturbing the show. He doesn't realize that they *are* the show.

resolved tension between the extravagantly performative skills associated with revue formats and the orderly world of narrative film.

Because the vaudeville aesthetic created a context in which audiences could read Dressler's unruly performances, her scene-stealing was applauded rather than derided. A fan profile gushed, "She has been accredited with stealing every picture in which she has ever appeared (even Garbo's 'Anna Christie') and not a single critic has ever written one derogatory word about her acting."[33] Norma Shearer was said to have sent Dressler a photo of her newborn son, Irving Thalberg Jr., with the loving inscription, "To Marie from Junior. My mama says you steal pictures from her, but we love you just the same."[34] Dressler's frequent costar Polly Moran complained, "That rubber face of hers makes me look like Dead-Pan Keaton when I'm in a close-up with her. All she has to do is make the slightest grimace and everyone else in the scene fades right out of the picture."[35] William Haines was pragmatic in his approach to sharing the screen with Dressler for his film *The Girl Said No* (MGM, 1930): "If anyone can steal my picture, more power to 'em. I still get credit for it, as long as I'm starred."[36] Dressler's scene-stealing was an effective strategy for garnering the attention of the audience without losing the goodwill of her nervous colleagues, or her audiences.

Even reviews that panned the other actors' work nearly always singled out Dressler for praise. The *New York Times* lauded her work in the clunker *One Romantic Night:* "The audience yesterday afternoon greeted Miss Dressler's comic expressions of anxiety and disappointment with outbursts of giggling and chuckling."[37] The *Outlook and Independent* gave this frank assessment of *The Girl Said No:* "As usual, Miss Dressler gives the best performance in the picture."[38] Reviews of *Let Us Be Gay* (MGM, 1930) were particularly effusive. The *New York Times:* "If one stands out among the rest, it is Marie Dressler."[39] *Variety:* "This one has a heavy cargo of virtues, not the least being Marie Dressler, whose first appearance brought forth a gasp of welcome recognition accompanied by applause that tells louder than fan mail or anything else how the character comedienne rates in New York, and probably all over."[40] The *Outlook and Independent:* "The really important person in this picture however—and in nearly every other picture Metro has made this year—is Marie Dressler, who sailing about as an imperious dowager under full canvas attempts to blast her way through every situation, to the audience's delight."[41] Clearly the positive attention helped set the stage for her return to starring roles.

Dressler's professional goals, of "upsetting the plot at least twice" in her transitional films, produced an ideological effect, the unruly disruption of class and gender norms enacted in the bodies of her characters. To counteract the stodginess of a Ruritanian romance like *One Romantic Night,* she would play her character with a robust sense of the ridiculous. To offset the heaviness of a social-problem melodrama like *Anna Christie,* she would play her character with a twinkle of humor. The mighty were brought low, and the lowly were raised up.

The Queen

> She's like one of those queens who chop people's heads off or send them to prison for life.
>
> —Jean Whitehall (Sally Blane) about her aunt (Marie Dressler) in *The Vagabond Lover* (1929)

Dressler first made a hit in the talkies playing an imperious queen. She had a standout role in *Hollywood Revue of 1929* (MGM), a film in which many of the studio's important stars, including Joan Crawford, Norma Shearer, Stan Laurel and Oliver Hardy, Conrad Nagel, Anita Page, Bessie Love, Marion Davies, the crooner Charlie King, the radio import Jack Benny, and even John Gilbert, that infamous casualty of sound recording, showcased their voices in songs and sketches loosely stitched together. Dressler played several small skits in the film, but the most interesting of these was a song, appropriately titled "I'm the Queen." The emcee, Conrad Nagel, introduces the bit by explaining that the recent war had so upended the social structure of Europe that royalty had been forced "into all walks of life," and there were even some royal folks in the company, including Queen Marie Dressler and Princess Polly Moran. He bids the chorus, "The queen approaches, friends arise," at which point the chorus, which had been standing, sits down in unison. Four muscular and bare-chested black servants carry out a royal litter, with Dressler apparently inside, though when she stops and the litter proceeds to the other side of the stage without her, it becomes clear that she had always been walking alongside the berth, rather than riding inside. The pseudo-African servants suggest the queen's imperial whiteness, while the joke about her weight renders that grandeur ridiculous. This mixture of high and low qualities is picked up in the song she sings, which announces the queen's dominion over both essential and trivial aspects of social life:

> For I'm the queen!
> (Chorus: She's the queen.)
> I'm the queen!
> (Chorus: She's the queen.)
> My subjects must remember I'm supreme—
> I can even take a life—
> Or a husband from a wife—
> I can eat peas with my knife—
> For I'm the queen!

The equation of murder and table manners is a clear jab at the pretensions of the ruling classes, which recalls the carnivalesque aesthetic of Bakhtin. Bodily necessity equalizes boundaries of class.

As Dressler sings, her body enacts a similar oscillation between majesty and buffoonery. After the first verse, the orchestra drops Dressler's tune to play a jazzy little interlude, which prompts the chorus girls to do a dance. Dressler looks over each shoulder sternly, freezing the chorus, and the original tune resumes. After each verse, there is a variation on this bit, with the music abandoning the main melody, suggesting a kind of loss of control, a series of ruptures in this song that is precisely about the necessity of submission to sovereignty. But the scowling Dressler finds herself as susceptible to the lure of the jazz as is her chorus of subjects. In the next interlude, the orchestra tries a little Charleston, and the queen herself gives in to the rhythm and starts to dance, but quickly catches herself, stamps a foot, and continues her song. In the final variation, the orchestra breaks into a snake charmer's tune. Dressler's right shoulder begins to twitch along with the music as though unintentionally. She regains control, gripping her left shoulder with her right arm to stop the motion, and continues with her imperious song. By playing this song as a series of ruptures—a refined character who loses control, sometimes in only one body part, and then regains it—Dressler draws out the comedy of the lyrics and achieves the kind of joke about class that was central to most of her performances. Under her elegant robes, the queen cannot control her unruly body.

This joke was also played out in her narrative films. When playing women of the upper classes, Dressler keeps her spine straight and her shoulders square, yet she finds ways to radiate an unruly bodily energy that defies the stilted logic of well-disciplined woman. Marie Dressler plays Mrs. Whitehall, a society matron, in the rather bad 1929 musical comedy *The Vagabond Lover* (RKO). Although the main narrative line of the film concentrates on the earnest young lovers played by Rudy Vallee and Sally Blane, Dressler is the best thing in the movie. While the young leads, clearly paralyzed by the microphone, speak their lines with awkward pauses, unsure what to do with their hands or bodies, Dressler whirls into each scene in a flurry of loud costume, fluttering hands, and confident voice. She steals scenes through constant motion—fiddling with her handkerchief, stroking her face, or fluttering her fingers in the air, even during the other characters' lines.

Among the most interesting of these gestures is a tendency to point at something as she speaks about it, followed by the horrified realization that it is impolite for a lady of her station to point, at which moment she stares at her hand in disapproval, as though it belongs to someone else, then hurriedly covers up the offending index finger with her other hand, or hides it behind her back. Unscripted, these moments demonstrate how Dressler acquires space through movement, exceeding the polite boundaries of the supporting actor in the same way her characters exceed polite rules of motion. Her body demands visibility, in violation of the hierarchies of the star system and the logic of narrative. The centrality of Dressler in this film creates a real tension between the forward trajectory of the narrative, with its values of youthful coupling and career success, and the spectacle of her performance, with its emphasis on bodily excess and affective pleasure. Bodily excess wins. Audiences responded to her lively performances: the *New York Times* movie critic Mordaunt Hall specifically noted in his review that Dressler "toys with a chiffon handkerchief, which amused the feminine element in the theatre last night. Miss Dressler's lines may not be witty, but they are comic. The dialogue for the other players, including Mr. Vallee and Sally Blane, is very poor."[42] Dressler's lively physicality easily overshadowed the beautiful and tuneful young leads.

In her 1930 hit *Let Us Be Gay*, Dressler plays another eccentric old dowager, Mrs. Bouccicault (Boucie to her friends), who hosts a weekend at her country house. Fearing that her granddaughter is falling for the rogue Bob Brown (Rod la Roque), Mrs. Bouccicault has invited the flirtatious divorcee Kitty Courtland Brown (Norma Shearer) to distract the inappropriate suitor, thereby preserving the granddaughter's virtue. Mr. Brown turns out to be Mrs. Brown's ex-husband, and she spends the weekend tormenting him with her flirtations with other men before the couple tearfully reconciles in the last act.

Dressler plays Mrs. Bouccicault as a crusty misanthrope, who declares her dislike for children and recoils when any of her guests try to kiss her cheek. Her class privilege is expressed through a studied control of the body—her own and those around her (figure 9). This character thrives on control and fights to maintain it, while the other characters wallow in the romantic excesses of the country villa farce. In the stage version of *Let Us Be Gay*, the actress who played Mrs. Bouccicault (Charlotte Granville) smoked a cigar through most of the scenes, expressing her disapproval of her young houseguests' antics with furious puffing. Because the Freudian implications of this behavior were unacceptable to the Hays office, the smoking was eliminated from the film.[43] So Dressler devised the substitute of knitting furiously in each daytime scene, in addition to a number of fidgety bits of business with her lorgnette and her walking stick, a series of scarves and shawls, as well as assorted teacups, spoons, and candies. Her character's big comic moment comes when Mrs. Bouccicault bursts into Kitty's bedroom dressed in a frowsy nightgown with a drooping, ruffled net cap on her head, determined to interrupt an imagined rendezvous. Again, it is the *rupture* of bodily control that is compelling. The simultaneously dowdy/covered up and undignified/exposed quality of this entrance accounts for its singular appeal. It is an inappropriate, impulsive bodily display, performed by a very appropriate, very buttoned-up character.

Throughout *Let Us Be Gay*, Mrs. Bouccicault also displays a tendency to look furtively away from the person she is conversing with. Dressler communicates Boucie's disconnection from the other characters by facing the camera

FIGURE 9. Marie Dressler is formidable in *Let Us Be Gay* (1930).

and betraying alarm, satisfaction, or pleasure at what they are saying. It is a habit halfway between a theatrical aside and a naturalistic film technique—letting the audience in on her emotional state in a highly conspiratorial way without breaking frame. Because Shearer was pregnant during the filming of this comedy, she spends much of her screen time facing partly away from the camera or assuming demure poses to hide her growing belly. The frame, then, is left open to Dressler, who is more than happy to fill it with her fidgeting.

The rather unpleasant comedy *The Girl Said No* casts Dressler as yet another imperious dowager, but one whose reserves can be broken by charm and a liberal dose of alcohol. Not a critical favorite, the breakneck romantic comedy starring fast-talking go-getter William Haines and the quieter, overmatched ingénue Leila Hyams was a solid financial success for MGM.[44] Haines plays Tom Ward, just home from a brilliant college football career and ready to live off his parents' money while he cavorts with his destructive and drunken college friends, squanders good jobs in big banks, and pursues pretty blonde Mary Howe (Hyams), who rejects his boorish attentions. When Tom's father dies suddenly, the family rapidly descends into relative poverty, and Tom is forced to take over management of the household. After months of struggle, Tom lands a job as a bond salesman. But a rival for Mary's affections sabotages his first day on the job by offering Tom a bogus lead on a bond sale: the wealthy but impossible hypochondriac Hattie Brown (Dressler). Posing as a doctor to get past the butler, Tom gains access to the lady's private study and prescribes his new patient a liberal dose of alcohol. Brown likes her first dose so much she insists on taking two, rapidly becoming drunk, falling off her chair, and giggling like a girl. As she sobers up, Tom confesses his true identity, and Hattie agrees to buy some bonds from him. He returns triumphant just in time to break up Mary's wedding and abscond with the furious bride.

Dressler has only one scene in this film, but it is a pivotal scene, carefully played. Dressler's presence turns a trite little accidental drunk routine, full of pratfalls and slurred speech, into a study of the female body as alternately grotesque and comforting in its excess. When Tom first enters, Hattie's stiff backbone and the fierce look on her face suggest a formidable spinster indeed, confident in her assurance that he is too young to be her doctor and he should leave. The wisecracking child of privilege is cowed by the woman's physical authority, and he persists only from desperation. When she relents enough to ask Tom if she should undress for examination, she already has her dress pulled half over her shoulders when he replies, "No, no," horrified at the prospect. Dressler makes her body the center of the scene; she reminds the viewer through gesture and expression that her body is the object of negotiation and diagnosis. When she is so shy about the nature of her illness that she can only whisper it in Tom's ear, Dressler's tiptoed posture renders the fearsome dowager childlike and vulnerable, appealing and ridiculous. Although the aging female body is the site of revulsion to Tom, something not to be touched, Dressler uses her body aggressively, forcing him to look at her, touch her, and even to pick her up off the floor when she falls, a feat that requires several rather graphic attempts. If the scene's comedy is based in the unattractiveness of her body, she plays that card as an advantage, a weapon against the avaricious and condescending gaze of the film's arrogant hero. She is utterly warm and endearing.

Although Tom uses her drunken state as a way to break down the frigid self-discipline associated with her class and marital status (rich old maids in the movies are always severe), Dressler's Hattie revels in her loss of control, putting her young con man on the defensive for the only time in the movie. He promises her that if she buys his Denver park bonds, she will forever be known as the "Mother of the Denver Park System." She hates Denver, and she hates parks, but Hattie sentimentally mumbles, "I always wanted to be a mother," turning his con into a moment of emotional ownership of Tom as her son. She agrees to sign the check. However, when the drunken patient takes Tom's pen, it drops down her dress. In the film's funniest and most risqué scene, obviously improvised, Hattie forces Tom to fetch the pen from her cleavage with long-handled forceps drawn from the medical bag. He gets the pen, gives her some coffee, confesses his real identity, and makes the sale to an impressed, amused, and suddenly sober client.

Hattie Brown recreates Tom as a new man. In the liminal state of alcoholic haze, the boundaries of identity become blurred, allowing for Dressler's transformation from bad spinster to good mother: the Mother of the Denver Park System. Tom fetches the pen from between her breasts with forceps in a bizarre parody of birth, the birth of a legal document, which renders Tom a wage earner, a man capable of finally winning Mary—putting the excesses of the indulgent jazz age behind him and regaining his place in patriarchy, claiming a bride. The descent into poverty and earned redemption are token nods to narrative necessity, a rather transparent allegory for the Depression itself, and the ease with which energetic people will overcome it. Dressler's performance of a physically bumbling millionairess, ever on the verge of losing control, not only lays bare the way class is constructed through entirely artificial rules of bodily comportment, but also disarms the cocky young man who had counted on the easy compliance of a hysterical dowager. He gets what he wants, but not before giving her what she wants—an experience of touch, companionship, and finally, oddly, motherhood, if only of the Denver park system.

The maternal aspects of Dressler's star persona were slowly developing over the course of these roles, softening the edges of her queenly persona and channeling the star's exuberant physicality toward a younger person in her care: Sally Blane, Norma Shearer, and finally William Haines. But the maternal side of Dressler's performances would come into far sharper focus not in her cartoonish queen roles but in the parts that cast Dressler as noble outcasts. For this, she would have to make a shift to melodrama.

Majesty in the Downtrodden

> Rags are royal raiment when worn by Marie Dressler.
>
> —Fan profile, *Photoplay*, 1932

In MGM's second adaptation of the Eugene O'Neill play *Anna Christie*, Marie Dressler plays Marthy, a broken-down waterfront hag, whose collapsed posture and bulldog face speak to years of hardship (figure 10). While her queenly roles brought out the clown in Dressler, this world-weary character inspired her most compassionate performance. A 1930 fan profile gushed, "For Marie manages to discover a streak of nobility in the lowest form of human life and, while making us laugh helplessly, also unexpectedly shames us into startled admiration as she so subtly, pitiably reveals these dazzling sacrificial streaks. She almost makes us feel that one must sink to the depths before one can rise to the heights."[45] The character of Marthy taps into Dressler's history with performing drunk routines, but it makes an extraordinary alteration to the generic context. Dressler's comic drunk routine works best when she plays characters who don't usually get drunk, or who don't realize that there is alcohol in the punch (or medicine, or tonic) they are drinking so eagerly. Marthy is the most knowing and most sad of the Dressler drunks, and she is wryly rather than broadly comic. Her constant motion betrays the twitchiness of an unhealthy body and the agitation of a troubled mind.

The film opens with a delightfully rich interaction between Marthy and Anna's father, Chris Christofferson (George Marion). Marthy, an old prostitute who has taken up residence with the sailor, sings drunkenly and is struck

FIGURE 10. Marie Dressler appears careworn in *Anna Christie* (1930). The actress always insisted that the hat was one of her own.

by an attack of the hiccups, whereupon Chris tries to help her by slapping her on the back. It is a scene that gestures toward slapstick comedy but is instead far sadder and wiser. *Anna Christie* is, in fact, a kind of funhouse mirror version of *Tillie's Punctured Romance*. In the Sennett film, Dressler's performance undermined melodrama with physical comedy. But the O'Neill adaptation is a film that finds melodrama in a kind of failed physical comedy. There is the same contrast of a large woman overwhelming a small man: outside the barge, Chris gallantly tries to help Marthy down the ramp, but he can provide no stability for her, and she pauses, sways, then runs straight down ramp like she's falling. And there is the same drunkenness. But where Tillie's drunken stumbling was naïve and exuberant, Marthy's is wry and knowing. The years had added pounds to Dressler's frame and soft wrinkles to her face, which she used to give dimension and history to this character.

In the sodden world of the docks, Dressler's Marthy carries herself with exquisite dignity and good humor. Joanna Rapf has pointed out that "there is something 'queenly,' or at least 'regal,' about all Dressler's screen performances, even when she plays a down-and-out waterfront reject."[46] Dressler's character acquires a poignant ridiculousness drawn from her costume: Marthy makes Chris hold the mirror while she puts on her hat—a sad old hat that Marthy carries with a peculiar pride. This hat was Dressler's own, and it marked the actress's identification with the character. She recalled, "After 'Anna Christie' was released, several persons wrote in to ask where on earth the studio found that 'broken-down hat Miss Dressler wore as Marthy.' One woman said: 'It was perfect. That hat alone was sufficient to establish Marthy as a besotted old hag.' Besotted old hag, indeed! That was one of my own hats. I still have it, and there's a lot of good wear left in it, too!"[47] Dressler's ready defense of the hat suggests a sentimental identification with the character. Dressler claims authorship of her character's complicated nobility.

As Marthy and Chris set off to the bar, Dressler emphasizes the play between Marthy's dignity and her dissolution. She teeters drunkenly through the damp, dark streets, supported by Chris, and has to swerve to avoid some oncoming horses. What begins as an evasive maneuver, however, quickly turns into a scamper and hop toward the bar—drama turned to comedy, in a way that restores the character's self-determination. As she tries to go through the main entrance of the tavern, Chris has to remind Marthy to stay at the ladies' entrance. Facing this ludicrous social nicety, Marthy mutters to herself, "Well, why not, said she, with all the dignity in the world," as she fixes her sweater and puffs out her chest. But the moment of dignity is lost when Chris leaves her waiting too long while he walks through the men's entrance and then opens the ladies' door for her. Demanding, "What's the matter with you, you old punk?" Marthy gruffly rolls up her cuffs as he apologizes and asks her drink order. But Marthy's selfless character is revealed when Chris explains that his daughter is coming to live with him, and she immediately sees the necessity of disentangling herself from Chris's life. The film uses a medium shot to frame her speech about how she's leaving him, pushing Chris entirely out of the frame—an image that suggests her agency in the choice, and her nobility. As she speaks, her body is animated and lively. She raises and lowers her eyebrows, twists her mouth to the side, and wipes her face with each sleeve. Although the dialogue suggests that Marthy is being forced out, her body language suggests that this world-weary woman is very much in control of the situation, pained, and deeply generous with her sacrifice.

When Chris repairs to the main barroom to sober up on coffee, the first meeting of Marthy and Anna takes place in the ladies' salon. This sequence is characterized by an extraordinary equity between the two women. The film's tag line, "Garbo Speaks," suggests that Dressler should have been only a secondary attraction in this, Garbo's first scene, so it is particularly extraordinary that Dressler was able to maintain such a tremendous presence throughout it. But when Garbo enters, the moment is framed in a long shot, showing the women on opposite sides of the barroom, and it switches to a relatively equitable series of alternating medium shots as they first converse. Garbo asks Dressler to sit with her, and the pair step into a democratic two shot. And as the barkeep puts down drinks, the audience cannot help but watch Dressler. Marthy reaches for her beer, withdraws her hand, reaches for it, and withdraws again, longing for a drink, but exercising the social grace of waiting for her companion to drink first. This little piece of business, besides artfully drawing the camera's gaze away from Garbo, again bespeaks the generosity and dignity of Marthy. It is a nice counterpoint to her finger-pointing business in *The Vagabond Lover*, in which a lady of elevated station tries to control her natural urge to point her finger. Here, a lady of reduced station makes the successful effort to control her nagging urge to drink. Suggesting the excesses of the body, Dressler's wharf hag exercises a hard-won control over her movements, where the society lady wrestles with a simple and empty social propriety.

But Marthy's self-control is incomplete. Anna tells Marthy her story of being abused, running away from her foster home, and becoming a prostitute out of desperation. Realizing that Anna is Chris's long-absent daughter, Marthy immediately grasps that the two are each hiding their real lives from each other; Chris is sobering up to meet the child he thought was safely tucked away in nursing school, and Anna is looking for a stable life her father cannot provide her. Marthy's agitated response to this recognition is betrayed in her fidgeting; in the course of this scene Dressler scratches herself, pushes up her hat, touches her curls, wipes her hand on one leg, picks up and puts down her drink, and fiddles with a loose piece of yarn that is beginning to unravel from her sweater sleeve. When she goes into the men's section of the bar to say goodbye to Chris, she touches her shirt, collar, and chest throughout. She does the same as she says goodbye to Anna. It is, on the one hand, a cacophony of movement, utterly consistent with her scene-stealing in light comedies. But on the other, this movement is an entirely new performance style for Dressler—tender, sensitive, and very much suited to the medium shots that were used so heavily in this scene. This character provides the cornerstone for Dressler's later stardom in films that liberally mixed melodrama and comedy, in order to create sentimental, folksy, highly theatrical vehicles that embraced both sides of Dressler's dual persona—as a common woman of exceptional nobility.

It is an ironic and fascinating aspect of the film that Marthy engages in a poignant act of self-erasure to protect Anna, while Dressler was engaging in a poignant act of self-promotion in stealing this scene from Garbo. Dressler's performance in *Anna Christie*, which was limited to this opening scene plus a brief reappearance later in the film, was applauded widely and praised as an act of virtuous theft. *Life*'s Harry Evans gave a typical appraisal: "Marie Dressler is so convincing as his hard-boiled, whiskey-sodden wife [*sic*] that there are times when it takes the combined efforts of Director Clarence Brown and the entire cast to prevent her walking off with the piece bodily."[48] *Variety* suggested that the audience was equally struck by the force of the performance: "Perhaps the greatest surprise is Marie Dressler, who steps out of her usual straight slapstick to stamp herself as actress with an affecting knack of genuine pathos. As a tipsy old street walker, superannuated at her trade but richly human, she accomplished the unusual feat of drawing applause at the finish of a scene."[49] *Photoplay*'s James Quirk added to the chorus, "It is no criticism of Garbo to say that it is lucky for her Marie Dressler was only in the first two reels. If she had remained throughout, it would have been a case of grand larceny."[50] Not only had Dressler successfully captured the character and exceeded the bounds of her small role, but she made the leap from comedy to drama with extraordinary success. The techniques of movement and gesture, sentiment and excess that had proved so useful in her slapstick comedy formed the basis of her sentimental performances. And the model of self-sacrifice, self-mockery, humility, and wisdom that formed the basis of the character of Marthy also became a formula for Dressler's starring roles.

Conclusion

> Marie Dressler regularly steals two-thirds of the pictures in which she appears—so every now and then they get tired of it all and give her a chance to do anything she wants as long as she wants—which just suits me perfectly.
>
> —Creighton Peet, *Outlook and Independent,* 1930

By refusing the marginality of the supporting actor's position, Dressler actively resisted the process of her erasure and quickly graduated to the category of star.[51] In order to contain her transgressive behaviors within the industrial logic of the studio system, MGM found it best to accommodate her in lead roles, rather than allowing her to rupture the films from the margin. But there were few ready-made vehicles for a woman who was too old, too loud, too big, too energetic, too funny, and too queer for conventional romantic leads. As a result, MGM's screenwriters found literary properties or invented new narratives that were very heavily influenced by Dressler's iconic role in *Anna Christie:* funny, sentimental, motherly characters sacrificing themselves for a young man or woman in need. The roles that were developed for the studio's best-loved star told stories about matriarchal families, towns and businesses, female friendships, and feminine heroism, and they always made room for the lush bodily energy of Dressler herself. The ideological richness of these unusual films are an outcome of the actress's vigorous performance style and her successful manipulation of the unstable industrial structure of early sound filmmaking. The next three chapters deal with the different ways that Dressler's feature films combined, bent, and distorted generic conventions to contain and channel the energies of this utterly unconventional lead actress.

3

Politics and *Prosperity*

The Body Politic

> Hey, Marie! Do you remember Bill Sykes? I'm the bum soldier whose hand you held the day they said they'd have to saw off the other leg. Say, you and Polly Moran were great in "Reducing." I laughed myself cock-eyed. How about sending me an autographed photo to brag to the boys about?
>
> —Fan letter, 1932

The most popular and profitable films of Dressler's starring years were her films with Polly Moran, a series of unpretentious manic comedies featuring broad slapstick that recalled the silent era: pratfalls, pies in the face, drunken stumbling. The low budgets and low-brow humor of these movies have contributed to their being eclipsed by the bigger literary properties of Dressler's career (and Dressler herself hated them), but they are among the most interesting of her films for their populism, their energy, and their portraits of feminine solidarity. Moran has a kind of shrill, nervous comic style that looks even more unbalanced next to Dressler's lumbering, deep-throated maternal gravity (figure 11).

The two women undertake comic physical antics together that often veer toward the trite and even the gross. They are often widows, unencumbered by marital responsibilities. When they do have spouses, the men are ineffectual, overwhelmed by the energy and physical bulk of these comediennes. At least one of the women always has an adult child, whose adventures complicate

FIGURE 11. Polly Moran and Marie Dressler in *Caught Short* (1930).

the lives of the older generation. And Dressler's character always comes out the hero, often at the expense of the boastful or carping characters played by Moran. Though these films lay the groundwork for striking explorations of the social agency of older women, they also articulate an ambivalence about matriarchal social organization. Moran's shrill comic style and unsympathetic characters often make her the object of derision, a foil for Dressler's appealing and humorous maternal figures, and Moran's characters derive from the most narrow stereotypes about feminine shrewishness: interfering mothers-in-law, class-conscious harpies, nagging wives.

But despite these drawbacks, the two middle-aged women at the center of a comedic narrative do allow for some spectacular assaults on female normativity in even their silliest vehicles. For instance, in *Reducing,* the pair tears apart a weight-loss spa in a series of cheap gags (Dressler accidentally backs into the treadmill on-switch, dumping Moran into the mud bath) that represent a clear revolt against the institutionalized pursuit of feminine slimness. The misuse of machinery like the steam bath and the electric vibrating belt shows the quackery of the spa and the masochism of subjecting one's body to these devices. The destruction of the spa is accompanied by Moran's shrill laments about how much each piece of equipment costs, increasing the childish giddiness of watching useless, expensive devices destroyed. These fleshy bodies simply cannot be subjected to these impersonal machines; Dressler's bulk and Moran's flailing are far too human for the regimented devices designed to transform heterogeneous body types into uniform compliant slimness.

Their first few roles together, from *The Callahans and the Murphys* through the stock-market comedy *Caught Short*, stuck to this formula with unremarkable fidelity. But the formula exhausted itself quickly, and critics began to demand more from the studio. Mordaunt Hall wrote of *Caught Short* that "though the rowdy humor is not without effect, one can't help thinking that both Miss Dressler and Miss Moran deserve a comedy of a higher order than this specimen."[1] Dressler's success in dramatic roles also helped effect a change in her public persona. A success story, a survivor, a proven actress, she was no longer perceived as a hammy old lady comic but as a figure of tremendous gravity, beaten down by circumstances, yet still dignified, courageous, and loving. A number of cloying newspaper pieces had completed Dressler's rehabilitation, and her film roles had little choice but to follow along. The MGM screenwriting team (especially Dressler's friend Frances Marion) and the fan press (especially another of Dressler's friends, the sentimental journalist Adela Rogers St. Johns) helped develop a new and highly successful star persona.

The most striking aspect of this transformation is how her new roles exalted Dressler's maternal characteristics: her characters were no longer spinsters, widows, bad mothers, or harridans; they became loving mothers, grandmothers, and surrogate mothers, usually to children who were teenagers or adults, blossoming under gruff maternal wisdom. A family melodrama was added to the plot of *Reducing*, to give Dressler the chance to shine as a sympathetic mother figure, wiping away daughter Anita Page's tears and forcing her boyfriend to marry the young woman who is carrying his child. The gawky old maid Tillie was thoroughly banished by Dressler's new incarnation as the nation's gruffly adoring mother, a woman who had known hard times but come up smiling, full of good humor and folksy optimism.

But despite this transformation, the films of her later career are not as high-minded as all that; they still rely heavily on slapstick, physical humor, and jokes about Dressler's body. Much of Dressler's appeal relied on her willingness to undergo physical humiliation in the interest of comedy, a trait carried over from her Broadway days. These two sides of her persona, rather than rendering her characters incoherent, enriched both aspects of her work; the slapstick comedy became figured as a generous humility that took the arrogance out of her characters' tendencies to hand down trenchant advice, offering instead generous, heroic acts and encouraging speeches. This unpretentious conflation of the maternal and the childlike, the philosopher and the clown, is the core of Dressler's final films. Bill Sykes's fan letter, quoted at the beginning of this chapter, points to this duality in Dressler's persona: Sykes makes a sudden, even unseemly shift between the memory of his amputation and his cock-eyed laughter at Dressler's antics. The emotional extremes associated with pain and pleasure, the maternal (hand-holding) and the infantile (laughter), are unified in Dressler's public roles.

Her films take on a double burden, to repair and distract the nation, to address both the ideological need for answers and the affective need for escape. The advertising campaigns of many of her later films articulated the ways Dressler herself was being marketed as an antidote to the culture of want associated with the Depression. One theater program for *Reducing* features the tag line, "You'll Laugh Yourself Fat!" as though the film would somehow physically nourish the spectator, a rich promise in the early days of the Depression. Next to an image of Dressler and Moran, mouths open and convulsed with laughter, a cartoon figure of an overweight woman stands on a scale, reacting in shock as the dial reaches two hundred pounds (figure 12). The film counters the problem of want with a comic representation of excess. An advertisement for *Prosperity* is printed on a counterfeit hundred-dollar bill, with Dressler's face in the place of Ben Franklin's. The copy reads, "Stop Hoarding Laughs!" and "Enjoy Prosperity" (figure 13). Dressler's offering to the country is figured as food and wealth. Her publicity and films treated her not just as a distraction but as a solution to the nation's problems. If "Depression" is read, as it often was in popular literature, as "depression," an emotional state as well as an economic one, then Dressler's emotional offerings—comfort and comedy—were more palliative than they may at first appear. When *Photoplay* labeled her "the great panacea for depression," the implication certainly was that she could cure, not just comfort, the ills of the motion picture audience.[2] Reaching the heights of her stardom during the depths of the economic crisis, Dressler spoke directly to the sufferings of the audience.

Dressler's star persona could render coherent the connection between the most intimate maternal care and the broadest clowning. Her films, even the silly ones, were figured in the public discourse as acts of love, presented by a woman whose own sorrows lend legitimacy to her apparent ability to

FIGURE 12. Dressler as nourishment: a theater program for *Reducing* (1931).

FIGURE 13. Dressler as currency: publicity material for *Prosperity* (1932).

channel the sorrows of the public. Her interviews are full of simple philosophizing and advice, offered as from a mother. "We have been going through lately what some people call a bad time. I cannot agree with that. It is the finest and the greatest time that has ever happened to the United States of America," she declared, emphasizing the lessons of hard work and community.[3] "Leave children free to choose for themselves," she instructed America's mothers, trying to bring harmony to the generations.[4] Other stars were asked for makeup tips or stories about their relationships. Marie

Dressler's interviews invariably turned to two main themes: how she had survived hardships in her own life, and how she had used those lessons of hardship to bring joy to millions.

Though Dressler was not herself a mother, this sentimental narrative placed her in a maternal position toward the public, a fact that was constantly referenced in her publicity. In one interview, she noted grandly, "It has been a great blessing to me—the opportunity to mother those who needed it and didn't have it. You'd be surprised how many grown-ups still need mothering."[5] On the rare occasions when the star was the subject of gossip, the topic was again hardship and mothering, as in this item from Cal York's gossip column: "Very few people know that Marie Dressler's great affection for humanity is the expression of a hungering and defeated mother love. Marie once had a baby girl of her own. The baby died a few hours after it was born and Marie has never quite reconciled herself to the loss. Marie seldom speaks about it and the studio does not want it to be known."[6] The absence created by the lost baby creates an invitation for a public in need of care. An article in *Modern Screen*, bearing the shocking title "Marie Dressler's Enemies," details how the star received so many letters from fans asking for money, imploring her to adopt illegitimate children, requesting her cast-off clothes, and demanding that she purchase their goods or services that her friends no longer permitted her to open her own fan mail because the outpouring of need and sometimes aggression was making her overwrought.[7] There is evidence that the audience responded to Dressler's maternal persona in a particularly personal way, expecting care or patronage from this woman whose star persona placed the audience in the position of child, whose burdens will be adopted by the good mother. If the public is a family, then the woman's power over the family can find a place in the organization of the state. Dressler occupied a kind of public position during these years that spoke to the fantasy of a familial national community.

Although Dressler had played a similarly active role in supporting the nation during the international crises of World War I, her films attained a new political relevancy in the Depression years precisely because the nation faced a *domestic* crisis. The country's interest had turned inward, and the household was a metaphor for the nation in a new way. Franklin Roosevelt's inaugural address of March 1933 insisted that the road to recovery began with "putting our own national house in order," so as to act as a "good neighbor" to our allies.[8] Amy Kaplan has argued persuasively for the ways that political discourse has constructed the "domestic" sphere in two ways, as the space of the home (feminine) versus the market (masculine), and as the space of the nation (men and women working together) versus the foreign (the alien or savage). These two constructions of the "domestic" are interdependent. Kaplan observes, "If domesticity plays a key role in imagining the nation as home, then women, positioned in the center of the home, play a major role in defining the contours of the nation and its shifting borders with the foreign."[9] By pointing to other nations as "neighbors," Roosevelt was drawing out the sphere of the home to embrace the second meaning. Indeed, many of the first steps taken by his administration furthered this rhetoric of domestication in public life. For example, he adopted the fireside chats, which connected his own home to the homes of constituents, and his own wife, Eleanor, took on a prominent public role. Further, his appointment of Frances Perkins as the first female cabinet member placed women in public offices more powerful than those available to previous generations. Roosevelt's administration crafted a new sense of intimacy in national politics that responded to the anxieties of the Great Depression by assuming a parental, familial political system, rebuilding the nation and building alliances with neighbors.[10]

Though they were released before Roosevelt's administration was put in place in 1933, Dressler's late films with Moran develop a similar logic regarding the domestication of politics, and they speak to some of the same concerns connecting the family and the state. Dressler's persona in these years had become so clearly connected to public anxieties about poverty that these films can be understood to anticipate the way the New Deal would reshape American ideas about the cooperative logic of domestic political and economic systems, the nation as family, and the leader as benevolent parent. The films present unexpected and challenging notions about the place of women in public life, creating maternal comic utopias from a Depression landscape.

Dressler's last two films with Polly Moran, *Politics* (released in July 1931) and *Prosperity* (released in November 1932), draw the maternal figure into the public sphere, where Dressler runs for mayor in the first film, and serves as president of a bank in the second. These films do not simply insert a woman into a masculine public space; rather, they use Dressler's maternal persona to redefine community around the institution of motherhood as an ideology of passionate social nurturance: she will clean up the city as she cleans her house, and nurture its citizens as she nurtures her children. The genre-bending narratives that were built around her late persona found ways to take seriously the business of maternal public authority, while maintaining a comic logic of physical exuberance, affective pleasures, and happy endings.

Motherhood and the Comic

> "No joke about a mother ever gets a laugh," he insisted most dogmatically. "We've tried that, and we know. You can't joke about a mother in even the lightest, mildest way. If you do, the audience sits there cold, and you get no hand."
>
> —Theodore Dreiser interview with Mack Sennett, 1928

It was no easy task to combine Marie Dressler's trademark slapstick comedy with the often-sentimental narratives of motherhood in which Hollywood (and even more immediately, Louis B. Mayer) tended to traffic. Dressler's transformation from old biddy to wise mother necessitated a rethinking of the maternal role. When Mack Sennett claimed that audiences will not tolerate maternal comedy, he was observing a trend that has held true through much of the history of American film comedy.[11] Feminist theorists of the comic have described in detail how comedy thrives on anarchy and pits itself against the kind of sociality and order that women have usually represented in classical Hollywood filmmaking. Molly Haskell pointed out in 1977 that the anarchistic ethos of slapstick comedy is boyish, specifically rebelling against feminine principles of order; comedy, she says, "instinctively sets out to destroy, through ridicule or physical assault, the props of an orderly society over which woman presides."[12] Joanna Rapf has argued persuasively, "If women are indeed primal earth mothers, sources of life and order, comfort and reassurance, apple pie, chicken soup, and everything that builds a foundation to give others the strength to grow, then comedy as Haskell defines it, is anathema to the feminine."[13] The feminine that both Haskell and Rapf (and many others) have described is clearly a maternal one, nurturing and life-giving and humorless.

While the sexual woman, the preadolescent woman, and the harridan have all found (admittedly ambivalent) places in the comic canon, the category of femininity that has been historically most at odds with the comic is the maternal. Lucy Fischer's influential essay "Sometimes I Feel like a Motherless Child" demonstrates admirably how, unable to reconcile the sentimental maternal with the anarchic comic, classical modes of comedy resist images of positive mothering. Drawing out Sigmund Freud's theory that comedy is a form of sexual bonding between men, designed to displace and humiliate the woman, Fischer demonstrates how women in film comedy tend to be "abandoned to the world of men" (in Stanley Cavell's phrase) or inscribed in a logical frame defined by the masculine erotic. Her article argues that from the silent era through the present, comedies of motherhood are extraordinarily rare. Where it appears, most notably in comedies like *It's a Gift* (1934) or *Throw Momma from the Train* (1987), mothers are nasty and controlling. In the parallel comedies of male motherhood, like *The Kid* (1921), *Mr. Mom* (1983), or *Three Men and a Baby* (1987), women have been forced out of the maternal role altogether.[14] Beyond these clarifying examples, all genres of comedy tend to participate in this effacement of positive mothering. In comedian comedies and buddy comedies, women are generally pushed to the periphery. In romantic and screwball comedies, mothers are often absent, dimwitted, or comically overprotective, necessitating the young lovers' primary attachment to one another.

Applying Fischer's insights to the thirties as a limited cultural moment, one finds the henpecking wives/mothers of *Judge Priest* (Fox, 1934), *The Awful Truth* (Columbia, 1937), *Fifth Avenue Girl* (RKO, 1939), or *Made for Each Other* (United Artists, 1939); the daffy, helpless mothers of *Dinner at Eight* or *My Man Godfrey* (Universal, 1936); and the frequently absent mothers in Deanna Durbin or Shirley Temple comedies. Adults in romantic comedies (as in fairy tales and Disney films) often had utterly delightful fathers but no mothers at all, as in *It Happened One Night* (Columbia, 1934, *Libeled Lady* (MGM, 1936), *You Can't Take It with You* (Columbia, 1938), or *Bachelor Mother* (1939). The charismatic supporting actors who filled these fatherly roles—Walter Connolly, Charles Coburn, Eugene Pallette, Jean Hersholt, Edward Everett Horton, and sometimes Lionel Barrymore—were among the most distinguished and endearing supporting players of the 1930s, many of them receiving billing equal to that of the romantic leads. The women of this same generation—Alice Brady, Margaret Dumont, Billie Burke, May Robson, Beulah Bondi, Mary Boland, Lucile Watson, Edna Mae Oliver, and Allison Skipworth—lack this charming understanding and bluster, specializing instead in playing comedic "dumb Doras," imperious dowagers, and shrill foils for male comedians.[15] Dressler herself had played bad mothers in several of the early comedies of her comeback, as in *The Patsy* (MGM, 1928), in which she steals the show while towering over her henpecked daughter, played by Marion Davies. But Dressler's career in the land of bad mothers was a short one. More notably, her contemporaries Kathleen Howard (often the wife in W. C. Fields movies), Margaret Hamilton (*The Wizard of*

Oz's Wicked Witch of the West), and Polly Moran (Dressler's frequent co-star) created memorable comic caricatures of carping, insufferable mothers, wives, landladies, and town gossips that played upon the worst stereotypes of threatening older women.

Compare this history of maternal anxiety in comedy to the ever-present function of the maternal in sentimental melodrama. The sound era was ushered in by Al Jolson's singing to his mother in *The Jazz Singer* (Warner Bros., 1927), a much-copied film whose prime features (music, Broadway, family melodrama) became the first staples of the sound cinema. In the *Jazz Singer* knockoff *Mother's Boy* (Pathé, 1929), for instance, Beryl Mercer plays a dying mother whose estranged son returns to her bedside and saves her life through song. The mother fad that helped inspire the song "Mammy" reached back a generation in popular song. Clyde Hager's lyrics for the 1918 song "That Wonderful Mother of Mine" speak directly to the genre's nostalgia:

> The birds never sing but a message they bring
> Of that wonderful mother of mine;
> Just to bring back the time that was so sweet to me,
> Just to bring back the days when I sat on her knee.[16]

These songs found a strong resurgence in the late 1920s, when a new crop followed in the wake of "Mammy." For instance, Charles King, in *Hollywood Revue of 1929* (MGM) (one of the watershed films of Dressler's comeback), sings a similar ballad to motherhood that treats the institution in maudlin, quasi-religious terms:

> Your mother, and my mother, too,
> You know that her heart was a shrine;
> And the one up above sent his message of love
> Through your mother and mine.[17]

However long they had been in the public consciousness, sloppy mother songs had become an epidemic in the late 1920s; Anita Loos's 1928 novel *But Gentlemen Marry Brunettes* contains the tossed-off observation, "And Dorothy says that if we could only manage to get all the song writers to meet Henry's Mother, it would be the quickest way to free the world of Mother songs."[18]

The Jolson character, his predecessors, and his imitators were not isolated in their expressions of exaggerated filial adoration for their mothers. Rather, they were symptomatic of a large-scale overdetermined veneration of the mother, who was invested with almost supernatural powers of perception, sympathy, and intimate understanding of her child. This sentiment was expressed in deliciously excessive melodramatic films such as *The Sin of Madelon Claudet* (MGM, 1929), in which a mother makes an extraordinary series of sacrifices for her son, eventually becoming a prostitute to put him through medical school. The mother was also often used as a signifier of the pain caused by social ills, as in *Mother's Cry* (First National, 1929), when the mother suffers the execution of her criminal son. Indeed, films of the early 1930s that took on political issues or social problems nearly always used the protagonist's mother to signal moments of poignancy, as in *All Quiet on the Western Front* (Universal, 1930), when the young soldier returns from the front for a tearful conversation with his bedridden mother, or in *The Public Enemy* (Warner Bros., 1931), when the criminal's body is dumped on his mother's doorstep. But the melodramatic function of the mother often undermined her political function. Thomas Elsaesser explains that "the persistence of the melodrama might indicate the ways in which popular culture has . . . resolutely refused to understand social change in other than private contexts and emotional terms."[19] In straightforward melodrama, the mother helps personalize, rather than politicize, injustice.

There were several sweet-faced character actresses of the late 1920s and early 1930s who became the familiar embodiments of America's maternal fixation of this time. Probably the most notable of these was Belle Bennett, who played the title character in Goldwyn's 1925 version of *Stella Dallas.* An accomplished actress with a knack for gentle corniness, Bennett played a resourceful middle-class heroine in *Mother* (FBO, 1927), followed by a sacrificing carnival-working mother in *Mother Machree* (Fox, 1928), a sad and mousy mother who nearly throws herself off a building when her husband falls for a younger woman in D. W. Griffith's *Battle of the Sexes* (United Artists, 1928), and the widowed mother of seven children in *Courage* (Warner Bros., 1930), among many other similar roles. Bennett's contemporary Louise Dresser often played a bad mother gone good, as in *Mother Knows Best* (Fox, 1928), in which she plays a pushy stage mother who learns to let her daughter have her own life; or in *The Madonna of Avenue A* (Warner Bros., 1929), when she plays a dissolute mother who takes poison to save her pregnant daughter from poverty; or in *Not Quite Decent* (Fox, 1929), when she plays a singer who finds a long-lost daughter but sends her away again in order to help her avoid the sordid life of the stage. Whether or not their past lives contain some stain of sin, these mothers are defined by passivity, sacrifice, and intense identification with the adult children they love. The heavy cycle of mother films in the late 1920s helped give form to the more glamorous maternal melodrama of the 1930s through the 1950s, populated by younger stars like Marlene Dietrich, Barbara Stanwyck, and Joan Crawford.

Although the maternal melodrama has recurred in each generation, there is reason to believe that the late 1920s and early 1930s provided a high-water mark for this particular cinematic form. The American Film Institute film database lists nineteen titles under the keyword "motherhood" in 1927, and a high of twenty-one in 1930, before dropping into the single digits for each subsequent year of the 1930s. These numbers point to a cycle of mother films immediately following *The Jazz Singer.* One of the first identifiable trends of the talking cinema, the sacrificing-mother film led into the 1930s on this regressive note, establishing an iconicity of the aging, sentimental, self-negating mother, who anchored these technologically advancing films in a comforting past. If talking films were a threat to the audience's sense of comfort, surely the mother songs of *The Jazz Singer, Mother's Boy, Hollywood Revue,* and others were the perfect antidote to the anxieties of sound and a counterweight to the talkies' transgressive potential for representing women's subjectivity through cinema.

This overstated deference to mothers and the institution of motherhood is clearly rooted in a sense of nostalgia, the connection of the idealized memory of life in mother's care with the idealized memory of a cultural past that never was. Melodramatic mother-love reaches into notions of the personal and social past, of conservative attachment to traditional familial arrangements. A Victorian characterization of the mother as the angel in the household, the woman on the pedestal, was at the center of patriarchal social thought. The simplified, sentimentalized representations of mothers of this era were, in some large part, a reaction to the upheavals of suffrage and the expansion of women in the workforce in the Depression. The ideology of separate spheres necessary to underscore this affection for the domestic mother figure was being challenged by the "New Woman" of the 1920s and the ways in which middle-class women were increasingly participating in the public sphere as workers, consumers, and political reformers. The saintly "mother" being celebrated in the sentimental rhetoric of popular film and music was a reference to a previous generation. Indeed, most of these films sanctify the mothers of adult men and women—not young mothers, but the mother whose relationship to her child is primarily based on a shared past. These films and songs represented a nostalgic repudiation of the ways women's public roles were changing the nature of middle-class feminine identity. The role of motherhood took root as a one-dimensional anchor to the conservative past in the film genres of sentiment and melodrama even while it was drained out of the irreverent world of comedy, replaced by fathering, mothers-in-law, and neurotic spinsters.

When Marie Dressler played a funny mother, she was drawing from two separate generic precedents. By inscribing the maternal in a comic frame, her films tended to repurpose the sentimental qualities attached to the institution of motherhood in order to make Dressler the moral center of a household, but also to endow the role of mother with an active and anarchic agency rare in the history of American cinema. Dressler's films reconcile the generic conflict of maternal melodrama and comedy by defining motherhood not simply as a social role, but as a physical one: the maternal shoulder/breast/lap become the sites of pratfalls and other body jokes. The mother's body is not sacrosanct but is constantly debased through physical exuberance. Her subjectivity is not self-negating but authoritative and politically engaged. The mother does not fade away in death and memory; she bursts out of the household into the public world.

Dressler's maternal comedies cohere around a cobbling together of the maternal melodrama and the slapstick comedy. These films preserve the moral authority and sacrificial trajectory of the mother, but they refuse the ideology of separate spheres, hurtling the sentimentally inflated mother into the public world. E. Ann Kaplan argues that melodrama's "contradictory impulses emerge . . . from the tension between a progressive social function—that of permitting expression of sufferings, contradictions, frustrations endured mainly by women within the constraints of the bourgeois family—and a reactionary impulse that has to do with allowing the level of familial relations to mask political/economic/racial conflicts."[20] By moving out of the home and into the marketplace, Dressler's characters bring the full potential of comedy as social criticism to the institution of motherhood, undermining its conservative social function and investing the role with a kind of physical exuberance and anarchic charisma that make motherhood a challenge to the community, rather than a sentimentalized pillar of the patriarchal state. All of Dressler's films of the early 1930s break down motherhood this way, crafting an active, blustering, aggressive mother, who draws her moral authority not from her willingness to give up her own life for her children, but from her willingness to change the political and economic structure of the town in order to make the world a better place for her children. The mayor's race in *Politics* and the bank failure in *Prosperity* demonstrate how Dressler's characters cannot fully care for their own children unless they take on equally the task of caring for the ailing community. These films offer a genre-bending, politically engaged vision of the maternal.

Politics: Marie Dressler and Maternalism

> I don't know a thing about politics. I haven't had time. I . . . I have all my preserving to do.
>
> —Hattie Burns (Marie Dressler) in *Politics*

The extraordinary little comedy *Politics* did not start out as a lesson in feminist civics. The scriptwriter, Tom Mahoney, turned in a story outline on March 9, 1931, that was consistent with the team's earlier vehicles, and so Marie Dressler and Polly Moran were cast as venal and ridiculous old biddies. Mahoney's treatment followed the adventures of a couple of scheming widows plotting to marry a policeman and fireman, run for office themselves, and award their husbands higher pensions. The author's note at the end of this synopsis encouraged, "You can't make this POLITICAL STUFF too big for these two women. They [*sic*] are a world of COMEDY SITUATIONS for WOMEN IN POLITICS."[21]

He was right, but a remarkable thing happened on the way to production for this film. *Politics* was gradually transformed from a little program about a couple of greedy old ladies into a script about the selfless transformation of a community. Joanna Rapf has detailed the process of successive screenplay drafts and reshoots for *Politics*, which slowly removed the drunk jokes, the pratfalls, the lingerie jokes, and the corny action sequences, replacing them with sequences that emphasize Dressler's maternal leadership of the community in need.[22] The film that was eventually released insists on Marie Dressler's iconic maternal presence as an anchor for the film's narrative and the moral compass for its understanding of just what "politics" should be. While Dressler's and Moran's comic antics in *Caught Short* or *Reducing* usually manage to destroy some of the symbols of patriarchal power, their comedic maneuvers in *Politics* actually usurp some of that power, and together the two actors establish a matrifocal community in its place. The film's utopian narrative valorizes women's participation in the public world and the nurturing values they bring to the community.

The new script for *Politics* adapts itself not only to the change in Dressler's persona, but also to the change in the national mood, which had begun to blame the greed and excess of the twenties for the economic disaster. Nick Roddick has argued that Warner Brothers films of the 1930s tended to replicate some of the central ideological tenets of Roosevelt's New Deal:

> The strongest of these was the need to deny that there was anything fundamentally wrong. The Depression, it was implied, had been a passing malfunction in an otherwise efficient system, brought on, perhaps, by greed. There were lessons to be learned from this, but they were lessons of adjustment, not radical change. What this meant in terms of movies was that the same values which had caused the crisis in the first place—rugged individualism; economic incentive as a basis for general growth—continued to be asserted as ways of resolving the crisis.[23]

The happy ending, one of the most abiding characteristics of American cinema, tempered the cinema's tendencies to point out social problems. It ensured that the audience would be presented with a ready solution, however provisional or temporary (the unemployed have found work, the lonely have found love, the business, bank, or town is rescued from evildoers, cheats, and scoundrels). There is no question that Dressler's films participate in precisely this simplistic logic, locating the problem of the community in a few greedy crooks and evicting them from their positions of power. But her films also go a step further, once the crooks are displaced, by replacing the institutional authority in her community with her own maternal presence.

The narrative frame of *Politics* is, in many ways, like a Warner Brothers gangster film, full of sleazy hoodlums, cops, and shooting deaths. But the centrality of Marie Dressler and her now-familiar form of slapstick comedy in this film displaces the individualist logic of the gangster film and imposes on the narrative the temperance logic of maternalist political leadership: the ideal that women's participation in public life will help bring maternal moral authority into the realm of public policy. The idea that the state should regard its citizens as a mother her children was a familiar one. It had formed the basic justification for women's participation in political life from the mid-nineteenth century. Women's moral authority, drawn from the ideology of separate spheres, became the guiding logic of the Progressive Era that stretched between 1893 and America's entry into World War I in 1917, and coincided with the suffrage and temperance movements. In 1919, Rheta Childe Dorr argued that "Woman's place is Home. . . . But Home is not contained within the four walls of an individual house. Home is the community. The city full of people is the Family. The public school is the real nursery. And badly do the Home and Family need their mother."[24] Taking on issues such as public education, the regulation of child labor and exploitative industrial practices, the regulation of contaminants in food, water, and milk, and the construction of parks and recreation centers, this generation of reformers put into place many of the benevolent faculties of contemporary government. Like Dorr, the women who joined the Progressive movement often argued that the logic of "separate spheres," which placed women in charge of nurturing children within the home, was precisely the impetus for women to participate in public life in ways that could spread the moral influence of middle-class motherhood to the city, state, or nation. Nancy Dye argues, "Many of women's reform efforts were directed at exploring and documenting the connections between the private world of the household and the political and economic institutions of the larger society."[25] Recognizing that in an increasingly industrialized economy, the home could not be isolated from the polity or the marketplace, those holding this political position argued that women's moral influence was more effective when undertaken collectively and publicly to improve conditions for the community as an extension of the family.

After suffrage came Prohibition. As women's access to the public sphere was legitimated in law, the doctrine of separate spheres had begun to dissipate. As the failures of Prohibition became visible through crime, unregulated liquor production, and a general disdain for law, they tended to call into question women's ability to influence the moral life of the nation through public policy. During the 1920s, much of the Progressive zeal faded. Yet the political logic of the Progressive Era lingered in public consciousness, and it would later underline many of the New Deal policies, particularly Roosevelt's unprecedented appointments of women to public offices, and the establishment of welfare and Social Security. In light of the economic devastation of the early 1930s, the tremendous success of *Politics* suggests that the public was once again ready to explore the idea that the nation needed its mother.

In *Politics*, directed by Charles Reisner (a regular of the Dressler-Moran films made in Harry Rapf's production unit), Ivy Higgins (Moran) and her stuttering, ineffectual husband, Peter (Roscoe Ates), live in a boardinghouse belonging to the widowed Hattie Burns (Dressler). Ivy neglects her household duties because she is always off at political rallies, so Hattie cheerfully does all the housework and darns socks for Ivy's husband, who spends his evenings at the local speakeasy. Meanwhile, Hattie's pretty blonde daughter,

Myrtle (Karen Morley), is secretly engaged to a bootlegger, Benny Emerson (William Bakewell). When Emerson is wounded in a gangland shooting that also kills the Burns's innocent young neighbor Daisy (Joan Marsh), Myrtle hides her beau in the attic of the boardinghouse, where she can treat his injury, undetected by her mother.

The shooting incident prompts Hattie to accompany Ivy to a rally of women who support Mayor Tom Collins (Tom McGuire), to ask him what he plans to do to protect the children of the town. When he gives an unsatisfactory answer (he is in cahoots with the bootleggers himself), the mild-mannered Hattie becomes enraged and makes an impassioned speech about the need for politicians to stand up to gang violence and protect the townspeople's children. The women in the audience throw Collins out on his ear and declare Hattie's candidacy in his place. The campaign becomes a take on Aristophanes' *Lysistrata:* the men all frequent the speakeasy, so they do not support Hattie's temperance ticket, and many of them raid a political rally in a drunken mob to reclaim their women. In retaliation, the women devise a plan to stop performing housework and other wifely duties in support of Hattie's campaign. Unlike the raunchy *Lysistrata,* however, Production Code mandates and American social mores dictated that this strike be articulated in ways that emphasized housework, rather than sexual congress. The film finds sly ways of hinting at the sex strike, though, as when Hattie describes the parameters of the action as "parlor, bedroom, and bath," or when a young newlywed sleeps over at Hattie's house to avoid her husband's advances.

The plan is effective, and Hattie's victory seems assured until the night before the election, when the wounded bootlegger in her attic is discovered and arrested for Daisy's murder. Hattie tries to resign her candidacy, but her supporters march to her door with torches to show their continued faith. They are met there by the chief of police, come to announce that Emerson is innocent of Daisy's murder. The chief further announces that the police support Hattie's candidacy, and the crowd cheers. The film ends with Hattie, as mayor, marrying her daughter to the reformed gangster, with Ivy—the town's new "Commissioner of Garbage"—as matron of honor.

Politics begins with an intertitle declaring the universality of the issues it explores: "This film is dedicated to women, who have been fighting for their rights ever since Adam and Eve started the loose-leaf system." The Eden theme is sustained throughout the film, most notably in the botanical names of most of the female characters (Ivy, Myrtle, Daisy), their flower-print dresses, and fruit-topped tables. Also, the dialogue explicitly recalls the opening title, as when Ivy asks her husband, "Without us women, where would you men be?" and he replies, "In the g-g-garden of Eden, eating apples." But it is the women in this film who are still in the garden; their homes are full of plants and birds, while outside is a gangster-film world of mean streets and speakeasies. Temptation comes not in the form of apples, but alcohol. The women have to tempt the men back into the home partly through the mechanism of sex (wholesome, marital sex), to return the men to their families and the feminine world.

Continuing the biblical theme, the name of the town, Lake City, recalls the story of Noah's Ark. The expulsion from the garden has given rise to a town inundated by sin and liquid, an association realized when the men raid Hattie's campaign in a drunken mass and a thunderstorm sends the whole lot home. There is evil in the world, and Hattie *Burns* is the figure of fire, an elemental contrast to water, and the answer to the town's problems. Fire recalls the domestic icon of the hearth, and Hattie's position as the bearer of values associated with the home. In the beginning of the film Hattie reassures Ivy that her pet bird cannot escape up the chimney, as the flue has been closed for the summer. The house is blocked off from the outside world; the hearth is cold; the isolation ensures there can be no fire. But with Hattie's political conversion, fire finally enters the frame with the procession of torch-bearing supporters who arrive at Hattie's door on the eve of the election. Fire has moved outside the home, to the street and the neighborhood, igniting the passions of the town's electorate. An ambivalent image of Hattie's force within the community, fire is comforting and domestic, but also the instrument of righteous cleansing and wrath.

Hattie Burns's competence in the public sphere is born of her moral competence in the private sphere. Her commitment to women's work is repeated ad nauseum in the film, as she is shown serving dinner, darning socks, folding up tablecloths, and plucking chickens while singing, "I'm only a bird in a gilded cage," reiterating the garden theme, but figuring the home as cage, the limited private sphere that temporarily keeps her out of the public square. But Hattie's moral authority is rooted in the fact that she derives significant moral satisfaction from her housework. The first time they discuss politics, Ivy boasts that she was born for "important things," to which Hattie, never pausing from her housework, replies, "Me, too—washing and darning and ironing." Dressler's performance as Hattie emphasizes her genuine pleasure in housework—she hums or sings as she moves about the house, and smiles when offering to do work for Ivy or Peter. Hattie's devotion to the domestic limits her political potential—she has "all her preserving to do," that is, keeping the status quo, which is corrupt, dangerous, and slowly intruding on her insulated household.

But Hattie's devotion to the domestic also shows the extent to which the personal truly is the political. Because of her mastery of nurturing and caring, she is immediately able to relate Daisy's murder to the political process, to see that the state is behaving negligently toward its children. She tells Tom Collins, "You'd get the vote of every woman in town if you'd only see that our children were being taken care of—that they were safe." She asks him to align the state's interests with the interests of the children. Her innate desire to nurture, which had previously excluded Hattie from public politics, becomes the very impetus to join, to mother the city the way she has mothered Myrtle, Ivy, and Peter, and to clean the city as she cleans the house. Hattie takes up the analogy of women's work and the public sphere, just as Lysistrata explains to the city councilor that the organization of the nation-state is like balancing a household income or spinning wool, a task that requires making order out of disorderly materials: "Say that the wool's a mass of tangles. Take it thus . . . / Draw it apart with spindles—make some sense of it. / That's how we'll loosen up this war—if we're allowed."[26]

But while *Lysistrata* is set in the public spaces of Athens, *Politics* is mainly set in the Burns home, a choice with radical implications (figure 14). In the beginning of the film, Hattie insists to Ivy that the town is fine, that good people should simply stay away from the speakeasies, to isolate themselves in their own homes (the garden, the ark). She wants to leave the public work to the men, but finds that the men lack the women's moral conviction. To show how the men of the town are incapable of true reform, the film feminizes the male characters, rendering them silly and powerless even before the women's strike forces them to take up mops and buckets. The first scene shows Peter looking for his pants, which he finds wrapped around Ivy's birdcage. The man of the family has lost his pants, a potent symbol in the Great Depression for the crisis of masculine roles as men lost the ability to earn money. The romantic lead, Benny Emerson, is wounded almost immediately upon entering the story, and he spends most of the film incapacitated, hidden, and in Myrtle's care. Tom Collins is humiliated in his political rally by the fervor of the women, who leap up onto the stage and begin celebrating in such an unladylike manner that one woman's hat comes off, and Ivy Higgins loses her skirt, prancing around the stage in a slip. The wild political fervor of Dressler's women frightens and shames the men. When the mob boss Jim Curango brings Hattie roses in an effort to lure her into his evil doings, he is summarily rejected. Hattie tells him to take the flowers to Tom Collins, an image of homosexual courtship meant to humiliate and emasculate the two leaders of the film's masculine criminal element. The only male character who retains his authority throughout the film is the police chief, a convenient but minuscule character whose approval guarantees the success of Hattie's candidacy. Women are on the side of law, and he is their ally in the enforcement of their moral will. It is a moral will determined by the feminine sphere of temperance law, but still requiring masculine legitimation in the gangster film world of Lake City's streets.

FIGURE 14. Hattie Burns undergoes a political epiphany within her own home in *Politics* (1931).

Because their conduct has put the town's children in danger, the men of Lake City must take over the duties of motherhood in order to learn the lessons of civic engagement. When Ivy throws Peter out of the bedroom and he goes to the barn to sleep, he wakes up with a brood of chicks on his chest and declares, "Ye gods, I'm a mother." When the women's strike forces the men to take over the maintenance of their households, nearly all of the images show men performing duties of motherhood or nurturing, rather than simple housekeeping. One man walks a tiny dog; another pushes a baby carriage. The man hanging out laundry is hanging out diapers, while his wife sits in the sun to dry her hair. The wife starts to get up when she hears the baby cry, but she then remembers the strike and keeps her seat, sending her husband to tend to the child. In one of the film's most fascinating ironies, the women give over the daily tasks of mothering in order to achieve a more perfect maternalist state, attentive to the safety of their children. Meanwhile, the film insists the men must learn the lessons of women's work, particularly the nurturance of the young. Ultimately, *Politics* shows the entire community embracing the values of motherhood.

When Hattie goes out into the world and finds her cause, she heals the public problems by bringing them into her own home for a political meeting. She is conferring with the other women when her daughter interrupts the meeting to ask what her mother would like at the store. Without leaving her supporters, Hattie asks her daughter to pick up some frankfurters and some cheese. Dressler delivers this line while holding Myrtle's hand, patting it comfortingly in sight of her political allies. This peculiar domestic moment further humanizes Hattie, and again Dressler's confident and seemingly unconscious gestures further locate her politics and her domestic concerns in the same spaces, the same scenes. Hattie and Ivy fold the tablecloth while singing "Happy Days Are Here Again," making the house a place of productivity, harmony, and political optimism. The film takes this utopian notion to its furthest point in the epilogue, when Myrtle is married to the former bootlegger. Hattie, as mayor, has reformed the masculine world of violence and alcohol and integrated it into the feminine sphere of marriage and domesticity. City Hall in this final scene is decked out in flowers for the wedding, a Garden of Eden welcoming the reformed gangster back into the culture of feminine home, seamlessly transported into the public world.

Prosperity: Dressler and the New Deal

> I am afraid of only two things in the world. Fear and Self.
>
> —Marie Dressler, *Photoplay,* October 1932

> So, first of all, let me assert my firm belief that the only thing we have to fear is fear itself.
>
> —Franklin D. Roosevelt, Inaugural Address, March 1933

Admittedly, there's something glib in my juxtaposition of these epigraphs. But I place these statements together not for comic effect or to exaggerate Dressler's political prescience, but because the similarities in language and sentiment are typical of the ways Marie Dressler's public persona of the early 1930s took on the role of public counselor, cheerleader, and mother figure, which is to say that Dressler's star persona anticipated the rhetoric of the New Deal. She was in the business of comforting the public, providing optimism and encouragement, castigating the greedy or venal, and preaching collective action from about 1931 onward, or sometime before Roosevelt accepted the nomination for the presidency in July 1932. The film that demonstrates this logic most directly is *Prosperity,* released in November 1932, just after the election of Franklin Delano Roosevelt.

Prosperity's publicity campaign rather shamelessly allied Dressler and Moran with Franklin D. Roosevelt's popularity and America's enthusiasm for change. Though Louis B. Mayer was a staunch Republican who had campaigned for Herbert Hoover, the fervor sweeping the country was so powerful that Roosevelt became the implicit backdrop of the comedy *Prosperity,* rendered visible in a publicity campaign that directly referenced the recent election. One MGM ad used a photo of the two actresses with FDR, emphatically proclaiming, "GIVE AMERICA 'PROSPERITY' MR. ROOSEVELT! Hooray for our new president! Sincerely Yours, Marie Dressler, Polly Moran, THE MGM 'PROSPERITY' GIRLS!"[27] MGM's campaign to sell the film to theater owners used the opening lines "PROSPERITY IS POSITIVELY NOT AROUND THE CORNER! Face the Facts! Don't be FOOLED! Metro-Goldwyn-Mayer dares to tell the TRUTH! IT'S HERE RIGHT NOW!"[28] More family comic melodrama than political satire, *Prosperity* is a film that relies on the sense of optimism being broadcast by the country's enthusiasm for its new president, and it plays with the slogans that would come to mark the discourse of the New Deal.

Sharing a similar optimism and popularity, Dressler was connected to

Roosevelt in a number of striking ways, even before the few years when her publicity presented her as an antidote to the national crisis. A reviewer describes Dressler's character in *Anna Christie* as having "a beaming smile as confident as Roosevelt's."[29] Dressler sold Liberty Bonds with Roosevelt as early as 1918, when he was assistant secretary of the navy, and they got along well from the start (by some reports she fell off the stage and landed on him, but all parties recovered well from the incident).[30] She served as chairwoman of his birthday ball in 1934 because he declared her his favorite actress.[31] Indeed, even the song "Happy Days Are Here Again," adopted as Roosevelt's theme song during the 1932 campaign, is featured in both *Politics* and *Prosperity*. MGM owned the rights to the song because it originated in an MGM film, *Chasing Rainbows* (which featured Marie Dressler in a supporting role). Dressler was a great supporter of the new administration, visited the National Recovery Administration headquarters in Washington, D.C., and gave a radio address in favor of the Mobilization for Human Needs. Her autobiography contains this gushing tribute to her friend: "The President is human. He has made some mistakes. No doubt he will make others. But there is one thing of which I am certain, as I am certain that God is Love. It is this: Franklin Roosevelt is ruled by one thought and one prayer—to lead the country wisely and safely out of what has been a hideous mess. He has made a heroic beginning. I believe he will take us all the way—if we have the courage and faith to go where he leads."[32] Dressler uses the rhetoric of faith and prayer to underscore her quasi-religious devotion to Roosevelt. Written at the end of her life (the autobiography was published posthumously), in sentimental language, this passage praising the new president is a logical extension of the ways Dressler's stardom had come to overlap with the rhetoric of Roosevelt's new presidency.

Roosevelt, for his part, had a talent for relating the affairs of state to the domestic sphere. His speeches were peppered with references to the Depression's impact on the citizen's home life: "See how the events of the past three years have *come home* to specific groups of people. . . . *Go into* the home of the business man. He knows what the tariff has done for him. *Go into* the home of the factory worker. He knows why goods do not move. *Go into* the home of the farmer. He knows how the tariff has helped to ruin him."[33] The repeated invocation of the home connects the masculine workers being described with the feminine space where their hardship has become evident. Roosevelt's promised leadership (abolishing the tariff, healing the relationship to the foreign) is presented as a solution to the nation's domestic problems. Roosevelt's "New Deal" speech of 1932 rather explicitly scapegoated a few powerful business interests for the economic disaster, locating them also in the logic of the familial, and casting the Republican leaders as bad and illicit fathers: "If they claim paternity for one [prosperity in the 1920s] they cannot deny paternity for the other [the Depression]."[34] Roosevelt, then, is the good parent, who will take responsibility for the national household and put it in order.

By emphasizing the domestic in this way, the rhetoric of Roosevelt's presidency risked feminizing the president (if the Republicans were bad fathers, was the more caring and attentive man more like a good mother?). His administration was particularly sensitive to this issue insofar as its members had worked extremely hard to conceal his disability from the nation for fear that it would make him seem too weak to lead effectively. Though Roosevelt's handicap was well hidden, the public did know that he had battled polio, and the fact was used as a humanizing element to appeal to women. A flier distributed by the Roosevelt campaign argued for "Three Reasons Why Every Woman Should Vote for Roosevelt and Garner," connecting national economic policy with domestic tranquility. The first two reasons to vote for FDR were traditional private-sphere concerns: the safety of children and the sanctity of the home. But the third reason further tied Roosevelt's disability to "feminine" virtues of heart and sentiment: "Roosevelt has known pain and hardship. He has fought a courageous and winning battle to health. He can understand the man and woman who is today struggling against terrific odds and he can be trusted to put heart as well as mind into the battle."[35] The flier explicitly associates his experience of physical illness with the feminine value of "heart," assuring women voters that his leadership will be compassionate and inclusive, and again emphasizing the imagery of the nation as a family, overseen by a patriarch whose experiences of pain lend him some feminine, even maternal qualities.

But the flier also places its strongest emphasis on the issue of recovery—Roosevelt's uncompromised masculinity, his readiness for leadership. The pamphlet uses the word "battle" not once, but twice, continuing the martial imagery that Roosevelt used in public speeches of the early 1930s. When articulations of the feminine and domestic aspects of Roosevelt's policies emerge from New Deal rhetoric, they are nearly always followed by some imagery of warfare, intellectual prowess, or masculine business leadership. Roosevelt's speechwriters, and the president himself, were very conscious of how the leader's disability would be understood as a sign of weakness in the leader, were it ever fully apprehended by the public or exploited by his enemies.[36] His speeches and public appearances cultivate a cooperative logic of domestic policy, underscored by assurances that the country will not be weakened by these potentially feminizing policies because they will be implemented with masculine discipline and courage.

Dressler's films articulate a similar paradox. Dressler shows the promise of female leadership in the public sphere, applying the "feminine" virtues of compassion and community to tough public roles. But her films battle a lingering ambivalence about the ways women's public work in the Depression years could serve as a reminder of male unemployment, and the ways America's traditional breadwinners were being feminized by their inability to provide for their families economically. Dressler's films of the 1930s fail to resolve the ways her competence disenfranchises the male leaders of the community. These films pay lip service to patriarchy, even while they demonstrate how masculine leadership has caused the ills from which Dressler must help the community recover. The displacement of male figures in her films is comic, and simplistic, but the very cartoonishness of these figures pointed to the lingering mistrust of maternal authority that kept Dressler's films from becoming truly radical. The nation was in a state of crisis, and Dressler's comforting maternal persona clearly touched a chord with a public that wanted to be reassured that everything was going to be all right. But this formula inherently infantilized not just the male characters in her films, but also the audience, which looked to Dressler for comfort and care. These films presented an exaggerated impression of Dressler's authority, tinging it with anxiety. Though this ambivalence is played for comedy in *Politics*, by the time of *Prosperity* the marginalization of male leadership has become a profoundly problematic displacement of gender privilege. Competitions for authority strain the relationship between the Dressler character and her son, and the son becomes a simpering and infantilized character. The film hits all its marks in papering over these problems, but in the end, the generic confluence of sentimental motherhood and slapstick comedy comes to a more awkward intersection than in *Politics*, leaving the viewer with the sense that all is not quite right in the cinematic polis.

In *Prosperity*, Marie Dressler plays Maggie Warren, the matriarch of a small town called Warrensburg, who has been president of the family bank since her husband's death. It picks up where *Politics* left off: with a wedding. The film opens in the prosperous year 1925, when Maggie relinquishes her job to her son, John (Norman Foster), as a wedding present, reminding him always to keep the bank's capital, $100,000 in government bonds, as security against runs on the bank.

The film cuts forward to 1931, when John and his wife, Helen (Anita Page), have two small children. As bank president, John decides to use the sacred bonds to make a loan to some shady builders. There is a run on the bank, caused by the hysterics of John's shrill mother-in-law, Lizzie Praskins (Polly Moran), and he doesn't have his collateral to stave it off. The bank closes for six months, until the building loan is repaid, and Maggie and her son sell their houses and possessions to tide over the townspeople. The whole family moves in with the insufferable Lizzie. Realizing that the building will run over schedule, and therefore jeopardize the return of the bonds, a desperate John forges a certificate of completion and leaves it in the care of the shady builders.

Clerking in the market to make extra money, Maggie struggles with the customers' lack of cash and her own sense of responsibility. Realizing that the town does not lack goods, only currency, she convinces the townspeople that they don't need cash to live, teaching them to barter goods and services instead. Her small-scale improvisation gives her a larger idea, and she recruits the townspeople to contribute their own labor to complete the building in which their money is invested. The building is finished under budget and ahead of schedule, and the town rejoices, while the crooked builders secretly catch a train out of town with the precious bonds, assured that John will not bring charges against them because they have evidence of his forgery.

Learning of her son's mistake, and that all their heroic efforts have been in vain, Maggie decides to kill herself to leave her insurance money for her son to reopen the bank. As she sits at home with her poison (which we, the audience, realize is not poison at all, but Lizzie's expensive diet serum, Prun-O-Lax, onto which she has pasted a poison label to prevent her poor relations from sneaking doses), her son catches the train, punches the crooks, and regains the bonds. The family returns to find Maggie's insurance policy out on the table, the woman herself already having emptied the bottle. They tell her of the recovered bonds, and she panics, thinking she's about to die needlessly. Lizzie soon discovers the bottle labeling error, and with great relief, Maggie steps out onto her balcony to give a speech to the cheering townspeople below.

> I'm awfully glad to be with you, so unexpectedly. How glad, you'll never know. We've been going through a tough time together, this town and this grand country of ours. It's a young country, and it's been having a bad attack of growing pains. But the worst is over and we've learned a big lesson. Yeah, we've learned that the stock market may go down, but the sun will always come up. But the biggest thing of all we've learned is this, that now we know that we can be just as happy with two rooms and a sink as we can with sixteen rooms and a marble bathroom . . . a marble bath . . . You'll have to excuse me.

With this, Dressler must run off the balcony to attend to her Prun-O-Lax emergency. The film fades to black, and the words "The End" appear under the music "Happy Days Are Here Again."

In the same year that Frank Capra made *American Madness* (Columbia, 1932), and placed Walter Huston outside a bank door to stave off the dangerous crush of panicky investors, and two years before King Vidor tackled a bartering economy in *Our Daily Bread* (United Artists, 1934), Marie Dressler stood outside a bank, reasoning with the townspeople about faith, hard work, and capital. Maggie takes over the town and organizes it with Rooseveltian optimism, spouting platitudes like, "This country has seen worse days than this, and she's come up smiling. Why? Confidence!" She supports Roosevelt's economic policies by encouraging her fellow citizens to spend their money and get the economy going again: "Oh, things would be all right if people would take their money out of their sock and stick their foot in it." She disavows the shady business practices that Roosevelt blamed for the Depression, telling her bank patrons, "We have learned that selling people out these days is bad business," and "I just want you people to know that not one penny of your money has been used dishonestly." She validates Hollywood's role in the national recovery, pounding her fist into her palm with politicized fervor as she counsels the crowd, "Go ahead, laugh! That's what this country needs is a good five-cent laugh!" This last quote is particularly remarkable, again insisting that an affective recovery is the real solution to "depression," but also tying in the economic end with the price tag reminding the listener that in the current age, all value is expressed in monetary terms. Late in the film, Maggie Warren even puts people to work under a barter system of her own invention, a local Works Progress Association, marked by her insight that "a man's much happier nursing calluses off a saw and hammer than he is nursing calluses off a rocking chair." The film is clearly an optimistic response to the nation's financial hardships, produced during one of the worst years of the Depression, pointing toward the policies that Roosevelt was endorsing for the nation as a whole. The body language with which Dressler punctuates these speeches—raised fists, fingers pointing, arms outspread—is the body language of politicians, selling ideas to an audience from a position of leadership. Standing outside the bank, Maggie convinces the townspeople not to panic. "You've got to have confidence," she implores, arms outstretched, "in me," she finishes, drawing her arms inward, and touching her own chest. This gesture offers up Dressler's own self, her body, as insurance against disaster, a promise that later comes to fruition when she takes poison to restore the bank's assets. It is after this moment in the speech that the crowd's attitude begins to turn.

Maggie's plump body, framed at the center of the crowd, comes to symbolize prosperity itself. There is enough of her, enough love, enough intelligence, enough mothering for the whole town. But despite the happy ending to the town's economic problems, the result of this expansive love this time is a city and a son who are spoiled and dependent. The film uses a milk theme to offer images of mothering gone sour. When Lizzie tells Maggie that her minister marries "the cream of society," Maggie replies, "Today's cream is tomorrow's cheese." When Maggie describes her husband's final illness to Lizzie, she notes that in his delirium the dying man asked for strawberries and cream, impossible to obtain in December. So she gave her husband radishes and buttermilk, and he never knew the difference. When John begins to feel sorry for himself, Maggie consoles him, saying, "It's no use crying over spilled milk." The images are of bad mothering: milk spoiled, the wrong milk, milk gone to waste, like Maggie's good advice that John must protect the bank's investment. And mothers are verbally derided in this film. When Helen tells Maggie on her wedding day, "I have two mothers now," Maggie breaks her embrace with the younger woman, touches her own hair in wonderment, and replies self-deprecatingly, "That's a double dose for any girl to start out in life with." When Maggie starts the crowd outside the grocery store to bartering, one man offers, "I have a mother-in-law I'll trade for a good pot roast." Too much mothering is suffocating, rancid. It is a moderation of motherhood that allows the family and the society to run properly.

Just as Roosevelt's feminine evocations of home, hearth, and heart were carefully tempered in his public rhetoric by the military metaphors and masculine charisma of his public life, Dressler's folksy maternity is tempered by the films' constant returns to masculine labor, pushing Dressler out of the way to make room for male heroism and male competence. The film creates from its overdose of mother's milk a nearly unsympathetic character in the figure of John, a profoundly indulged young man who is entrusted with the bank at too young an age, and who makes terrible mistakes in its management. His mother cleans up after him each time, handling the crowds in his place during the run on the bank, masterminding the completion of the building, and ultimately offering her life for his welfare through the suicide attempt. A guardian of the patriarchy, she gives up the bank far too soon, granting her son unearned power and responsibility in order to invest him with the masculine authority that she believes he requires as a married man, but she does not ever really leave. When Lizzie starts the run on the bank by demanding her whole account be closed, the teller responds that he'll have to check with the president. Maggie and John sit together in the president's office, and it is Maggie, chosen for her diplomacy, who goes out to oversee the transaction and gives the teller permission to close the account. She still acts as president, performing a duty that only the president is authorized to perform, using feminine skills of negotiation and a calm, motherly voice, while John calls Lizzie foolish names ("turkey" "worm") from the impotent privacy of the president's office. John's adolescence is prolonged by her indulgence.

John whimpers and apologizes, one minute sheepishly admitting that it must take up all her time cleaning up after his mistakes, and the next minute arguing that the family should just give up on the bank and on their responsibility to the townspeople. "The Warren name can rot for all I care!" rages John. Maggie, finally pushed beyond her maternal forbearance, slaps him. Dressler performs this as a backhanded slap; shocked stillness follows as John rushes from the room. Her body communicates horror and ambivalence, a rage born of her "masculine" identity as guardian of the bank, the Warren name and the city, followed by a paralysis anchored in her "feminine" identity as John's mother, who cherishes even her unworthy son. Maggie is torn between her loyalty to the patriarchy of her husband and his ancestors and the child she is trying to integrate into their legacy. And she takes that responsibility seriously, arguing always for male privilege in her defenses of her son. When Maggie instructs her minister on how to conduct John's wedding, she tells him that he should stick to the traditional ceremony: "put all the love, honor, and obey that you can cram in there—we want this to last!" Mother-in-law Lizzie, meanwhile, asks her own minister to leave out the "obeys," as John tends to be "bossy" anyway. Similarly, one of the arguments that pushes John out of his mother-in-law's household has to do with his son Buster's hair. At the age of about four or five, the boy still has old-fashioned aristocratic long curls. John and Maggie think it's time to cut his hair short, while Lizzie swears that it would break her heart to see his beautiful hair cut off. While Maggie tends to take the side of allowing men to maintain the social markers of privilege, Lizzie aggressively fights against them. But both women show up on Christmas Eve dressed as Santa Claus, spoiling John's delight in his own Santa Claus costume. The three Santas, with their long white beards, are a striking visual reminder that there are too many heads of household, that the women are taking on roles that undermine John's attempts to clarify his masculine privilege.

Lizzie Praskins, perhaps Moran's least likable character, a mother-in-law to justify any joke ever made about mothers-in-law, is a demonized parody of female heads of households, and of women who don't want to accept the mandate to "obey." She carps, whines, and boasts, nearly destroying the bank, the town, and her daughter's marriage in the process. She is used throughout the film to represent the dangers of pessimism, selfishness, or despair, all of which produce real economic consequences like the closing of a small town's only bank. The film enacts its revenge on Lizzie according to the logic of comedy, by subjecting her to an almost ritual humiliation at the end of each scene. At the end of the wedding scene, she stumbles into the cake, gawking into the camera with icing all over her face. At the end of the Christmas scene, the cotton beard of her Santa Claus costume catches fire. At the end of the bank run scene, she crawls through the crowd to reach the locked door, hitching her skirt up past her waist. At the end of the breakfast scene, she accidentally bites down on a caterpillar that has crawled onto her pancake, and she jumps up, causing Maggie to spill coffee into her lap. At the end of the haircutting scene, a rather complicated narrative coincidence results in a tooth being accidentally extracted from her mouth. The humiliation of Lizzie is a form of aggression against the bad mother, the bad mothering that threatens to emasculate John and his curly-haired son.

And yet, Maggie tries to reconcile Lizzie with the rest of the family and with the community many times during the film. Dressler performs these moments very physically, usually drawing Moran into an embrace as she recites lines about how they were girls together, assuming a girlish posture of intimacy to emphasize their mutual history. Dressler flutters around Moran in these scenes, trying to calm her as she would a hysterical child, often patting Moran's shoulders, straightening her collar lovingly, or even placing her hand near the other woman's heart as she speaks to her of love and solidarity.

Dressler performs the role as though she is trying to draw Lizzie into the body politic, to quell her antisocial tendencies by encircling her physically. Dressler's body stands in for the community, and Maggie tries to inspire a greater communal spirit simply by holding Lizzie in a series of cajoling embraces.

But while Lizzie holds too much back from the public trust, Maggie gives too much. She sells all her possessions to pay the bank's debts, keeping only sentimental things: an oil painting of her late husband, a photo of her grandchildren, the napkin ring her son used to cut his teeth, and her mongrel dog. She embodies a charismatic combination of high and low culture: she participates in ideals of leadership and history based on her class background, without the entitlements, disproportionate wealth, and pretensions of the upper classes. Dressler's character in this film, as in many of the Moran films, exists in a kind of class limbo that replicates the vacillations of high philosophical rhetoric and low bodily humor in the films. She is the bank president but wears frowsy print dresses and keeps her knitting tucked in a desk drawer. She lives in a big house, but seemingly without servants. When she moves in with Lizzie, she cajoles her friend to let her cook to earn her keep. She is shown working at four different jobs in the film—running the bank, cooking for Lizzie, clerking in the market, and participating in the construction crew that completes the building. She strides through the film with palpable physical energy and confidence. She does too much work. Her class mobility creates the possibility of her labor, and her competence at these jobs is specifically tied to her son's experience of Depression-era crises of masculine privilege and self-esteem. The comically feminized men of *Politics* are succeeded by one dramatically, dangerously infantilized young man in *Prosperity*, whose failures of responsibility lead to terrible hardship for others.

Only Maggie's transformation from accepting, forgiving, nurturing mother to angry, disciplining mother drives John to action. After his mother slaps him, in the last reel, he takes responsibility for his mistakes, and in a very masculine narrative sequence that is played mostly without dialogue, in slightly accelerated film speed, John drives his car alongside the train, jumps to the ground running, jumps aboard the caboose, kicks in a stateroom door, punches the crooks, grabs the bonds, and makes a break for it out the train window. It has been a very talky movie up to this point, marked at intervals by Dressler's impassioned speeches. Her son is a man of action at last, in an undercranked sequence straight out of the silent era, a genre shift to miraculously bring the film out of the thick narrative tangle that his own mistakes and his mother's comic improvisations have created.

But as Maggie nurtures the son who will replace her, she prefigures her own removal from the public world. She fights that removal, staying to mother long after her usefulness has ended. Yet the child has to grow up, and in *Prosperity*, John's adulthood is marked by a genre change from small-town comedy to adventure film—a manly form that excludes and derides feminine influences. His act of independence, however, also rescues Dressler from maternal melodrama; the result of her successful mothering looks like it is going to lead to her own erasure, the threat of her death. The poison undergoes a magical metamorphosis into a laxative upon his return, a striking metaphor for gross physical humor and the genre change back to comedy. In the final moments, Dressler resumes her role as both a mother and a community leader, glad that the "young country" she loves has "learned a big lesson," as though she is speaking to a child, rather than a town (or, from the movie screen, a nation). The generic conflicts between the maternal melodrama and the family comedy necessitate a seesaw action between Maggie's optimistic, comic acts of leadership, which infantilize her son, and John's criminal or heroic acts of leadership, which push her out of centrality and toward the ultimate threat of self-sacrifice. The comedy genre insists on happy endings; the film must conclude with a speech of Rooseveltian optimism, a joke, and a song. But the joke is finally on Maggie. As each previous scene had ended with a ritual humiliation of Lizzie, the final scene ends with the humiliation of Maggie, her body overwhelming her rhetoric and dragging her off the stage and to the toilet. The film never resolves whether Maggie's role is to take charge, as in a comedy, or step aside, as in a maternal melodrama. The conflation of genres here presents a fascinating conundrum, a Depression parable ambivalent about its own message of maternal moral authority, and finally expressing that ambivalence in its comic humiliation of Maggie Warren.

Conclusion

> If you took any comic strip joke about a mother-in-law, multiplied it by two, added a bank failure, four platitudes about the silver lining, and a vaudeville fox terrier, you would have all the ingredients of Prosperity except the one which makes it human and amusing. This ingredient is Marie Dressler, who always impersonates grunting, sympathetic, noisy, witty, violent, immensely courageous old ladies but somehow manages to do it with enough vitality to make them seem alive.
>
> —*Time*, December 5, 1932, review of *Prosperity*

It is easy, and even tempting, to romanticize the extraordinary political logic of the late Dressler/Moran comedies. Certainly audiences of the time responded to these optimistic and sentimental parables with real fervor. However, it is necessary to admit that her bold film taking on bootlegging was made in the very year Prohibition was repealed, and her film on the banking industry offers a solution that involves punching the crooks' lights out in order to restore the bank's assets. Her films tended to have these easy politics, convenient scapegoats, and simple solutions.

In each case, the generic trajectory of the film branches into two paths. The maternal melodrama asks for the mother's sacrifice (the resignation of her candidacy in the first film, and the suicide in the second), while the comedy seeks reconciliation and celebration. The films have it both ways, demonstrating Dressler's willingness to sacrifice herself, then drawing back the necessity at the last minute to accommodate a comic ending. But the stakes are much higher in *Prosperity* than they are in *Politics*, showing how the maternal melodrama is starting to win out over the comedy, and how the Depression landscape exerts a gravity on the comedy that makes Dressler's efforts at lightness more and more strained. The next chapter will demonstrate the point at which this tension causes the generic balance of comedy and melodrama to break. Marie Dressler's films with Wallace Beery, relieved of the easily scapegoated Moran, are weighted down by the children's problems in ways that require real, not imagined, sacrifice.

4

Min and Bill and *Tugboat Annie*

The Mythic Body

> Her face is like a god's come back to life—
> A face that shows the pain of mortal man;
> And happiness that centuries have known—
> A god who speaks as only idols can.
>
> Perhaps she learned the truth when Time was young,
> And comes again with Heaven-songs of mirth;
> And leaves her god and goddesses alone,
> To live with us a little while on earth.
>
> —poem by Joel Keith

When a fan clipped the above verse from a newspaper and mailed it to Marie Dressler, claiming it "exactly expresses how I feel about you," the star was so touched by the tribute that she had the poem engraved on a small metal plate and carried it around in her handbag. When she died, the poem was read aloud at her funeral, and the engraving was placed in the casket with her body.[1] It is likely that most stars of the 1920s and 1930s were compared in the press, explicitly or implicitly, to gods or supernatural beings.[2] Dressler's own studio, MGM, promised the public "more stars than there are in heaven," intentionally conflating the movie screen, the night sky, and the eternal resting place of the virtuous. But as Marie Dressler transformed herself from a slightly tawdry slapstick comic to the nation's adored surrogate mother and Oscar-winning thespian, these heavenly tributes began to accrue to her public image with unusual force. This chapter will investigate the mythic Dressler, drawing from the folkloric figures of the trickster and the frontier hero to analyze her two films with Wallace Beery, *Min and Bill* and *Tugboat Annie*.

The two films that were the subject of the previous chapter have a rather literal, often simplistic relationship to the sociopolitical world of the early 1930s: *Politics* is about an election, and *Prosperity* is about a bank failure. The Beery films are not the stories of community leaders doing great deeds. They are the stories of little people, social outsiders who stand up and make heroic sacrifices for the good of their children, at great cost to themselves. Rather than prescribing specific social solutions to the widespread suffering of the Depression, these films speak in the language of allegory or parable. The plots are circular, dealing with the cycles of nature and the continuation of families. As Joanna Rapf has argued, they are "about how to endure."[3] And by privileging the personal over the social, these films show a different attention to scale than the Moran series. When the world around her shrinks, Marie Dressler grows. The public Dressler may be a leader, but the private Dressler is a hero. These films frame Dressler's body differently, letting the wind blow through her hair, letting her dwarf the characters and landscapes she inhabits. They mythologize the heroine by framing her against the sea, or by placing her in her rocking chair with a shawl over her shoulder, an unmistakable maternal archetype.

The crisis of the Great Depression inspired a search for heroism and the nobility of daily life in America. WPA murals remain in post offices and other public buildings all over the country depicting heroic, larger-than-life farmers, steel workers, carpenters, pioneers, and other emblems of America's grassroots strength. Writing about the creators of these figures, Erika Doss argues, "In both their private paintings and their public commissions, these modern artists generally depicted American wage laborers as figures of action and autonomy, and thus as exemplars of the work ethic."[4] Many of these images fetishized the strong male body, the Herculean man whose work is a testament to his nearly superhuman might. "Ironically, when social and industrial progress seemed inert," Doss says, "many American artists chose to depict sturdy, strong, muscular, and dynamic laborers, as if these painted and sculpted symbols of manly might and movement might actually propel America out of its economic slump."[5] The creation of a dynamic male hero was a direct response to the sense of helplessness gripping the country. The visual arts depicted the working man as a hero, precisely because a crisis of unemployment had undermined the cultural normalcy of masculine work. A WPA poster from the 1930s conveys one such image, a burly blacksmith standing over his anvil, his right hand over his head, clutching a hammer poised to strike the hot metal he holds by the tongs in his left hand (figure 15). It is an image of almost godlike power, transforming the blacksmith into a massive, bull-like figure, manipulating fire, a modern-day Vulcan. The image mythologizes the American worker.

Few such images depicted the heroic working woman. While "Rosie the Riveter" would become the symbol of working women during World War II, the Depression suppressed such images of women doing paid labor. Barbara Melosh argues that "without exception, wage-earning women are excluded from the monumental and heroic imagery associated with the

FIGURE 15. The Worker as Hero: Works Progress Administration poster (Harry Herzog, c. 1936). Courtesy of the Library of Congress, Prints and Photographs Division, image number LC-USZC2-1116.

manly worker."[6] But compare the figure of the blacksmith with that of Marie Dressler in a publicity photo (figure 16). Broad-shouldered, thoughtful, one stubborn hand on her hip, her jaw set, she leans into the wind. The diagonal positioning of her torso emphasizes dynamism, but the way her body fills the frame suggests solidity. Set against the backdrop of some kind of boat or dock apparatus, Marie Dressler is out among the working people, demonstrating strength and leadership. The framing of her body uses some of the same visual conventions of the heroic working class as the WPA poster. Dressler's comforting maternal persona, discussed in the previous chapter, was buttressed by the ways in which her stardom also attributed to her a kind of monumental character. While the powerful female body at work may have received little attention from the painters of the 1930s, the movies presented precisely such an extraordinary figure in the stardom of Marie Dressler.

Dressler's publicity in these years tended to cast her as a figure of tremendous public stature, expressed literally. On dealing with fame, the *New York Times* emphasized her modesty when confronted by the sheer *size* of her stardom: "Miss Dressler is still skeptical, and a bit confused, like Alice when she found herself a giantess."[7] At the time of *Min and Bill*, Dressler's body became a national fetish object, a colossal mother from whom to draw strength. One critic called her "a magnificent mountain of energetic sorrows and impulses."[8]

FIGURE 16. The Star as Hero: MGM publicity photo (c. 1933).

The poem that opens this chapter claims she has "a face that shows the pain of mortal man." These tributes suggest that she became for fans a kind of archetypal mother during these years. To her admirers, she was larger than life, and she embodied an essential quality of womanhood, transcending the particularity of her time and place. Her films accommodated the star's position by adopting the form of tall tales, stories of an impossibly big hero.

Her costar, Wallace Beery, was also a big, powerful person. Fifteen years Dressler's junior, he lived a wild life, working first for P. T. Barnum as an elephant trainer, and later coming to the movies in 1913, just a year before Dressler's debut in *Tillie's Punctured Romance*. Beery's most popular recurring character in these years was "Sweedie," a dimwitted Swedish maid he played in drag. Although Beery was an accomplished comedy star, the combination of his size and his rubber face also made him an excellent villain, which became his stock-in-trade after the popularity of Sweedie diminished.[9] A skilled character actor with a gift for comedy, Beery worked steadily through the 1920s in supporting roles and slapstick comedies, often playing the lumbering simpleton opposite the smaller, shrewder Raymond Hatton. (Their team comedy is mostly forgotten, but the pair made six features together for Paramount in the late silent era.) His gravelly voice was also an asset when the talkies came along, and Beery earned a supporting actor Academy Award nomination for his first role at MGM, the illiterate murderer Butch in the gritty prison drama *The Big House* (1930), directed by George Hill.

Dressler and Beery were as familiar as the family dog by the time they were teamed in *Min and Bill*. They both had histories that suggested a combination of respectable dramatic training and all-out comic shenanigans. The film was very successfully publicized with the tagline "America's New Sweethearts," a label that captured their oddly sentimental comic chemistry. Unlike the manic Moran films, which paired two comediennes and therefore lacked cultural gravity in the sexist logic of the movies that persists to this day, the Beery films cast Dressler in a fondly chaste partnership with an actor who also embodied a paradoxical associations of lowbrow humor with and skillfully nuanced drama. Higher on the studio ladder than the Moran programmers, these films drew far more prestigious directors, bigger budgets, and better publicity. *Min and Bill* was given to Hill, who had already seen Dressler through *The Callahans and the Murphys* and Beery through *The Big House*. He was also screenwriter Frances Marion's second husband, a D. W. Griffith alumnus, and a former assistant to King Vidor. *Min and Bill* was a runaway hit, earning MGM's best grosses of the year and a spot in *Film Daily*'s list of the top five films of the year. With this film, Marie Dressler became a star of the first magnitude.

America's New Sweethearts having robustly proven their appeal, it is perhaps surprising that it took MGM two years to pair them again, years in which Dressler won her Oscar for playing Min and Beery won one of his own for playing the drunken boxer who tries to redeem himself for son Jackie Cooper in *The Champ* (MGM, 1931). A reunion of two Oscar winners, *Tugboat Annie* was given to Mervyn LeRoy, recently come to MGM from

FIGURE 17. *Tugboat Annie* (1933): Wallace Beery is scared of Marie Dressler.

Warner Brothers, where he had directed some of the best films of the early sound era, including *Little Caesar* (1931), *I Am a Fugitive from a Chain Gang* (1932), and *Gold Diggers of 1933*. Bringing with him some of the populist sentiment and quickness of the Warner Brothers product, LeRoy emphasized the folksy values in this story. The great Gregg Toland contributed extraordinary cinematography, which captured the Puget Sound environment and Marie Dressler's expressive face in gently worshipful detail. The products of talented collaborators, the two films with Dressler and Beery together were *bigger* movies than her Moran films—with bigger budgets, bigger names, bigger publicity, and bigger audiences.

To promote their second collaboration, Dressler and Beery gave silly interviews together, playing the devoted pals for the reporters. "Wally is such a baby," Dressler told the *Los Angeles Times*. "I have to pet and coax him along all the time. I almost have to wipe his nose and change his bibs. I'm the only one he'll let fix his bibs."[10] What a gigantic mother Marie Dressler must be to change big Wallace Beery's bibs! The impression that she towers over him in stature was exploited in both films, which show Dressler scolding, cajoling, and even physically beating Beery. When she is angry with him, as in several scenes from *Tugboat Annie* (figure 17), Beery cowers as though he is physically afraid of her. The tagline for his 1932 film *Flesh* announced, "Women love this dumb, good natured giant!"[11] By casting this big man to play opposite her, and then giving Dressler the advantage in all their many altercations, these two films increase the impression of Dressler's size, her strength, and her maternal authority. Beery encourages that impression by playing these roles as though he were an overgrown child, speaking in slow, drawn-out sentences and incorporating childish physical humor in his parts, like spitting watermelon seeds, or stealing a piece of cake when Dressler isn't looking. As an actor, he made liberal use of a facial expression that suggests a hopelessly naïve and possibly naughty child. Contrasted with the infantile but powerful Beery, the already monumental Marie Dressler is revealed as a mother of mythic proportions.

Min and Bill: A Trickster Tale

> Gee, Min, but you're a hellion. I guess that's why I likes ya.
>
> —Bill

The title card of *Min and Bill* indicates that the screenplay, by Frances Marion and Marion Jackson, was "suggested by the novel *Dark Star*, by Lorna Moon."

Marion later claimed in her autobiography that the screen credit was a ruse to secure her friend Moon some money to pay for the treatment of her tuberculosis. Marion enlisted the help of her friend Kate Corbaley, head of MGM's "reading department," and the two agreed that Moon's gothic story about a betrayed young Scottish woman would never make a Hollywood blockbuster. But realizing that the MGM producers rarely actually *read* the stories they put under contract, Marion and Corbaley devised a scheme to deceive their bosses. At the next production meeting, Corbaley recommended the new novel *Dark Star* to Harry Rapf and his team, and Marion narrated a comic tale about a couple of Puget Sound old-timers who save a young woman from her dissipated mother. Telling the studio heads that it would be a perfect vehicle for Marie Dressler and Wallace Beery, Marion and Corbaley secured a generous $7,500 fee for their sick friend.[12] Lorna Moon used the money to move to a new sanitarium in Arizona where she hoped to recover from her tuberculosis. Sadly, she died of the illness just a week after her arrival.

This film, then, was born out of an act of feminine tricksterism—a knowing deception of the MGM brass by one woman who was a writer and one woman who was a reader. The two used the weaknesses of the powerful against them in order to benefit their fellow women. True tricksters, they turned the subordinate position to their advantage through deception. Marion's autobiography narrates the astonished reaction of Moon, a Scotswoman, when she got her check: "'Lassie! The devil will bite off the tip of your deceitful tongue! Out with the truth!' She threw back her head and laughed merrily. 'Here's proof of the devil in the chimney pot!' It was a letter from Harry Rapf, assuring her that he would make a very good picture out of her comedy though he admitted it was a bit on the wild side. 'I've heard about those men who sell iceboxes to Eskimos but I take off my bonnet to you, lassie.'"[13] According to Sam Marx, the women's sense of victory lasted through the shoot; "Frances sat on the set beside [her husband, director George Hill] throughout the production. She and Kate were ecstatic about the way they had put over their friend's wish; it was part of the fun, a joke on their bosses, adding flavor to their working routine as well as a triumph for their sex."[14]

The trickster is a stock figure in comedy, often the character whose mischief creates the chaos from which comedy emerges. The term "trickster," coined by Daniel Brinton in *The Myths of the New World,* his 1868 study of Native American myth, but now widely used in folklore and anthropology, is common to the mythologies of many cultures. Ancient Greece's Hermes, the

French folk hero Reynard the Fox, the Ashanti spider Anansi, the American South's Brer Rabbit, the Norse god of mischief Loki, and the Arabian Nights' clever Sheherezade are all tricksters, figures who use wit and deception to prevail in impossible circumstances. In *Min and Bill,* Dressler's maternal persona creates a cover for her trickster tendencies, for tricksters are rarely women, even more rarely mothers. She looks harmless, sounds harmless, and her primary achievement in the film rests in convincing those around her that she is *not* motherly. But by successfully hiding her relationship with her surrogate child, she is able to protect her.

Like her joining of comedy and melodrama, Dressler's combining of maternal and trickster characteristics permits her to occupy a curious ideological space; she is a defender of the home, but a breaker of rules, a comforting and sentimental figure, but a challenging and comic one. Confronted with crisis, Min both bears up in maternal fortitude and schemes her way out of it. Dressler's association with the trickster challenges the rules of melodrama, with its emphasis on the melancholy and passive heroine. But her tricks are all tricks of self-sacrifice, lacking the joyful exuberance of the conventional trickster.

Marion's adaptation of Moon's novel was a tricky business indeed. The screenplay did use some elements of Moon's gothic novel, though most of the plot points were fabricated to suit Marie Dressler in the role of Min, a character who is a combination of several characters from the book. Marion shifted the location from Scotland to an unspecified American port town on the West Coast; she took the narrative focus off of the romance of the young orphan and placed it instead on the older generation; and she made the tragic novel into a comedy-melodrama hybrid. Unlike the Dressler-Moran films, which clearly began as comedies and slowly developed melodramatic plotlines to suit Dressler's persona, *Min and Bill* has its roots in gothic gloom, with a couple of rip-roaring slapstick scenes thrown in to appeal to the studio bosses. The result is a wildly unbalanced, utterly unconventional sentimental comedy shot through with anguish and loss.

The film opens on a shot of Bill's ship coming into the harbor. The hatch is opened and a load of giant tuna is revealed below. The film is a big-fish story, set on the harbor in the world of sailors, prostitutes, and dock workers. Min (Dressler) waves to the sailors, and Bill (Beery) takes her aside to show her a secret treasure he has smuggled in: six bottles of vodka. This is the first of many tricks—the lower-class life on the docks requires deceptions but also other coping strategies like superstition and storytelling. Altogether, it adds up to a tall tale, a portrait of how Dressler as trickster transforms the maternal melodrama from a strategy for managing loss into a strategy for physical power.

Min runs a wharfside hotel, where Bill is her tenant. Being nervous about the dangers of the world, Min is superstitious. Walking from the dock back to her home, she steps around a ladder, rather than under it. She gasps and covers her mouth in horror when she breaks a mirror. She tells Bill that she had a dream that a canary flew in the window, a sign of bad luck. The objects in her boardinghouse suggest a house of prostitution (an idea that was explicit in early drafts of the film, but only suggested by the final mise-en-scène of the film), with flowered wallpaper, paper fans, and heavy tassels decorating the doorways, making Min's room a gaudy showplace.[15] Downstairs in the common rooms, a statue of a naked woman is unobtrusively displayed on the far side of the front desk, and a perfume dispenser shaped like a bull's head hangs on the wall. These are markers that the house is or once was a brothel, but they also are totems: they give Min's lair a quality of having built up these objects over the course of many years by the sea, where people come and go and leave things behind (figure 18). These objects suggest a history

FIGURE 18. *Min and Bill* (1930): The cluttered mise-en-scène of Min's bedroom.

and a superstitious power: Min collects things, draws them into the net of her house. Netting, in fact, is the most noticeable element of her home's décor. Min's bedroom is hung with fishnets and dangling decorative fish. Min is a fisher; if you read the net as a web, she is even a spider, ensnaring those who threaten her child.

The child is an orphan girl, the teenage Nancy (Dorothy Jordan), who does housework for Min and is just beginning to receive attention from the lecherous sailors in the boardinghouse. Early in the film, Min defends her right to raise Nancy to the truant officers and school officials who several times raid her boardinghouse to check on the girl's treatment and working hours. Later, she agonizingly surrenders the girl to Mr. Southard, the school superintendent (Frank McGlynn Sr.), and his wife (Gretta Gould) to protect her from the perils of rough seaside life, particularly the attentions of a rather shifty young sailor named Alec. When the girl's real mother, the trampy and drunken Bella (Marjorie Rambeau), arrives at Min's home looking for the child she hopes will support her in her old age, Min lies and says that Bella's daughter is dead. But as soon as Bella leaves, Min begins plotting to get the girl away from the harbor altogether. She goes to the Southards to give them her life savings to pay for Nancy to go to boarding school, far from the mother she knows nothing about.

Several years later, Nancy returns from boarding school engaged to the gallant, wealthy Dick Cameron (Donald Dillaway). On the same boat, Bella also returns, convinced by seaside chatter that her daughter is still alive. Bella plans to crash Nancy's wedding, make a scene, and demand money from the daughter she now despises. Desperate to distract Bella from the yacht whistles announcing Nancy's wedding, Min offers to read her rival's cards. Their conversation toys with the idea of fate, superstition, and luck. Min sees good news: "You're gonna meet a rich guy, gonna wear diamonds, ride in a big car." But Bella is not fooled, and replies with prescient sarcasm, "A hearse?" Min's hands start to shake while she shuffles the cards, and Bella reveals that she knows about the yacht, the wedding, and the kid. Their argument continues to follow the theme of the cards. "I'm gonna have those diamonds you seen in my cards," Bella promises, outlining her plan to leech her fortune from the kid or else to reveal her tawdry origins to the whole town. "When I call a spade a spade," Bella boasts, "nobody forgets."

Min finally has to leave the trickster's world of con games and beat her rival through sheer physical force. Min stands in the doorway, immobile, and stares Bella down, using her big maternal body as a weapon against the woman who threatens the child's happiness. A closeup shows Min's eyes narrow, her nostrils flare, and her mouth set itself in a line as she declares to Bella, "You're not going to leave this room." Bella shrinks from Min's fierce gaze and begs her, "Aw, gee, Min, don't look at me like that." Bella bends over in apparent defeat, then suddenly grabs a hot curling iron and slaps it across Min's face. Min is knocked down by the blow, but she scrambles for the gun she keeps in a bureau drawer. Rising, she shoots Bella dead.

Summoned by the noise, Bill enters the room. Knowing the police will be on their way soon, Bill packs a suitcase for Min and tries to take her aboard his boat to Mexico. But Min refuses to leave until she's seen the wedding procession, now taking place out on an adjacent dock. With a kind of stunned, silent determination, Min pushes her way through the crowd, until she watches a radiant Nancy emerge from a limousine, kiss Mrs. Southard goodbye, and board the yacht with her new husband, never noticing Min among the crowd. As a policeman taps Min on the shoulder and starts to lead her away from the dock, Min slowly begins to smile.

The narrative similarities between *Min and Bill* and *Stella Dallas* (Samuel Goldwyn/United Artists, 1937) are striking.[16] In both films, the woman sacrifices herself for the child's class rise and romantic happiness. The painful scenes of rejection that the mother must perform to convince the girl that she really doesn't want her, the emphasis on the wedding ceremony, and especially the triumphant final tracking shot of the heroine smiling through her pain, having secured the child's happiness at the expense of her own, all translate directly from one film to another. Frances Marion had written the screenplay for the 1925 film adaptation of *Stella Dallas*, so the story was clearly familiar to her. Even the name of the daughter's suitor is similar, Dick Cameron and Dick Grosvenor, a couple of rather bland Prince Charmings who have little function in the narrative except as objects of the mother's desire for her daughter's class rise.

The similarities between the quintessential maternal melodrama and the film that garnered an Academy Award for Broadway's broadest comedienne point to the extent to which the maternal melodrama and the trickster tale are not that far apart. The maternal melodrama has long relied on the mother's act of sacrificial deception—a trick that permits the daughter to leave her mother behind. In *Stella Dallas*, the mother decides that her own working-class garishness is a liability to her daughter's happiness, so she pretends to be tired of motherhood and tells her child she is planning to move to South America to marry her fun-loving alcoholic boyfriend. Though the daughter is crushed by her mother's emotional abandonment, the trick works, and the film ends with the daughter's successful marriage to an upper-class suitor. Though the conventional trickster is a figure of fun and adventure, or the "productive chaos" of "creativity, play, spontaneity, inventiveness, ingenuity, and adventure," the trickster mother is a far more ambivalent figure.[17] She may be rowdy or adventurous or a social outsider, but she typically uses her wit unselfishly to ensure her child's happiness even if it costs her own. While the male trickster is often a loner, the maternal trickster has a primary connection to the family.

The closest antecedent to Hollywood's maternal trickster is probably Sheherezade, the heroine of *A Thousand and One Nights*, who is married to the tyrant Shahryar. Because his beloved first wife had been unfaithful to him, King Shahryar no longer trusts women. He takes a new wife every day and has her executed the very next morning, thus ensuring he will never be betrayed again. Finding herself next in line for this marital doom, and her beloved younger sister also in the queue, Scheherezade realizes she has to think of a trick that will save them both from the executioner. By telling her new husband a story each night, and ending each of her stories with a cliffhanger, Sheherezade is able to divert her husband from his murderous plot. Unwilling to sign his wife's death warrant until he has heard the rest of the story, Shahryar spares Scheherezade night after night, until she has borne him two children and he finds himself in such a state of marital comfort that he calls off his outrageous scheme.

Sheherezade is often treated as the archetypal female trickster, a woman who uses her feminine wiles to keep the story going until her family is safe.[18] She concocts a story, which is to say, a lie. Between the beginning and the end of that story, she extends the period of liminality, keeping the middle going and going and deferring closure long enough to bring about her desired result.[19] In the same way, the trickster mother creates a story (a deception, a ruse, a lie) that pushes away a dangerous closure for her child. When the child is safe, like Scheherezade and her younger sister, the deception can end.

The maternal melodramas of the late silent and early sound eras were full of trickster mothers. The mother (Ruth Stonehouse) in *Poor Girls* (Columbia, 1927), for instance, pays for her daughter's education by leading a double life as respectable Katherine Warner and notorious Texas Kate, a nightclub owner. The rich mother (Alice Joyce) in *13 Washington Square* (Universal, 1928) goes undercover as a poor cousin in order to prevent her son's marriage to the wrong woman. She doesn't succeed in stopping the marriage, but she does manage to foil a gang of jewel thieves. The mother (Adele Dayton) in *Modern Mothers* (Columbia, 1928) finds that she and her daughter are in love with the same man. Because the mother is a celebrated actress, she is able to feign indifference to the boyfriend so he is free to marry her daughter. In *Not Quite Decent* (Fox, 1929), a nightclub-singer mother (Louise Dresser) conceals her identity from her daughter and then saves her from a life of degradation by summoning her daughter's virtuous sweetheart to take her away from nightclub life. In *This Mad World* (MGM, 1930), the mother (Louise Dresser again) of a French secret agent conceals her son's identity and completes his mission for him after his death. In *Mother's Millions* (Universal, 1931), a rich mother (May Robson), who worries that money will ruin her children, treats them coldly in order to test their character and loyalty. When they have proved their worthiness, she becomes warm and loving.

These trickster mothers use deception, impersonation, and disguise to parent their children. In nearly every case, it is the child herself (and these are mostly daughters) who is being deceived. These melodramas articulate an extraordinary ambivalence about motherhood: the bond between mother and child is idealized to the point that the mother is driven to make extraordinary sacrifices, but the foolish children must be duped by the wise and wily mother in order for her clever scheme to save them. William J. Hynes argues that trickster narratives can create a space in which to explore the "shadow" of dominant values: "breaking through into the world of normalcy and order, the trickster plays out subterranean forbiddens in dreamlike fashion."[20] The "subterranean forbidden" of motherhood is vast, including realms of resentment of the children, terror at their loss, and overidentification with their desires. This emotional landscape of the maternal is repressed in sunny Hollywood sentimentalizations of motherhood, but it comes to the surface through performance and deception in the trickster melodrama.[21]

Unlike Stella Dallas, who must reject her child only one terrible time, Min sends Nancy away four separate times, putting greater distance between herself and her child with each painful interaction. As in all of Dressler's roles, her body is the anchor of the film's emotional landscape. Matthew Kennedy argues, "She never looked more perfect for a role. That great shelf of a bosom became the resting place for so many comforting nights with her beloved adoptee Nancy."[22] And the actors take advantage of Dressler's maternal physicality to clarify their characters. Dorothy Jordan was twenty-three when she took on the role of the teenaged Nancy. Partly in order to make herself seem younger, she presses her body up against Dressler's in the early scenes, and leans her head in toward the older woman's chest as she speaks. Like a very small child, clinging to her mother, Nancy's posture suggests dependence, adoration, and filial devotion.

The challenge of giving up the child is framed as a series of encounters in which Min lies about her feelings for the girl in order to put distance between Nancy and her maternal body. When she sends Nancy away to protect her from the sordid boardinghouse environment, she lies outright: "I'm sending you away 'cuz I don't want you to make me no trouble. You know I don't care nothing about you, just me." Nancy is hysterical with grief, clinging to Min and begging to stay, but the older woman pushes the child off of her body and holds her at arm's length to break the embrace. When she leaves the girl at the superintendent's house, Nancy gazes longingly after her through the barred window of a heavy wooden door. She is visibly grieved by her isolation from the physical comfort of her surrogate mother. Min, walking home, kicks a can off the street in idle frustration, then sits slumpingly down on the edge of the dock. Framed by two tall wooden posts, Min, too, is imprisoned by isolation.

Later, Nancy runs away from her new foster parents and returns to the dock, so Min is forced to increase the severity of her methods in order to prevent the child's return. She calls the girl "an ungrateful little brat" and throws a tin can after her to hurry her retreat, and to increase the distance between the child and her comforting maternal body. The third time she sends Nancy away, when she fears that Bella might find the girl, Min takes her own nest egg and makes up a bald lie about the money's being a legacy from Nancy's mother. Giving the money to Nancy's new foster parents, Min insists that it be used to send the girl away to boarding school, where she will be safe from her tawdry mother. When Nancy tries to embrace Min, she pushes the girl away, directly into the arms of her new adoptive mother, and hurries out the door. The fourth and last time Min has to reject Nancy, the girl is all grown up and stops by the boardinghouse to invite Min to her wedding. Min feigns disinterest and turns away from the girl, so Nancy has to follow her around the beauty parlor, speaking to her surrogate mother's back. These episodes each speak to the ways Min must trick her child into believing that her feelings for the girl are *not* maternal. Her most protective instincts paradoxically require her to walk away from her child.

By playing the bad mother, Min is able to shield the girl from her true bad mother. But because Nancy has not two but three prospective mothers—Min, Bella, and the school superintendent's wife—the film reflects interestingly on the question of exactly what a "good mother" might be. Both Bella and Mrs. Southard can be read as Min's doubles, as women who each embody a different shadow figure of Min herself.

Lori Landay argues that the double is an essential characteristic of the trickster, who often leads a double life, or disguises herself in order to gain access to power. "Doubles in cultural texts often show two sides of the same coin—the dualities that the imagination conceives of as opposite and irreconcilable. Because the public discourses about femininity are riddled with contradictions, most revolving around polarized notions of 'good' and 'bad' women, the creation of the double is one way to achieve complexity in representations."[23] In *Min and Bill*, this complexity is played out in triplicate. The good woman, the bad woman, and the ambivalent trickster woman who can play both roles all compete for the role of mother.

Min and Bella have a strong physical resemblance. The ample body of Marjorie Rambeau makes her an obvious double for Dressler (an association exploited more fully years later when Rambeau took over the role of Tugboat Annie Brennan in *Tugboat Annie Sails Again* in 1941 for Warner Brothers). Similarly, both women wear thick, patterned bathrobes and walk down the boardinghouse steps barefoot in strikingly parallel sequences thrown away at different corners of the film: Min goes downstairs to meet the truant officers near the opening, and Bella goes downstairs to ask Min for some hair tonic very near the end. Both are unashamed of their bare feet and bathrobes, entering the public space of the boardinghouse lobby with the comfort of women who have long since given up caring about propriety. They are both resourceful and violent: Bella's surprise attack with the curling iron is met by Min's surprise attack with a gun, weapons produced from the clutter of Min's bedroom. Their fates are linked, like the cards that Min reads for each of them, finding spades for herself (bad luck) and diamonds for Bella (wealth). Although Min and Bella stand at opposite sides of the film's moral spectrum, they share the bond of this wharfside culture and the social-outsider status of its inhabitants. Both of them must be removed from the scene of the wedding in order for Nancy's future to be secured.

But the superintendent's wife, Mrs. Southard, is also a double for Min. Though she is such a minor character that she appears in only a few scenes, this good mother takes Nancy into her home and into her arms when Min sends her away. More important, she is the mother who links arms with Nancy on her wedding day, taking the place that Nancy had invited Min to occupy. As Min watches Nancy embrace her adoptive mother, kiss her full on the lips, and wave goodbye, it is clear that Min is mentally trading places with Mrs. Southard through the whole ceremony. Min is mute at this point of the film, and nearly catatonic with shock. She lumbers toward the wedding party slowly, speechlessly, with an expression of confused fascination on her face. Earlier in the film she had told Nancy that her new life sounded "just like a dream," and it is easy to read Min's insensibility as that of a sleepwalker. She watches the pretty scene as though it is a dream, enjoying a fantasy identification with the middle-class mother who fits into this scene in a way that Min never would. Unlike the ending of *Stella Dallas*, in which the mother refuses to leave the wedding scene until the groom kisses the bride, this ending does not show the young couple kissing each other at all. Instead, Min watches the girl kiss her adoptive mother before stepping onto the boat, an acknowledgment that the child's class rise and secure future were obtained through Min's successful selection of her replacement. The wedding is explicitly framed not as a heterosexual romance, but as a triumph of mothering.

If it were told from the perspective of Nancy, *Min and Bill* would be a Cinderella story, about a girl caught between wicked stepmothers and fairy godmothers. Nancy makes her first entrance in the film in a coarse cotton dress, holding a big bucket of laundry, snapping gum. She ends the picture as a bride, in an elegant gown, holding flowers, sailing into the sunset on her wealthy husband's yacht. The agent of this transformation, the fairy godmother, is Min, who disguises herself as a wicked stepmother when she is within view of the girl. But her ability to control the child's destiny, to bring about her fairy-tale ending, is magical. In narrative time, two years pass between Min's insisting that the child be sent away to boarding school and Nancy's triumphant return to the wharf, gleefully betrothed to Prince Charming. In screen time, however, the change is virtually instantaneous. When Nancy drops by the boardinghouse to invite Min to live with her and her new husband in Boston, she narrates a future life for the little family that is as fantastical to Min as a fairy tale; it is, in fact, a description of the lifestyle Hollywood movies often used to tantalize Depression-era spectators, complete with a garden, a little cottage, a limousine, and complete ease. To preserve the child's fantastic future, Min must remove herself from the scene. While the film lingers in the muck and grime of Min's daily struggles, it asserts the possibility of fantasy and wealth and beauty through the story of Nancy. When Nancy achieves that magical transformation, the mother's trick is successful.

Wallace Beery and the Problem of Genre

> It is evidently a law unto Min . . . that what is loose is meant to be thrown, that a broken mirror is bad luck only because the vase she hurls at Bill's head misses him and crashes into the looking glass, that a pickaxe is a very handy weapon with which to punish a male who has revealed a tendency to be unfaithful.
>
> —Mordaunt Hall

One might wonder why this story about mothers and daughters is called *Min and Bill*, or indeed how it could ever have been understood as a comedy.[24] Bill functions only as Min's moral support and sparring partner. His presence is hardly relevant to the narrative, but it has an affective function. He and Min enact a kind of rough companionship that compensates for the loss of Nancy. He rubs her neck when she has had a rough day, listens to her read a letter from Nancy out loud, and lovingly leads her down to his boat when he knows she is in trouble. Bill is also fun. He tells Min dirty jokes, smuggles booze to her joint, and teases her about her age (figure 19).

When Bill enters the frame, there is often an almost-palpable generic shift from melodrama to comedy. His presence creates the conditions for Min's defiance of the conventions of self-erasure that usually accompany maternal melodrama. Min's pleasure in her sparring with Bill creates the backdrop, the context for Min's trickster wit. None of the comic sequences is especially integral to the plot, and they drag on for several minutes each, luxuriating in Dressler's performances of panic and rage as privileged moments of cinematic pleasure. The pleasures of laughter are dissociated from narrative, and in this case narrative represents an inevitable progression toward loss and tears. Because these episodes show Dressler's ongoing association with the comic, they prepare the audience to read the ending as a triumph, rather than a tragedy. Dressler's rubber face and restless energy resist the melodramatic and the maudlin, even when they are matters of narrative necessity.

Bill's role is most prominent in the film's two major slapstick sequences. The first is a very early scene, which shows Min and Nancy caught in a runaway speedboat. Bill dashes out of the barber's chair to join the coast guard's rescue boat, half his face still covered in shaving cream. The second is a full-out brawl in Bill's bedroom, which is probably the most famous scene in the film. Coming home one day, Min finds Bella perched on Bill's lap, both of them drunk. Enraged, she throws Bella out and turns on Bill in

FIGURE 19. The incompatibility of motherhood and comedy in *Min and Bill* (1930): Min will not let Bill finish his dirty joke until Nancy is out of earshot.

a violent temper. A slapstick brawl ensues, in which Min wrestles Bill to the ground, forces him behind the bed, chases him into a closet, and then breaks down the closet door with an ax. When Bill finally collapses in the corner, unconscious, covered by a fishnet that has fallen off the wall, Min cradles his head against her shoulder and mutters repentantly, "Aw, Bill, you make me so mad." It is a cartoonish, virtuosic, utterly delightful slapstick scuffle, enacted by two veterans of the form.

Nearly every newspaper review singled out this extraordinary scene as the film's most memorable. *Variety* was typical in claiming that the film "gathers its interest" through the relationship of Min and Bill, "rough, tough, and slam-bang admirers of each other. Min breaks up every loose article in a room in giving Bill a licking after catching him with Bella on his lap."[25] Most reviewers struggled to describe the lowdown dust-up in language that didn't replicate the slangy coarseness of the film's setting. Their descriptions tended to sound prim, as when the *Outlook and Independent* praised the film for its scenes of "fisticuffs and furniture throwing."[26] *Time* rather delicately identifies the most fragile of Min's weapons, noting that she "hits Bill with a variety of objects, including porcelain bedroom utensils."[27] Mordaunt Hall disliked the film, and used his fussy language to mark his disapproval: "After having smashed up the furniture and thrown everything at him that will break, this robust woman seeks to give Bill the coup de grace with a pickaxe, and only because of her inability to throw straight is Bill's life spared."[28]

It is no wonder that the critics were confused. Born of a generic muddle between gothic melodrama and slapstick comedy, *Min and Bill* plays outrageously with the boundaries of genre. The oscillation between pain and joy, both achieved through rather cheap emotional effects (the weeping closeup, the bottle broken over the head), creates a populist aesthetic that draws on familiar cinematic conventions but revises them through unfamiliar combination. "Some of the gags were outrageously far-fetched, [and] the sentiment ran like treacle," confessed screenwriter Marion.[29] The combination of these two elements of broad comedy and sloppy sentimentalism connect the film back to popular art forms like music hall melodrama or the "vaudeville aesthetic." It was a film aimed at the common folk, to a far greater degree than many of the sophisticated pictures Hollywood was producing for urban audiences. This film is simple, even childlike, in the ways it pushes the boundaries of the narrative until it becomes a tall tale. Bruno Bettelheim argues that fairy tales deal in magical extremes of joy (a fairy godmother), and sorrow (the loss of parents), and fear (the big bad wolf), because "this is how the young child experiences the world: either as entirely blissful or as an unmitigated hell."[30] The maternal Dressler guides the viewer through these extreme affective experiences, positing the viewer as a kind of child—easily frightened, easily amused. In the process, she is rendered large, as a mother is large to her children.

Dressler's physical dominance of the burly Bill also allows the film to point out the fierce physicality of her maternal instincts, her willingness for fight or flight in protecting her young. This dominance points to the ways that Min, in the end, is not a self-destructive martyr but a woman who is willing to commit murder on behalf of her child. She is associated with violence in several comic sequences before the film turns tragic. She gives Bill a shave and mockingly holds the razor to his throat when he makes a joke about her age; she pokes him with a letter opener to punish him for peeking through her keyhole; and she gives Nancy a gentle kick to the rear end to prevent her from eavesdropping on a dirty joke Bill is trying to tell. When the truant officer contends that Nancy's life lacks discipline, Nancy defends her surrogate mother by arguing that "if I don't walk a chalk line, Min whales the life out of me." When Bill charges Min ten dollars for the vodka that he's bought from the bootlegger Ivanovich, Min complains, "I'd kill a Russian for ten bucks."

The violence of comedy, particularly of the slapstick comedy in which Dressler had achieved her earlier successes, ruptures the comic frame in Bella's death and Min's arrest. Though she wouldn't really kill a Russian for ten bucks, Min would kill to protect her child. In this film, Marie Dressler uses her iconic body quite expertly, to suggest both maternal archetype and raging slapstick harridan. But in the murder scene, those two personas collide forcefully with the necessity of committing real violence. When it is over, Min's body collapses, and she begins to walk with a slow, shuffling limp. This loss of her aggressive energy is perhaps Min's most striking capitulation to melodrama. Bill has to drag her out the door; she only shuffles as she leaves his side to watch Nancy's wedding. And as the police officers lead her away from the pier, she is dead weight against their arms, beginning a journey through the legal system that is entirely likely to end with her execution. By killing off her shadowy double, Min sacrifices her own life as well—her ferocious body has already been brought under submission to the law in the last frame. But the ambiguous smile on her face—so weird, so sublime, the smile of a martyr or a saint—is also the smile of a trickster. The child is safe, and the story can come to an end.

Tugboat Annie: The Folk Hero

> Boasting—the epic brag—has always been part of the trappings of the hero. The strong man would gird himself for combat and inspire confidence in his followers by rehearsing his exploits in big talk.
>
> —B. A. Botkin, *The American People*

> Anytime the *Firefly* shows her heels to the *Narcissus,* I'll swallow the anchor.
>
> —Tugboat Annie Brennan

Tugboat Annie was based on the series of short stories by Norman Reilly Raine for the *Saturday Evening Post.*[31] The stories feature the adventures of a salty widow, captain of the tugboat *Narcissus.* Raine's Annie is an exuberantly comic trickster, using her wits and her knowledge of maritime law to foil her underhanded rival, Horatio Bullwinkle. For instance, when Bullwinkle tries to cheat Annie out of a towing contract by getting an unfair start to the boat, she uses a high-speed passenger ship to tow her tugboat to the prize first. When Bullwinkle steals her next towing job, Annie recommends Bullwinkle to a client who never pays his bills, and thereby sticks her rival with a huge job for which he will never be compensated. In the end, after Bullwinkle discovers her clever tricks, she always trades insults with her competitor. In the story "No Cure, No Pay," she finishes by counseling Bullwinkle, "And now ye'd better go and stick that head o' yours in a pail o' water, for if it ain't due to bust into flames any minute, I'm a man-eatin' canary."[32] Her salty language suggests the outlandish idioms of the docks.

Tugboat Annie's serial adventures place her in the company of eighteenth- and nineteenth-century American tall tales, whose heroes' accomplishments would be recounted around the campfire or in town gatherings. She is a heroic figure, a big woman on a tiny tugboat, whose exploits are known for miles around. For generations before, this type of hero was the subject of the American oral tradition. B. A. Botkin describes these folk characters: "A composite picture of the American hero would show him to be a plain, tough, practical fellow, equally good at a bargain or a fight, a star-performer on the job and a hell-raiser off it, and something of a salesman and a showman, with a flair for prodigious stories, jokes, and stunts and a general capacity for putting himself over."[33] Tugboat Annie, with her legendary exploits, her serial adventures, and her boasting, was a mass-media incarnation of an old folkloric tradition: the larger-than-life hero.

These tales were regional, and usually based on a real person, but later expanded to legendary proportions. Johnny Appleseed traveled the country in bare feet, sowing life in the soil. The giant lumberjack Paul Bunyan carved the Grand Canyon by dragging his ax behind his blue ox, Babe. The Pennsylvania steel worker Joe Magarac could put his hands straight into the fire and grab the hot steel, molding four rails in each hand. The Massachusetts sailing legend Stormalong piloted a ship so big that he had to keep a stable of horses aboard, so the crew could get from one end of the boat to the other.

While these eighteenth- and nineteenth-century folktales did not die with the urbanization and media explosions of the twentieth century, it was inevitable that American mythologies would take on new forms. In 1936, the literary critic Clemence Dane argued that America had begun to look to its pulp literature for mythologies because "it is a modern state, a machine-run state, a state whose wonders are material, 'scientific.'"[34] The sense of wonder that had once been associated with folk tales, fairy tales, and legends became attached to mechanically reproduced popular media, like movies, magazine serials, pulp novels, and the radio. Tugboat Annie was part of the new generation of heroes emerging from popular fiction. And she was in good company. Edgar Rice Burroughs cut his teeth on magazine fiction and detailed the adventures of Tarzan of the Apes in *All-Story Weekly* before he published the first Tarzan novel in 1914. *All-Story* was also the birthplace of California's heroic Zorro, created by Johnston McCulley in 1919. Edward O'Reilly wrote *The Saga of Pecos Bill*, about a giant cowboy raised by coyotes, for *Century Magazine* in 1923. Buck Rogers emerged from the pulp serial *Amazing Stories* in 1928, before migrating to the comics page in 1929.

Here, Buck Rogers was not alone. By the late 1920s, newspaper comic strips and comic books had already eclipsed pulp and magazine fiction as the home for popular heroes of serial adventures. *Popeye the Sailor* joined the comics page in 1929. *Dick Tracy* comic strips first appeared in 1931, followed by *Flash Gordon* in early 1934, *The Phantom* in 1936, and *Prince Valiant* in 1937. The first *Superman* comic book was published in 1938, followed by the *Batman* series in 1939, fully launching the era of the modern superhero, who more or less took the place of the folk hero in the imagination of the public. Female comic-strip heroes, such as the reporter Brenda Starr and the Amazonian Wonder Woman, wouldn't appear until the World War II era brought women's heroism into more beneficent focus.[35] This delay seems particularly stark, given how cinematic adventure serials with heroines, such as *Hands Up!* and *The Perils of Pauline*, had found success in the 1910s.

Modern folk heroes had a talent for shifting easily from one vehicle to another. The serial nature of their adventures allowed the stories to morph from page to comic book to screen in a way that replicated the transformations of folk tales as they move from teller to teller. These new heroes also reflected the new conditions of twentieth-century life in America. Media-age folktales were often set in urban landscapes, rather than rural ones. And the modern heroes' powers were usually born of tremendous intelligence, technology, or supernatural forces, rather than being side effects of their sheer size. So Tugboat Annie's heroism was already a bit of an anachronism; a blue-collar, rural character, she was big, tough, intransigent, and sly, in the tradition of a frontier hero, rather than fast, street-smart, privileged, or futuristic, in the style of a mass-media hero. Finally, Tugboat Annie's heroic actions were often aimed to safeguard her own professional standing in the harbor, or to help out one of her salty and eccentric pals, threatened by Bullwinkle, who was a bully but not a true villain. She was legendary for her competence and tricky wit, not for her altruistic service to the community.[36] Her successors often traced a wider arc, bringing down enemies of the people.

When Norman Reilly Raine's series was transformed into a film vehicle for Marie Dressler and Wallace Beery, the plot changes widened the gap between the folk hero and her cohorts. In the films, three major changes radically altered the heroic logic of Tugboat Annie's adventures. First, Dressler's Annie is not a widow. Very much alive, the movies' Terry Brennan, Annie's husband, is a lovable buffoon, and a serious alcoholic. The cinematic Annie is still the true captain of the tugboat, constantly compensating for her husband's drunkenness and incompetence. Second, this being a Marie Dressler film, Annie is also a mother. Her grown son, Alec, is played by the charming-but-bland Robert Young. This sudden family exerts a kind of gravity on the Tugboat Annie character, so that she is no longer the carefree adventurer of Raine's stories. With the family, sentimental melodrama enters the generic frame, and the *Narcissus* is now not only a professional tool, but a family home. Finally, the literary Annie's rival, Horatio Bullwinkle, is gone from the film. Instead of spending her energy battling a bully, Annie uses her talents just to earn a living and protect her family from the natural and social disasters of the harbor. This change in plot created a remarkably ambivalent narrative structure, one that reflected a Depression era when male breadwinners were struggling to maintain the social roles they had previously occupied.

In her transformation from frontier hero to domestic hero, Tugboat Annie enters the realm of maternal melodrama typical of a Dressler character. Annie is still a character of mythic proportions, but Terry's appalling behavior sucks the life out of her heroism. He secretly sells lengths of hawser (hauling rope) for drinking money until one inevitable day, Annie throws the line to a ship and finds it doesn't reach. Beery's infantilism was used in *Min and Bill* to playfully liberate Dressler's character from her misery. But in *Tugboat Annie,* his immaturity is the primary cause of that misery. He alienates Annie from their son and drags her to the brink of financial ruin before redeeming himself and reuniting the family through his self-sacrificing heroism. The movies' Tugboat Annie, then, cannot match the exploits of her newsprint counterpart, because her heroism must always be focused on holding her own family together.

In this way, *Tugboat Annie* traces the overlap between melodrama and myth. Peter Brooks has argued that melodrama's emergence in the eighteenth century was an attempt to compensate for the increasing secularization of public life in the wake of the Enlightenment and the French Revolution.

According to Brooks, "Melodrama becomes the principal mode for uncovering, demonstrating, and making operative the essential moral universe in a post-sacred era. . . . Melodrama represents both the urge toward resacralization and the impossibility of conceiving sacralization other than in personal terms."[37] Melodrama does the work of myth by ritualizing cultural values, but it frames those values in terms of the vulnerable body of the social subject. The suffering individual, in this genre, becomes the sacred figure.

Tugboat Annie is sacralized both by her capacity for work (the frontier myth) and by the injustice of her suffering (the maternal melodrama). Like *Prosperity*, *Tugboat Annie* explores how a woman's competent work upsets conventional gender roles already threatened by the Depression's economic instability, tying women's heroism to the suffering, unstable family. The film expresses this ambivalence by focusing Annie's considerable heroic energies not on her work (which she does well), and not even on her child (who makes a very early and seamless transformation to the middle class), but on her husband. One of the few films that shows Dressler as a married woman rather than a widow, *Tugboat Annie* presents a family run through with cyclical problems of alcoholism, dependence, and resentment. Annie's strength becomes a liability to her marriage, and the film finds its happy ending only when Annie finally steps out of the way and lets Terry be the hero. Like *Prosperity*, it never really resolves its ambivalence about this transfer of power, leaving the family imbalance open for the next installment of the series, which was never produced.

The opening scene shows Annie (Dressler) helping her young son, Alec (Frankie Darro), with his homework. Reading from what she calls his "book of knowledge," she helps Alec learn the following facts, struggling over the unfamiliar words:

> "Who was So-crates? A Greek Philosopheer."
> "What was the first wonder of the world? The Peer-eye-mids of Egypt."
> "What did Sampson slay the Philistines with? The jawbone of an ass."

When Annie then quizzes Alec on what he has learned, he finds he can't remember the answer to the third question. Annie gives him a hint, by pointing to her own face.

> "What's this?"
> "Your chin, Mom."
> "That's the jawbone of an ass."

The opening inscribes Annie into this ancient context as an ass, a fool. The film plays with the notion of myth and legend, even as it mocks these traditions. Annie is both powerful and ridiculous, a figure writ large yet extraordinarily ordinary. The name of her boat, the *Narcissus,* is an ironic reference to vanity, while Annie's labored pronunciation of it ("Nar-siss-US") points to her alienation from any such high-toned nonsense. She is a working-class hero, lacking vanity or pretension, who knows nothing of her mythic predecessors but performs great deeds.

And in the beginning of the film, Tugboat Annie *is* powerful, able to change events through her will in quasi-miraculous fashion. At the end of the opening sequence, Annie extols the value of education to her son, explaining to him that he has to stay in school so he can become captain of a big steamship. Her speech ends with the wistful pronouncement "Alec Brennan, Master Mariner," to which the young Alec responds with a salute. The film then dissolves to a newspaper photo of an adult Alec (Robert Young) saluting beneath the headline "Glacier Queen, New Liner, Due Here on Maiden Trip" and the caption "Youngest Captain." Annie here is an oracle, foretelling her son's future and also drawing it into existence through her guidance and will.

Annie's salty maritime expressions trade in oversized images that are the stuff of myth. They often imply Annie's awesome physical powers, "Anytime the *Firefly* shows her heels to the *Narcissus,* I'll swallow the anchor," she boasts. She tells her rival Red Severn he won't beat her, "not unless you sprout fins and a tail," linguistically transforming her opponent into an animal. She often uses this verbal gesture, calling Severn "horseface," and labeling her husband, Terry, "you big ox," "you big ape," "fish ears," and a "good-for-nothing seagoing cockroach." B. A. Botkin argues that this sort of tall talk implies a "totemic transfer of traits" between human and animal figures.[38] With language, Annie echoes the mythic antecedent of Circe, who used her magic to turn Odysseus's men into pigs. Seeing the men around her as an assortment of degraded animals, Annie announces her dominion over them with her salty expressions.

Judith Yarnall argues that Circe's power to turn men into beasts is also a mythic reference to women's reproductive powers, "the awe-provoking female ability to give shape to flesh and blood."[39] The movies' Annie has heroic powers that are clearly related to her function as mother. For instance, Annie gives a locket holding a photo of a very young Alec to his fiancée, Pat (figure 20). When Pat asks if she won't miss the locket, Annie replies, "Oh, I don't mind. I've carried him for nigh on twenty-five years. Past time I've given him up." The viewer is left with the almost unavoidable impression that Annie has literally carried Alec, as a mother in her womb, for his entire lifetime. The film is full of references to Annie or her tugboat carrying, pulling, holding, or hauling others. The *Narcissus* is both her home and the engine of her work, merging the public and the private spheres of her heroism like no other of her films. Dressler's maternal power draws along the younger generation, the economy of the harbor, and the imperfect husband.

The name of the ship, *Narcissus*, implies that the boat is a reflection in the water, a double that Annie loves. And of course her name, "Tugboat Annie," also merges the captain's identity with that of her ship. When the engines begin to fail, Annie visits several banks on shore to obtain a loan to repair the boilers. Calling her boat "she," Annie's rhetoric substitutes her own body for that of the boat; they are feminine workhorses of similar ages and in similar battered states. The first banker reminds her that the boat is forty years old, to which Annie replies, "That's nothin. I'm more'n that myself." And later she says, "The *Narcissus* nor me ain't ready for the boneyard yet."

FIGURE 20. *Tugboat Annie* (1933): Annie presents a locket to her future daughter-in-law, Pat (Maureen O'Sullivan).

As a monumental worker created in the model of the folk heroes of the last century, she fights obsolescence, insisting on the power of her own body in the face of impersonal financial institutions that fail to see her lingering worth. Again switching genders in her working life, she proclaims, "I'm as good a tugboat man as ever I were."

This masculine noun is a clue to how the film plays with gender roles in the characters of Annie and Terry. Dressler's tough performance emphasizes that Annie becomes awkward when she is away from her tugboat. At a grand reception honoring the crew of the *Glacier Queen*, she wears a frowsy print dress and elaborate flowered hat, a parody of middle-class feminine garb. The clothes are fussy and excessive on Dressler's ample frame. Trying to keep Terry away from the spiked punch, she grabs his cup and drinks it several times in a row, until Annie herself becomes drunk, and dances with a second mate with a lumpy, self-conscious gracelessness. Her girlish flowered hat bobs crazily around the dance floor. When she visits the bankers in town, Annie wears an even more eccentric hat, bedecked with an elaborate feather. Just as the *Narcissus* is clearly a joke about vanity, this enormous, drooping feather makes Annie look like a cockeyed peacock. As she lumbers wearily home from town, the delicate accessory sways raggedly on her head. Her deportment does not match her attire; when Dressler wears feminine frippery, it is always a joke.

Aboard the *Narcissus*, Annie wears work clothes, often accessorized by a man's cap and a matronly shawl. This combination of masculine and feminine attire points to her position as both maternal keeper of the home and blue-collar working hero; she is both mother and father to Alec. Marie Dressler's performance as Annie is touching and broad; her androgynous posture matches her clothing. Several times she sits on a crate or a ledge on the deck of her tugboat, legs spread far apart, one or both elbows propped on her knees, and chin resting in her hand. She adopts this posture to suggest frustration, thoughtfulness, and determination in the face of adversity. Its striking refusal of feminine propriety, particularly the unabashed openness of her legs, suggests her position as worker and captain of the small ship. When she stands on deck, as in a scene where she is watching her son through binoculars, she also stands with her legs far apart, a good, balanced stance to counteract the motion of the boat, and one that is rare indeed for a female MGM star. Annie often speaks in a voice that is often just a little bit too loud for the social occasion, implying that she is more comfortable shouting orders across the deck than she is chatting in close quarters. And she punctuates her exclamations with broad physical gestures, like punching Terry in the shoulder, or embracing Pat tightly against her body. Her body language suggests a woman who is physically accustomed to hard work, and the hard life of the harbor.

As in her other films, Dressler's androgynous power infantilizes the men around her, particularly her alcoholic husband, Terry. The film's first scene shows Terry asking Annie for fifty cents' drinking money; he is like a child looking for his allowance. When she refuses, he shuffles away, muttering glumly, "There's more ways of killing a cat than kissing it to death." Terry's infantile behavior throughout the film implies that Annie is undermining his masculinity with her maternal protection. A later episode shows Terry getting too drunk to attend his son's homecoming ceremony, so Annie locks him in his cabin. Escaping, Terry shows up at the celebration, visibly plastered, wearing only his shirt, suit jacket, and long johns, grinning like a child. As in *Politics*, the man is missing his pants, but this time he is out in public, for everyone to see. When Annie later throws a dinner party, he steals a bite of cake while her back is turned, his eyes shifting around the room to make sure he is not caught. Before the dinner guests arrive, she has to tell him to wash his hands. The handwashing conversation is explicitly infantilizing, as Terry whines, "Aw, do I have to?" before shuffling off to comply. Later, she tugs his hat off at the dinner table. The film makes much of this contrast between Annie's heroic physicality and Terry's juvenile irresponsibility.

The very bourgeois, upstanding son, Alec, tries to remake his family to reflect the middle-class values his mother helped prepare him for when she told his future. Hoping to transform his father into a breadwinner and his mother into a housewife, Alec secures Terry a position at the steamship company. Annie reluctantly prepares to leave the *Narcissus* in order to take up life in a small apartment, but Terry is fired before she can even pack. When he shuffles home, drunk, Annie begins to swipe at him, while he ducks and hides. The pathetic scuffle is like the dissolute shadow of the rip-roaring fight in *Min and Bill:* halfhearted, spiritless, and short. Chasing her husband around the table, Annie trips. Alec walks in to see her fall and assumes that his father has been beating his mother. This is an extraordinary moment in the film, one that reveals the class differences between the son and his parents. Alec's middle-class values cause him to misread the scene of violence and to see his mother as a victim. His bourgeois sensibilities dictate that someone should "take care" of Annie, and if Terry is not up to the task, then Alec should take over. But faced with an ultimatum from her son, Annie slaps Alec. She cannot tolerate his attempts to unseat her husband, and she also seems to resist the idea that she requires a caretaker. After the slap, Annie stares at her own hand in disbelief. His ultimatum rejected, Alec leaves his family.

Annie and Terry try to get on with their lives, but while Annie is in town to secure a loan to repair the boat's boilers, Terry takes the *Narcissus* out by himself. Reaching into the water for a wooden crate that he hopes was dropped by bootleggers, Terry steers the *Narcissus* into a ferry boat, wrecking it. The tug is sold at auction and is bought by the garbage contractor, who hires Annie to tow garbage scows through Puget Sound. Terry brings Annie to despair and economic ruin, causing her to lose everything. Annie's singular heroism is placed in contrast to her husband's dangerous incompetence. As they walk away from the boat they have lost, Terry looks back, like Lot's wife or Eurydice, while Annie, stronger, though hunched and despairing, walks purposefully away. This scene makes it clear that the gender roles in the Brennan household remain reversed. The disempowered husband has become a force of destruction in their domestic lives.

The film gives evidence of this slow destruction through metaphors of dirt and pollution. Terry is always dirty in this film, and Annie's attempts to reform him are nearly always framed as attempts to clean him up. Annie asks him to put on a clean shirt for Alec's homecoming, and he winds up finding alcohol in his hair tonic. She asks him to wash his hands before welcoming Alec and Pat to dinner, and he drops the soap in the sauerkraut, ruining dinner. When he crashes the tugboat, their final degradation is to take a job using the *Narcissus* to pull a garbage scow. Though Annie keeps up a brave face, she confesses to Pat that the smell nauseates her: "I can't seem to keep anything on my stomach, except my hand." In a ragged dress, she sits on the deck of her once-proud boat and darns socks, her body slumped in defeat. Terry has reduced them to a life of filth, stench, and disrepair.

Where soap and water always fail to clean him, Terry is finally cleansed by fire. The only tugboat in the harbor willing to risk a terrible storm to rescue Alec's ship, the *Narcissus* is weakened by the leak in its boilers. Protected only by a covering of water-saturated burlap, Terry crawls into the ship's furnaces to plug the holes that are letting the steam escape. Gregg Toland's cinematography in this sequence creates the impression that Terry is almost literally descending into hell: smoky darkness punctuated by intense flames envelops him. Annie frets and wails as Terry crawls away from her into the pit. The film rehabilitates Terry through this sudden and total act of sacrifice for his family. When Alec and his crew notice that the tugboat has gained power, Alec shouts, "She's holding us!" Though it is Terry who has enabled the rescue, the conflation of Annie and her tugboat again produces the remarkable impression that Annie herself is holding, as a mother a child, the entire crew of the *Glacier Queen*.

But Annie at this point is not at the wheel. After Terry's tremendous act of heroism, she holds not her son, but her husband as he loses consciousness, blackened and soot-stained from the furnace. Annie tearfully tells Terry he shouldn't have done it. "It was for our kid, wasn't it?" replies the barely conscious Terry, before passing out. Annie nods and snivels, "Terry," as the shot fades quickly to black, suggesting the possibility of Terry's death. At the fade-in, Annie is still perched above Terry's supine body, but he is wrapped in white bandages and safely lodged in the hospital. Terry's improbable recovery from a life-threatening act of sacrifice also recalls the old adventure serials, where a character would be seen driving off a cliff in the end of one installment, only for it to be revealed in the next installment that the character was able to escape from the car only seconds before it flew over the edge. The adventurer is saved so that the adventure can continue.

This magical transition also echoes the opening of the film, where Alec transmutes from young boy to grown steamship captain. Here, Annie's oracular power transforms Terry from dirty, sooty hero to a white-clad invalid in the sterile hospital room. Where water has failed to clean him, fire succeeds. And where Annie had earlier wished her son into manhood, she seems here to have effected a similar transition for her husband. When he is healed, Terry receives a medal for bravery. He stands proudly on the dock and is praised by the steamship owner, Red Severn, who has bought the *Narcissus*, repaired it, painted it a clean white, and returned it to the Brennans. Inspecting the medal, pinned on her husband's chest, Annie grumbles, "Heaven help me from now on. Pretty, ain't it? Well, I oughta get it for living with ya." Patting her husband's chest, she finds a bottle hidden in the sling. Terry's heroism was fleeting. Annie is once again alone in her leadership of the reunited family.

The film ends with a medal, pinned on the wrong chest. Though Annie was able to raise her son to middle-class manhood with one quick pronouncement of his future, her husband's transformation was only temporary. The film cannot award the family its final conquest of Terry's alcoholism because his incapacitation is necessary to the next installment in the series. Though Dressler's death prevented MGM from immediately pursuing the sequel, Matthew Kennedy reports that Beery and Dressler both had heard there was to be a second film and discussed it when the actress was on her deathbed.[40] Several later films tried to pick up where Dressler left off, notably Marjorie Rambeau's *Tugboat Annie Sails Again* (Warner Bros., 1940), and even further down Hollywood's food chain, Republic Pictures' *Captain Tugboat Annie* (1945), starring the terrific Jane Darwell, a few years after her Oscar-winning portrayal of Ma Joad in John Ford's *The Grapes of Wrath* (20th Century Fox, 1940). Even later, Raine's stories became the basis for a one-season 1957 television series, *The Adventures of Tugboat Annie*, starring hawk-eyed Minerva Urecal. This is an extraordinary history of a serial that just couldn't get out of the harbor, despite four capable performers in the lead role, and a beloved and well-known central character. This impulse toward seriality is part of the ethos of the frontier hero. Repetition, cycles, and returning are all central elements of the heroic folktale, and they stayed with the form as it transformed itself into the mass-media adventure serial.

But the impulse toward *return* here in Dressler's *Tugboat Annie*—the way the film cycles each character back to an earlier state of being—also betrays the conflicting demands of comedy and melodrama. The first return, Terry's return from the dead, expressed in his improbable survival and recovery, responds to the demands of comedy. The family is healed and reunited in a happy scene that even points to the conventional comedy device of the wedding—Terry, from his hospital bed, tells the story of how he married Annie, and he cajoles his son to marry Pat. Even the recurring use of white—in Terry's bandages, in the hospital walls, in the freshly painted *Narcissus*—suggests a nuptial theme in this ending. These elements of renewal and harmony comprise a fitting resolution for a comedy.

But the second return, Terry's return to the bottle, is an ending that evokes melodrama. Though the moment is treated as a joke, it restores the family to its disordered state, setting the stage for the next crisis. Tania Modleski has argued that repetition and stasis are keys of the melodramatic form. She writes, "Unlike most Hollywood narratives, which give the impression of progressive movement toward an end that is significantly different from the beginning, much melodrama gives the impression of a ceaseless returning to a prior state."[41] Because melodrama is concerned with scenes of trauma, the heroine is often focused on a point in the past, rather than one in the future. Melodramatic forms like the adventure serial or the soap opera even permit a repetitive cycling through a series of crises that defer a final state of equilibrium. The child has grown up and sailed away, but the husband is stuck in a kind of grotesque infancy that keeps Annie anchored to one spot.

Conclusion

> I love any role which shows that if you aren't afraid of life, life can't hurt you. That is what Tugboat Annie does. She licks fate because she can look it in the eye and not be afraid. . . . I think that's the kind of stimulant that we need in American life right now.
>
> —Marie Dressler, 1933

Marie Dressler characterizes *Tugboat Annie* as a parable for Depression America.[42] If this ambivalent film suggests that "life can't hurt you," it does so precisely because the film is about cycles, about surviving rather than conquering hardship.

Though the classic frontier hero roamed the American West, finding new adventure and new space, Tugboat Annie's location on the Pacific Coast suggests the end of expansion, the enclosure of the hero in the narrow harbor. Because the age of the tall tale had passed, Dressler's folk heroes are touched with ambivalence. Far from carving the Grand Canyon or riding a cyclone, Annie's Depression-era feat was just to survive, and to keep her family afloat. Rather than fighting off the dangers of the frontier world, Min and Annie are able to protect their children only by absorbing the pain themselves. The world seemed to have narrowed in on the hero, so that at the end of the film, the medal winds up on her husband's chest instead of her own. Her claim that "I oughta get it for living with ya" points to the film's subversive message: just "living with" hardship is an act of tremendous heroism. These two films dignify survival, offering a new kind of tall tale for an anxious time.

5

Emma and *Christopher Bean*

The Sexual Body

> I firmly believe that I owe whatever good fortune has come my way largely to the fact that I was born without a pretty face. Sour grapes? Not on your life! I can admire another woman's beauty with all the detachment of a Cook's tourist beholding the Coliseum by moonlight. It's grand. But thank the Lord I don't have to live up to it all the time.
>
> —Marie Dressler

By 1930, Marie Dressler had long since traded her vanity for the pleasures of comic stardom. A reviewer wrote of her 1910 appearance in *Tillie's Nightmare*, "The show is dominated by an actress whose sole aim is to make herself a monstrosity that she may use ugliness as a bludgeon to wallop the ignorant into blithering and painful laughter."[1] Dressler's unruly body was similarly castigated as an unwholesome form of comedy in *The Callahans and the Murphys*. Her first autobiography was called *The Life Story of an Ugly Duckling*, and Dressler often spoke about her homeliness. Her two autobiographies are full of self-deprecating anecdotes: she used to tell people, "I never owned a picture of myself until I was old enough to pay the photographer!"[2] In the early part of the century, she often went out on the town with the lovely Lillian Russell, and the pair were called "Beauty and the Beastie."[3] Will Rogers once found himself in a bind because he had been asked to give out a gold laurel to the most beautiful woman in the room. Not wishing to offend any of the young ladies, Rogers elected to make a joke of the award, and presented it to Dressler.[4]

It marked a real shift in her star persona when Dressler entered her sixties being praised sincerely for her beauty. *Photoplay* gushed, "Facing sixty, Marie Dressler remains younger than a flapper and modern as next year's hat."[5] *Photoplay*'s Barrett C. Kiesling described Dressler's arrival at the premiere of *Min and Bill:* "She turned around, showed to the crowd a beautiful face, wrinkled, age-worn, filled with experiences which have never embittered."[6] The unabashedly sentimental journalist Adela Rogers St. Johns produced this gushing tribute: "I thought—gee, she's a swell person. There are not many like her. She makes you feel good. Troubles don't look very big. Get your confidence back, while you're talking to her. Life warms up. It's good to be with her. Her eyes are so bright. Why, she's younger and more beautiful than any woman I know. I love to look at her."[7] *Photoplay* reported in 1931 that a letter had arrived from a "gentleman farmer" from Minnesota who explained that he had heard Dressler was a widow, and he wondered if she would marry him.[8] Llewellyn Miller of the *Los Angeles Record* confessed, "There is no use setting out on the hopeless enterprise of describing in print the charm of Marie Dressler."[9] As Mollie Merrick described her, "She is 60 years of age and has more real vim, vigor and vitality than any 20-year-old," and "her skin is as soft as a baby's and almost wrinkleless."[10] Eleanor Packer published a posthumous tribute that insisted, "Marie was beautiful. She liked to call herself an ugly duckling, to laugh about her homeliness. But hers was a beauty which defied description."[11]

In this odd way, it is clear that Marie Dressler had become an object of desire to the film audience by the end of her career. Chapters 3 and 4 have shown the ways in which her body—her heroic maternal body—is figured in her films as a kind of salvation not just to her suffering children, but also to the suffering communities she upheld. The films access a unique kind of desire in their spectators. They construct the spectator as a kind of surrogate child, one who is ultimately reassured by the good mother's humor, self-sacrifice, and optimism. She saves communities by offering her own maternal body for the pleasures of laughter, the comfort of consolation, or the work of rebuilding. These films posit the ideal spectator as a child in need of mothering. This chapter will explore the ways that regressive quality of Dressler's implied spectator also slips over into the realm of the erotic, not least through the very physicality of her mothering.

Patricia White has argued that some of Bette Davis's films, particularly her governess melodrama *All This and Heaven Too,* construct their ideal viewer as "a girl with a crush."[12] They make the star powerfully sexual, and reinforce her singular screen presence by matching her with a young girl who is overwhelmed by her caring attentions—her lover's daughter Tina in *Now, Voyager* and the schoolgirls in *All This and Heaven Too.* Her lover taken away from her, Davis finds a new outlet for her erotic energies in the passionate parenting of an adolescent girl. It is also possible to view Dressler's later films, particularly the two that are studied in this chapter, as similarly addressing themselves to a child with a crush—both male and female spectators are invited to receive her cinematic embrace, accepting the position of child to her maternal care. That the eroticization of this bond is not perverse, but comforting, is evidence of how the bond can work only one way. The audience is invited to nurse a crush on the lushly physical Dressler, but Dressler displays no pedophilic impulses toward the infantilized spectator. Her films therefore ingeniously eroticize the star, while on the surface they render her sexuality invisible.

Her constant touching, stroking, patting, and clinging are part of Dressler's career-long scene-stealing technique. As long as she is in motion, the audience watches Dressler rather than her costars. Whenever another character has a big emotional monologue to deliver, Dressler usually spends the scene touching that character comfortingly on the shoulders, hands, or face. By stealing away the emotional center of such scenes, Dressler had managed to gather more and more stardom for herself over the years of her comeback. But this technique also put her in constant contact with other bodies, young and old, male and female. Using her body to link the other characters, and to bring them connection, pleasure, and comfort, Dressler became the erotic as well as emotional center of her films. Figure 21 shows how even objects take on a kind of erotic charge in Dressler's presence. Her tactile exploration of the world and expressive use of her body imply an experience of touch that exceeds the shadowy disembodied nature of the film medium. In this scene from *Christopher Bean,* Dressler lovingly clutches the back of a leather chair as she remembers her late husband. While the three other characters are physically isolated, their upright bodies expressing coldness and judgment, Dressler's body, half-pressed against the chair, suggests warmth, connection, and sexuality.

This chapter will deal with two films that use Dressler's affectionate physical relationship to the world as the basis for unusually frank explorations

FIGURE 21. *Christopher Bean* (1933): Marie Dressler's touch sexualizes even everyday objects.

of middle-aged sexuality. In *Emma*, the Dressler character is a housekeeper who marries her employer shortly before his death. When his embittered children challenge the legality of the marriage, a protracted court case ensues, centered around the legitimacy, even the very possibility, of Dressler's sexuality. In *Christopher Bean*, a museum representative contacts the Haggett family to find out whether they have any paintings by the late artist Christopher Bean, whose work has suddenly acquired significant value in art circles. Only late in the film do the Haggetts discover that Bean had secretly married their cook, Abby (Dressler), shortly before his death, and that she has saved many of his canvases.

Both films turn on the question of genre. Kathleen Rowe has argued that "romantic comedy usually contains a potential melodrama, and melodrama a potential romantic comedy."[13] Both genres explore feminine worlds of desire and domesticity, but they differ in their approach to the dramatic possibility that the couple will not find each other. In the romantic comedy, misunderstandings and poor timing delay the couple's union until the end of the film.

In the melodrama, misunderstandings and poor timing threaten the couple's happiness. *Emma* and *Christopher Bean* address this generic tension by killing off the hero (the latter film dispenses with him before the film even begins), thereby ascribing a successful and loving union to the Dressler character but forcing her to suffer the loss of her beloved. Being hybrids of comedy and romantic melodrama, they then create a happy ending out of something other than a marriage. The Dressler films never end with a kiss, or a clinch, or a wedding. They end with her finding happiness by channeling her energies into surrogate motherhood rather than romance. Her own romantic impulses thus extinguished, Dressler becomes an available object for the "crush" of the spectator, who occupies the place of the children in her care.

These two narratives of sentimental, impulsive, and short marriages are particularly germane to Dressler's personal history. The result of a teenage infatuation with a fellow actor, her first marriage was painful and brief. Then, in the 1910s, she began referring to a man named Jim Dalton as her husband, and he managed her business affairs as well. At the time, Dressler knew that Dalton had not obtained a divorce from his first wife, but they brazened out a charge of bigamy launched at him in 1914 by a theater owner, angry about Dalton's management of Dressler's contract.[14] Sometime in the late 1910s, Dalton apparently stole the money Dressler thought he had spent on his divorce; he staged a fake wedding for the two of them, and for several years Dressler was happily fooled.[15] When he finally confessed to his deception, she threw him out of her home. But as she reportedly confessed to Frances Marion, "The cards were all stacked on his side. He had a stroke and lay there a pitiful, helpless creature. What could I do? Up to that moment I had loved this man, and the human heart clings, even to its pain."[16] She nursed him through his final illness, and when Dalton died, Dressler suffered the final indignity of letting his legal wife bury the man the actress had thought was her husband.

Perhaps understandably, Dressler was always quiet about her "marriage" to Dalton, and she hardly mentions him in her autobiography. In *My Own Story*, she offers this cryptic tribute: "I have always liked men. Many of my stanchest [*sic*] friends have been of the male persuasion. But in all my life I have loved only one man. He has been dead for many years. I will not tell you about him, for our love belongs to me alone."[17] So her actual personal life remained a cipher, and the audience could fill it in with the information provided by her publicity, which continually stressed her love for all human kind. In an interview with the *Los Angeles Times*, Dressler insisted that the romantic pangs of youth bring terrible heartache but eventually give way to more satisfying intimate friendships: "When you're fifty you know a different kind of love. If you've been fortunate enough to get over love with someone, to graduate from all that hysteria into a sane and sensible companionship, then you have a romance which is greater than anything youth brings you. . . . I have always valued and treasured my friends, but never with the great depth which I have learned the last ten years."[18] Dressler's interviews and autobiography are filled with these kinds of intimate addresses, which include the audience in her meditations on the importance of close companionship. By collapsing friendship and romance, Dressler developed a star persona that implied an intimate attachment to others, and that intimate attachment implicitly extended to her audience. But slyly, the language "have loved only one man," of course, leaves open the possibility that she has loved women. Judith Mayne has argued that "lesbian spectatorship is concerned with that space between visibility and invisibility."[19] This space is legible in both Dressler's life and in her films.

Biographers have disagreed on the exact nature of Marie Dressler's relationships with other women, but it is clear that many of her dearest friends and confidants were part of the lesbian subculture of New York and Hollywood. She was friendly with women who were fairly open about their lesbianism in the 1920s, such as Elisabeth Marbury, Elsie de Wolfe, and Mercedes d'Acosta.[20] She relied on the counsel of a gay astrologer, Nella Webb, and often credited her success to the confluence of stars that Webb had predicted. When she came to Hollywood in the 1930s, she counted the lesbian comediennes Patsy Kelly and Thelma Todd among her friends.[21] And from 1927 to 1932, Dressler lived in what was clearly a domestic partnership with a younger actress named Claire DuBrey. Dressler's biographers Betty Lee and Matthew Kennedy have carefully documented the partnership of these two women. DuBrey was a visible element of Dressler's publicity at this time, a constant quiet figure in the background. A fan profile in *Photoplay* labeled her Dressler's "close friend and secretary, Claire DuBrey." *Screen Book Magazine* carried a photo of Dressler playing the piano at a 1932 party, surrounded by friends and colleagues. The caption clearly identifies the young woman sitting prettily on top of her piano as Claire DuBrey.[22] The younger actress even has a small role in *Politics*, as the most vocal of the rebellious wives.

A far more frank analysis of DuBrey's position in Dressler's household was offered just after the star's death, when her young companion was in the process of shopping around a book manuscript describing their years together. (The manuscript was never published but was discovered in the early 1990s by the elderly DuBrey's caretaker and forwarded to Betty Lee.)[23] The *New York Times* described the young authoress: "She said she was in the closest association with the actress during the last seven years of the actress's life, and was thoroughly familiar with her affairs. She declared that she was always assistant hostess when Miss Dressler entertained, and that Miss Dressler's friends always entertained her whenever they entertained Miss Dressler."[24] As with so many gay stars before and after her, Dressler's

FIGURE 22. Marie Dressler at home. The photographs on the mantel are of women only: her sexuality is hidden in plain sight (MGM publicity photo, c. 1932).

homosexuality was visible if you knew how to look for it, but invisible to most. Figure 22 is a studio publicity shot of Marie Dressler relaxing in her own home. On her mantelpiece are photos of four women; the image announces the ways her intimate attachments were almost exclusively feminine. But like Edgar Allan Poe's purloined letter, these women are hidden in plain sight—the very fact that they are visible implies that there is no secret subtext to their presence. In this same way, Claire DuBrey was hidden in full view of the world.

Matthew Kennedy characterizes the star's relationship with Claire DuBrey as one that was kept safe under the guise of asexuality: "Marie's matronly looks and aura served to shield her personal life and private happiness."[25] The same sentence could be applied, quite aptly, to either *Emma* or *Christopher Bean.* The central conflict in both is the fact that none of the other characters can believe that Marie Dressler can be either object or subject of desire. These two films deal precisely with the ways Dressler's sexuality is invisible, and her erotic energies are repurposed into a very visible mode of parenting meant to relegate her romantic impulses to a fond past. But this is a variation on the same model employed in the Bette Davis films that Patricia White cites to demonstrate how the films use this pseudo-parenting as a mode of eroticism. Having proven her status as an object of desire (in *Emma* an actual court of law is convened on the issue), Dressler's move back to surrogate motherhood acknowledges that her caretaking had always been tinged with the erotic energies of her intense touch. As in many of her other films, these pictures construct the ideal spectator as a jealous child, needing Dressler's care and affection. But by transferring the erotic energies of the older couple's bond into a younger generation's love of Dressler, the films make room for that eroticism to become visible.

Cinderella

> I was too homely for a prima donna and too big for a soubrette.
>
> —Marie Dressler

Hollywood has long cherished an affection for the Cinderella story, the narrative of a poor but virtuous heroine who loves and later marries a wealthy hero.[26] Like Cinderella, these young brides generally earned their marital admission to the upper classes by being able to masquerade successfully as a member already. In comedies like Clara Bow's *It* (Paramount, 1927) Mary Pickford's *My Best Girl* (United Artists, 1927), or Janet Gaynor's *Sunny Side*

Up (Fox, 1929), the heroine's clothes, language, and manners are tasteful and attractive. The marks of their working-class backgrounds are manifested through positive personality traits like spunk, compassion, and an absence of snobbery. Their minor social faux pas are charming, comic, and easily overlooked. It is an important element of the story that in each of these films the young heroine is a shop girl, purveying goods to those wealthy enough to consume them.

Other Cinderellas also tend to have white-collar jobs, many of them requiring that they perform a professional service for the man they will eventually marry. They can be his secretary, as in the dramas *Companionate Marriage* (First National, 1928) with Betty Bronson, or *Restless Youth* (Columbia, 1928) with Marceline Day. In these, the young professional and his able secretary eventually discover that the daily intimacies of taking dictation, scheduling appointments, and paying bills have fostered a pleasant dependence, and the employer declares that he cannot live without the woman with whom he shares his office. These secretary films tend to demonstrate the ways in which wifehood can often be read as a job—the secretary moves into the hero's home, gets a better wardrobe and social standing, and continues her duties taking care of the small details of the professional's life, so he can think about more important things.

More intimately, the cinematic Cinderella can also be the governess to the hero's child or children, taking a job that places her in the position of living in his home and occupying a quasi-maternal position relative to his offspring. The governess occupies a delicate class position. Her labors confer upon the children the education, manners, and morals that will enable them to occupy their parents' class. And yet the governess herself does not belong to the class she teaches, and she becomes a kind of shadow figure to the ruling classes. The erotic charge of this liminal position within the master's household has been explored in literature at least as far back as Charlotte Brontë's *Jane Eyre*, which was first published in 1847. The novel was adapted to the silent screen at least six times between 1910 and 1921, and it made its first appearance in the talkies for Monogram in 1934, with Virginia Bruce in the title role and Dressler's own partner Claire DuBrey as the mad wife, Bertha Rochester. The melodramatic possibilities for cross-class romance in the governess film were further exploited for films like RKO's *Devotion* (1931), in which shy Ann Harding nurses such an intense crush on Leslie Howard that she disguises herself as an old woman in order to take a position as his children's governess. By the time he discovers her true identity, he is already enraptured with the ways in which her presence in his home makes his life richer and easier. Later iterations of the theme, such as the Bette Davis vehicle *All This and Heaven Too* (Warner Bros., 1940) and the classic *The Sound of Music* (1965), demonstrate the enduring fascination of the governess as a romantic subject.

But while Hollywood clearly regarded showgirls, secretaries, and governesses as progressive erotic objects of cross-class romance, precious few films showed the master falling in love with the housekeeper. Although the housekeeper occupies the position closest to "wife" in a conventional sense—she cooks, cleans, and manages the household—the class status of the master is maintained precisely by having someone other than his wife perform all those menial tasks. That is, by the time one is rich enough to have a housekeeper, one is rich enough to spare one's wife such tasks. The line between white/pink-collar and blue-collar labor is important here. While the shop girl, secretary, and governess manage goods and information for the employer, the housekeeper hauls, cooks, and cleans. She gets her hands dirty in the daily performance of her tasks. This domestic pollution places her in a different category of laborers, one that is less bound up with the erotic charge of the pristine white-collar working girls. Marie Dressler's history of cinematic bodily "pollution," registered in *The Callahans and the Murphys*, *Anna Christie*, *Min and Bill*, and the whole ethos of slapstick comedy, further contributed to her status as unclean object of desire.

On the rare occasions when Hollywood films of the late silent and early sound periods treated the subject of romance between a blue-collar servant and an employer, they always included some way of removing the stain of domestic pollution from the woman, often through extraordinary means. One of Hollywood's few forays into this territory was in its three adaptations of Israel Zangwill's 1903 play *Merely Mary Ann*, one in 1916, one in 1920, and one in 1931, the year before *Emma* was released. A romantic drama about a composer who reluctantly falls in love with the young drudge who cleans and serves in his boardinghouse, the play was itself an adaptation of Zangwill's much darker novella of the same title. The novella describes the hero, Lancelot, in his first encounter with the maid: "The first time Lancelot saw Mary Ann she was cleaning the steps. He avoided treading upon her, being kind to animals. For the moment she was merely a quadruped, whose head was never lifted to the stars."[27] This brutal description of Mary Ann places her on her hands and knees, scrubbing the dirt beneath Lancelot's feet. The work of domestic labor is written on her body, and it is overcome only with great effort. Most tellingly, when Lancelot begins to fall in love with her, he asks Mary Ann to wear gloves, so her rough hands will not irritate his refined sensibilities—essentially transforming the rough front paws of the quadruped into the fit limbs of a bipedal equal.

The novella ends with the two lovers going their separate ways, but the play and film versions of *Merely Mary Ann* tacked on a happy ending: though the composer briefly considers turning Mary Ann into his mistress, her inheritance of a large fortune renders that scheme impractical, and they are briefly separated before being reunited at the premier of his opera. This deus-ex-long-lost-uncle is typical of the strategies used in the movies to erase the stain of domestic labor from potential spouses. The happy ending could not be achieved until the identity of the maid was fundamentally altered to make her a suitable companion to the employer.

But the supply of rich dead uncles being finite, many of Hollywood's other films about a romance between the maid and the master posit the domestic as a person in disguise, so the stain of household labor simply falls away with the revelation of her former identity. The attractive housekeeper in *Pleasure Crazed* (Fox, 1929) turns out to be a crook, whose plot to steal some jewels is abandoned when she falls in love with her intended victim. The beautiful cooks in *Honey* (Paramount, 1930) and *The Runaway Bride* (RKO, 1930) turn out to be, respectively, the impoverished landlady and a socialite on the run from a gang of jewel thieves. Later versions of the story reversed the genders of the domestic and the employer. Most famously, the handsome butler in *My Man Godfrey* (Universal, 1936) turns out to be a dispirited Boston blue blood. The copycat comedy *Merrily We Live* (MGM, 1938) transforms the butler into a famous writer doing research. In a later variant, the domestic became a symbol of democratic ideals by lifting him- or herself into public life, as when the butler wins a seat in parliament before proposing to his employer in *The Baroness and the Butler* (Fox, 1938) or the maid wins a congressional seat before marrying her boss in *The Farmer's Daughter* (RKO, 1947).

But in *Emma* and *Christopher Bean*, no such magical or civic-minded device undermines the class status of the two housekeepers played by Marie Dressler. They are just housekeepers. So when the other characters are simply unable to perceive the romantic relationships that they form, they are behaving in ways consistent with the genre: Marie Dressler is an extremely unlikely Cinderella. In a kind of meta-cinematic sense, it is possible to see the younger characters behaving as though they are the stars of the picture, while their maid is a supporting actor, as would be the normal hierarchy of a Hollywood feature. They go about their business, expecting Dressler's support. With the revelation of the housekeepers' marriages, the rest of the characters behave as though they are surprised to discover that they are the supporting actors, and Dressler is the star. In this moment of shock, the logic of Hollywood's marginalization of mature female sexuality shifts into view like the hidden figure in a gestalt puzzle. The marginalized woman's sexuality, hidden in plain sight all through the picture, becomes suddenly visible to all.

While these films do not fully suggest her erotic attachments to other women, they do make visible the kinds of devices that keep the erotic attachments of queer old broads out of the public eye, devices that often use class difference as a shield against threatening sexualities. An unnamed reviewer for *Time* criticized Dressler's Oscar-winning work in *Min and Bill* rather strangely: "Miss Dressler, who, made a star because of the extravagant praise given her for her work in bit-parts (*Time*, July 28), has now kept on making bit-parts out of roles in which she was supposed to star."[28] The author does not elaborate on how a starring role can become a supporting one, but the quotation seems to mean that Dressler plays her roles with a series of disconnected scene-stealing tricks to suggest the character's noble outsider status, rather than settling into a confident and unified performance as the star. The vaudeville aesthetic lingered, even after Dressler began to play lead roles.

More interestingly, the *Time* reviewer's remark also suggests that Dressler's starring roles still cast her as the *kinds of people* who were usually supporting characters: aging mothers, aunts, wise old crones, dowagers, and most radically, maids. Patricia White has argued that "the supporting character—at once essential and marginal to classical realism and its narrative goals—is a site for the encoding of the threat and the promise of homosexual difference."[29] So the most obvious lesbian presence in classical Hollywood cinema has been relegated to memorable supporting roles played by actors like Judith Anderson, Agnes Moorehead, Thelma Ritter, Eve Arden, or Ethel Waters. These wry, deep-voiced stars sometimes played characters who made slyly overt references to lesbian sexuality, like Anderson's Mrs. Danvers in *Rebecca*, or Moorehead's prison warden in *Caged*. But most often, they played characters whose sexuality was supposed to be irrelevant: housekeepers, nurses, aunts, and best friends. From the margins and usually veiled by class difference, they would comment on and judge the heterosexual doings of the leads, sometimes aiding and sometimes obstructing the course of straight love. According to White, "They were the types who were meant to remain invisible so that the codes of Hollywood's heterosexual contract would also remain invisible."[30] When Dressler's marriages betray her place in the sexual economies of these films, the codes of that "heterosexual contract" are both revealed and critiqued. They are, in this sense, profoundly interesting films.

Emma

> I bet there isn't a bed as good as that in the whole of Niagara Falls.
>
> —Emma

The advertisements for *Emma* tried to posit the film as a sentimental romance. A photo that ran in the *Los Angeles Evening Herald Express* showed Jean Hersholt lovingly holding Marie Dressler's face, while she turns her eyes shyly away from his adoring gaze. The caption read, "Marie Dressler and Jean Hersholt are caught in the bliss of romance in this scene from 'Emma' at the Criterion."[31] But the reviews of *Emma* nearly all used language that suggested that the romantic relationship between Dressler and Hersholt was sexless or pitiful, rather than romantic and emotionally rich. *New York Liberty Magazine* suggests "the wealthy old inventor and the housekeeper marry, more out of loneliness than anything else."[32] The *Philadelphia Record* treated the marriage as a melodramatic "weakness," a "divergence from her fated lot in life . . . one for which she pays almost too dearly."[33] The *Portland Oregon Journal* explains the marriage at length: "He's the inventor in whose home Emma . . . is housekeeper, whose children she mothers, whose comfort and health are constantly in her thoughts, who, finally, finds her so much a part of his life that he marries her. Perhaps their marriage is not a love match, in the sense marriages of younger folks usually are, but it has the foundation of sincere affection."[34] No reviews I have found described the film as a romance or love story. Yet the film hovers around the romantic nature of Dressler's attachment to the Smith family with an almost obsessive constancy.

Based on a screenplay by Frances Marion, *Emma* demonstrates an interest in the hidden nature of human sexuality from the beginning. It opens in New York, during 1911, as Mrs. Smith is giving birth to the youngest child. The other Smith children sit around the table as Emma scurries through the kitchen looking for blankets and water. Bill asks, "Will the stork bring the baby in a blanket, or just wrapped up any old way?" Isabelle rejects the stork scenario, asserting that the doctor brings the baby in his medical bag.

The youngest, Gypsy, simply cries, though when Emma asks why she is crying she confesses that she does not know. The children, each in his or her own way, are working through their anxieties about sexuality. Emma is busy trying to save their mother's life and does not correct them. When the scene moves upstairs to the mother's bedroom, the woman in labor is of course not shown, due to strict Production Code regulations. The camera is placed behind the headboard of the bed, so the camera captures frontal images of Emma and the doctor looking into a kind of black chasm, with a large, dramatic window behind them. The sufferings of the dying woman are excluded from this oblique shot, emphasizing the unseen, drawing a line around the unrepresentable reality of the female body in reproduction and in pain. The film thus begins on this painful note, with the mother's death, the children's ignorance, Emma's wisdom, and the chasm of human sexuality clearly placed in the center of the screen. The tragedy that befalls the family with the loss of the mother is clearly inscribed around the dark danger of sexuality and reproduction, the realities of which are transformed into fairy stories by the children and forbidden to the audience. When the doctor despairs that the baby is not breathing, it is Emma who slaps it on the back to make him draw breath. She guards the door of life and death, while the doctor simply observes.

She also guards the door, literally, to the mother's bedroom. Emma brings the baby out to meet its siblings; she sits down on the kitchen stairs so the children can peek at the little bundle without entering their dead mother's bedroom. Stopping Mr. Smith on his way to his wife's bedroom, Emma shakes her head wordlessly. Understanding, Mr. Smith withdraws in despair. This extraordinary moment on the stairs, a liminal space between the warm family kitchen and the dark maternal deathbed, points to Emma's position between the two locations. Keeping the rest of the family always in the sunny kitchen, she stands guard at the door of death. And she does so by setting her bum right down on the stairs, as though she is a child herself, sharing life with the children, and death with their father. Like Zangwill's Mary Ann, scrubbing the boardinghouse steps, Emma is associated with dirt, and that which is beneath our feet. But she can also be understood as being somewhere between high and low, ready to climb the steps at any time. The older Smith children will always regard her as being beneath them, reading her generous physical humility as a marker of her debased class status. But Mr. Smith, a step back from the tableau, recognizes the powerful position she occupies.

After this tragedy, the narrative picks up in 1931 with a scene that establishes Emma's special relationship with Ronnie, the baby she saved, now a handsome young man. The darling of the family, Ronnie is played by Richard Cromwell, a boyish blond actor who made a modest hit two years before in *Tol'able David* (Columbia, 1930). Dressler had met Cromwell outside the studio because he was a close friend of Claire DuBrey. Though he worked for rival Columbia, Dressler made up her mind that the baby-faced twenty-two-year old must have the role of Ronnie. Betty Lee reports that Dressler cornered the casting officer, Louis B. Mayer, and finally Nicholas Schenk himself, in her determination to have her choice.[35] The casting of this charming young man was a capitulation to the star's desire, a condition that underscores his character's function as the sentimental heart of the film. The chemistry between Cromwell and Dressler is apparent, underscoring the ways in which this film is about fond attractions between characters who would not be conventional romantic leads. It also contributes to the ways the film conflates Emma's intimate affection for Ronnie's father, Frederick, with her intimate affection for the son. While the middle-aged object of desire is tame, sweet, and frankly paternal, the young object of desire is dangerous, demonstrative, and frankly flirtatious. The film merges these two as it gradually reveals and then obscures again Emma's erotic function in the household.

Twenty years have passed, and the family is now fabulously wealthy as a result of Mr. Smith's clever inventions. The scene opens with Emma in the linen closet, gathering towels. The spoiled older children each summon Emma with a note, Isabelle's (Myrna Loy) explaining that it's a matter of life or death. But when Emma discovers that Ronnie is home from school, she ignores the other three and runs right to her favorite, who greets her with a kiss on the cheek and his nickname for her, "Beautiful," to which Emma, habitually and with mock severity, replies "Don't call me 'Beautiful.'" Turning to his father and holding Dressler's arms so that he is literally presenting the older woman to the elder Smith, Ronnie insists, "She is beautiful, isn't she, Dad?" Distracted with his inventions, Mr. Smith does not respond. When Ronnie is present, he participates in a mock romance with Emma that is touched with ambivalence. Ronnie seems to be making a joke of her sexuality, though he is the only one who appreciates and draws out the Dressler character. This favorite child makes overt what is one of the film's most interesting insights into the relationship between the loving domestic and the family she cares for. Her relationship to the Smith family is undeniably a very intimate, very physical one. Several times she is shown in the linen closet, counting sheets and bath towels, regulating what will touch the bodies of the family. She refuses Isabelle's attempts to plan the menu for a dinner party, insisting that she, Emma, has been feeding the family for years and is capable of selecting appropriate foods. She regulates Mr. Smith's diet with particular care, reminiscing about how she has had to stay up "half the night" with him in the past because of his indigestion. This imagery of bathing, feeding, and nocturnal oversight of the family connects Emma to the most intimate aspects of their physical care. That the rich are able to delegate such tasks to servants is unexceptional. It is extraordinary, however, that this film makes a point of sexualizing that delegation, not in the person of a sexy young soubrette, but in the person of Marie Dressler.

Insisting he has a date with a "high flyer," Ronnie runs off to the airfield. Thinking he may be mixed up with a chorus girl, Emma follows him. The conflation of aviation and sexual adventure is one way the film sublimates the sexual connection of Emma and Ronnie into a form of danger. He likes to fly airplanes; she likes to stay firmly rooted to the ground. Out of place at the airport, Emma has to grab her hat to keep it on her head, while her skirt is lifted a bit by the strong drafts off the planes. When she expresses worry about his safety, Ronnie insists on strapping Emma into a flight simulator, even pushing her rear end with his hands to encourage her to climb the stairs to the platform that holds the contraption. Uncertain, Emma requires a lot of persuasion, and the flight mechanic insists twice, "You're as safe as you are in bed," while hustling her toward the cockpit. When he touches her to help move her along, she calls him "fresh" several times. This scene subjects Dressler's body to the usual indignities of slapstick comedy, and contrasts them with Emma's reserve and propriety. The child forces on her a kind of adventurous bodily experience that is out of line with her safe domestic life. The comedy of this scene is born of her unsuitability to the anxiety and physical exuberance of flying. The simulator tosses her back and forth and flips her upside down, while Dressler responds with facial contortions, hoarse yelps, and much flailing of her arms. Her romance with Ronnie's father will be quieter, more domestic, and more harmonious with her age.

Back at the Smith home, Emma goes up to her bedroom to pack for a long-overdue vacation. Rolling up a giant corset, the film makes a joke both about Dressler's size and about the intimacy of the things that touch our bodies. When Smith comes to her door to say goodbye, Emma tries to hide the corset behind her back but fails more or less to conceal it. Mr. Smith admits that he has never seen her room before and remarks on the photos on the wall, particularly the fact that there are more of Ronnie than the other children. The combination of Ronnie and the bedroom, its strangeness to Mr. Smith, and the pesky corset lend the scene a striking intimacy. Smith frets over how the family will manage without her, particularly with Isabelle quarreling with her husband. Emma's extraordinary response to this problem is to defend the marriage, noting that Isabelle loves her husband and, after all, "Women are queer. I knew one who was crazy over a pet mud turtle." This striking comment is simultaneously innocuous (it comes off as a homespun bit of parenting advice, as though Isabelle's husband is an odd pet she picked up somewhere) and perverse. The casting of Myrna Loy as the sour daughter Isabelle emphasizes the character's sexual neurosis.

This was Loy's first film at MGM, after a six-year period of multistudio work in which she was often cast as exotic foreign temptresses. Her makeup nearly always emphasized her lovely almond-shaped eyes, which filmmakers used to signify the mysteriously and erotically foreign. She had played the Arab girl Azuzi in *The Desert Song* (Warner Bros., 1929), the gypsy temptress Nubi in *The Squall* (First National, 1929), the Indian princess Yasmini in *The Black Watch* (Fox, 1929), the Mexican siren Lolita in *Under a Texas Moon* (Warner Bros., 1930), and the treacherous Arthurian queen, Morgan le Fay, in *A Connecticut Yankee* (Fox, 1930). While MGM would eventually reinvent Loy as "the perfect wife," two of her most outrageous exotic villainesses were still ahead of her when she made *Emma.* Later in 1932, she would appear as Fah Lo See in *The Mask of Fu Manchu,* and as a murderous half-Indian mystic hypnotist who systematically murders the women who had rejected her at boarding school in *Thirteen Women.* Loy was right in the middle of this (decidedly precode) string of sexually transgressive roles when she was cast as a class-conscious young socialite opposite the kind and tolerant Marie Dressler.

So when Emma calls Isabelle "queer" and facetiously marries her off to a box turtle, it is a reminder of this erotic disturbance in the Smith household, the young woman who resents and betrays her. Given her marital difficulties and frankly immoderate resentment of sweet Emma, it is not a particular stretch to regard Isabelle's nastiness as a symptom of sexual jealousy at the housekeeper's preference for Ronnie. This unease in the household sets the stage for the film's representation of Emma's expansive sexuality and suggests how the child with a crush fits into the film's narrative framework. Because of her crush on Emma, whose attention the children fight for, Isabelle resents both her spoiled brother and Emma's marriage to her father. The women reconcile only when both men have died, and Emma is again in a position to mother the motherless.

The fact that Emma is going to Niagara Falls for her vacation suggests a honeymoon; she seems to cherish no further hope for a husband, so she will go herself. Or, as she tells Smith, "I've been wanting to go all my life and I'm gonna go." But she is reluctant to leave the family that is her true source of pleasure for the compensatory pleasure of a nonhoneymoon. Of course this sentiment is expressed in terms of the bedroom. "I bet there's not a bed as good as that in the whole of Niagara Falls," she notes wistfully. The final item she packs is her alarm clock, which she announces she will set every night just for the pleasure of ignoring it each morning when it rings and she finds she does not have to get up. This moment plants in the viewer's head an image of Emma in bed, both at home and in Niagara Falls, and emphasizes her experiences of sensual pleasures associated with the bed.

When Smith takes her to the train station, the film continues to explore its fascination with the bedroom. Insisting that Emma needs some magazines for the train ride, Smith chooses some serious political and scientific literature from the newsstand. Emma, on the other hand, chooses women's magazines on the subjects of love and fashion. Picking one up, she sees a photo of a scantily clad lingerie model and puts the magazine down in alarm. Asked if she has remembered to pack everything, Emma replies, "Worst comes to worst I can borrow a nightgown from the engineer." These two moments certainly invite a queer reading. Dressler's anxiety, even panic, at the sight of the lingerie ad points to both an experience of covert desire and a sense of alienated identification. Her own bulky corset has been the object of blatant display in the film, standing in for the size, age, and even the vulnerability of her body. Her offer to borrow a nightgown from the engineer further marks her alienation from conventional femininity, but also accesses the pleasures of cross-dressing, of masquerade, of wearing another person's clothing. Emma's attempt to kid about her unfeminine body again points backward to her own sexuality, as it has throughout her career. By using her body for comedy, Dressler has put it into evidence in ways that permit and even invite sexual desire.

The scene emphasizes exposure, the ways in which the domestic Emma is suddenly vulnerable out in public. Carrying her bag for her, Smith does not notice that a piece of the suitcase has ripped and Emma's things are falling out, including her corset and the sweater she has been knitting for Ronnie.

Following behind him, Emma notices with horror that her possessions are being scattered around the train station. She begins gathering them up, winding her knitting yarn back into a ball as she tries to track Smith through the labyrinth of people. It is a lovely moment, creating a comic connection between two old people whose lives are threaded together by the sweater, a gift for Ronnie, the child whose birth put Emma in the place of parent to the children. Walking past the fallen corset, Emma refuses knowledge of it, and she snorts in disgust at a passerby who picks it up and offers it to her. The accident with the suitcase further binds Emma and Smith together, demonstrating her employer's affection for her, but also his incompetence in small tasks, his need for her. Recognizing his need, Emma reminds him, "Your heavy underwear is in the bottom drawer of your bureau." But Smith is unable to tolerate the prospect of her absence and proposes, "Let's be alone together, Emma." A touching, flustering scene follows in which he sits very close to her on a bus station bench and has to work very hard to convince her that he is serious, that his feelings for her are genuine and romantic. Emma admits, "It doesn't seem to be real somehow. It seems as if I was dreaming." At this moment, the alarm clock in her bag goes off, presenting a gag on the word "dream," a word that has always had a sensual connection to the voluptuousness of sleep and bedrooms. The suddenness of the alarm jolts them back to the present and the realization they are about to miss the train, so they rush off to the platform, Emma's bag ringing all the way, which draws the mirth of the crowd. The film has these antiromantic impulses—let the characters enter a reverie, and then the comedy kicks in, breaking through the sense of dream, or emotional seriousness. With Ronnie, Emma's sexuality is sublimated into comic gestures: fluttering, nagging, pushing, pulling, and flailing. With Smith, the romantic moments are quiet and touching, but usually deflated by these sudden alarms and the unkind gaze of strangers.

The scrutiny of others is particularly brutal in Niagara Falls, where the other honeymooners regard them with suspicion. Smith and Emma are next seen spending a happy afternoon in a rowboat—Emma is rowing. Smith asks Emma if she's happy. She replies that she's happier than she ever thought she would be. Two young men and a young woman vigorously paddle by in a canoe. They heckle Smith and Emma, calling them "ancient honeymooners." "Why doesn't he row her?" one of the men demands, to which the young woman replies, "Aw, she's too chivalrous to let him." This remark riles Smith, who insists on taking the oars from Emma. Explaining that he was on the rowing team in college, Smith draws the rowboat past the young scamps in a vindicating display of manliness. Then he collapses from exhaustion. Again, this scene holds the aging lovers up to ridicule and demonstrates their acute self-consciousness about their age and the nature of their relationship. The confrontation of melodramatic love plot (the sentimental honeymoon) and comedy (the large woman is rowing while the small man reclines) has created a conflict that adds poignancy to the moment, strikes the characters with agonizing self-consciousness, and leads Smith to exert himself to the point of endangering his life. The film plays up this generic conflict with extraordinary precision during the first half of the film.

Smith's frail health is unable to withstand his efforts to perform the role of protective husband in public. Back in their room, he reclines on a

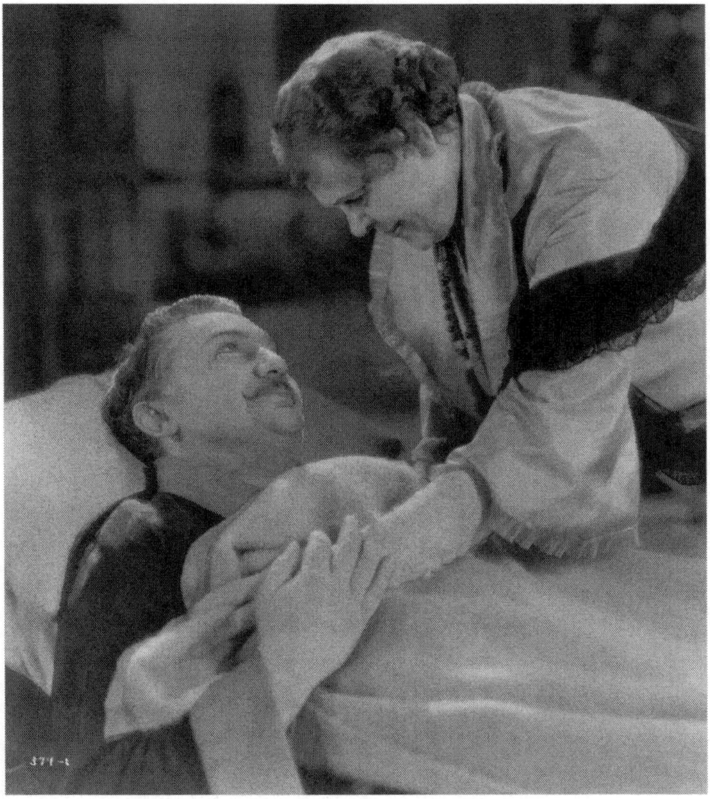

FIGURE 23. The bedroom scene sexualizes the marriage: Dressler and Jean Hersholt in *Emma* (1932).

couch while Emma bosses the hotel maid. When she leaves, Emma turns tender, insisting that Smith keep his arms under the blanket. Smith's position in a makeshift bed suggests the sexuality of their relationship—she has already speculated about the beds in Niagara Falls, and now she tucks her husband into one; the scene looks like one from a marriage (figure 23). Smith asks her to sing to him. She demurs, insisting, "I have a voice that only a deaf mother could stand." "Or an affectionate husband," counters Smith. He asks her to sing the song "that Ronnie likes," again conflating her love for Ronnie with her love for Smith. "Don't you mind it honey if the world goes wrong, 'cause I'll still love you," sings Emma, sitting at the piano as the light in the room begins to fade. Unseen, Mr. Smith's arms slip out from under the blanket, his head slumps to the side, and he is gone. Emma, unseeing, plays on.

There are, then, three scenes of romantic happiness for Emma before she enters the dark third act of the film, when she inherits Smith's fortune but loses all the things that had brought her happiness—caring for the Smith children, the devotion of their father, and even Ronnie, who is killed in a plane crash. When the family lawyer reports the details of Smith's will to the children, and they realize that the former housekeeper will receive the whole fortune, the elder three begin to fume, eventually insisting that their father was not in his right mind when he made the will. Emma had been prepared to turn the money over to the children, but when she hears them maligning their father, she becomes furious and throws them out of the house. Ronnie is pleased and bemused, congratulating Emma on her spunk and hitting her up for money to buy a plane. Distractedly, Emma consents.

Walking back into the house, Emma is confronted with the physical impression of her isolation. She sees a ghostly image of Bill sliding down the banister. He falls, and calls to her, but disappears before she reaches him. She sees a ghostly image of little Gypsy reading a book and crying. Emma goes to comfort her, and she too disappears. The world contains little warmth or physical comfort for Emma in these scenes, and Dressler is uncharacteristically dwarfed by the big, stark, empty sets. Her widow's black sets her off against the sterile white of the patrician manor. The fact that she cannot touch the remembered children is painful to her, and her loneliness is expressed as bodily isolation. Dressler's characters always express anxiety by a kind of anxious physical movement. In this case, Emma hugs herself and touches her face as she confronts the loss of the people she has loved.

The Dressler technique of touching all those around her is turned inward, magnifying the isolation of the character.

The spoiled children, led by Isabelle, bring murder charges against Emma in an attempt to break the will, using as a witness the petulant housemaid from Niagara Falls who observed Smith complaining about having to take his medicine, and Emma insisting that he should take it. Like the Smith children and the young boaters, this maid is unable to perceive the tenderness between Emma and Smith and interprets their teasing as genuine discord. Emma, befuddled by the proceedings, is unable to remember precisely how many pills she gave to Smith, and the prosecution makes much of the maid's inflectionless transcription of a line Emma had originally delivered with teasing affection: "Do I have to hold your nose and put these pills down your throat?" The court case is based on the misperception that old folks are incapable of romantic banter.

The court case proceeds on the basis of this testimony, with the Smith children essentially arguing that it would be impossible for their father to love Emma because her class status and body type are ill-suited to the cultural norm of romantic love. Their ridiculous interpretation of the events, that she somehow entrapped their father into marriage and then poisoned him, is a melodramatic murder plot befitting a much younger villainess. Their charges depend on two conflicting scenarios: the Hollywood convention of working-class gold diggers taking advantage of addled old millionaires and the children's insistent conviction that Emma could hold no romantic charm for their father. Emma's lawyer has two grounds on which to defend Emma. Instead of arguing that it is entirely plausible that Smith could love this homely middle-aged woman, he takes the narrower path, insisting that the jury recognize that Emma Thatcher Smith is too naïve, too old, too loving to fit the absurd logic of the gold-digger narrative. Regaling the jury with stories of the Smith children's craven moments, the lawyer tricks Emma into leaping to their defense, which she does in the film's most melodramatic episode. Dressler plays this speech to the rafters, clutching her chest, then spreading her arms wide and putting a hoarse moan in her voice as she insists that it no longer matters what happens to her, but the lawyer must not accuse the children. Drained, she collapses into the defendant's chair with the urgent plea to her lawyer, "No, it's an injustice—you've got to take it back!" The lawyer then turns to the jury and asks if this woman could really be a murderer. It is a moment that is designed to undo the humorless maid's testimony by allowing the jury to see Dressler's emotional capacity. If the case turns on the reading of a line, it is also possible to understand the film as allegory for cinema: what role will the jury assign to this woman? Clearly, she belongs in the role of mother.

The evidence used to acquit Emma, then, is a demonstration not of her genuine romantic attachment to Smith, but of her maternal attachment to the children. The film never does "prove" that Frederick Smith was in his right mind to desire and marry his housekeeper. What it does prove is that Emma was Smith's true wife insofar as she fits into the model of a nuclear family. He is the children's father, so the lawyer gives the jury a way to read Emma as the children's mother, proving that her marriage to Smith made sense. Claire Van Ens points out that the word "Emma" comes to sound oddly like the word "Mama" when spoken by the characters in this film.[36] This strategy bypasses the question of desire, in fact emphasizing her maternal qualities as a way of desexing her. While it is a reasonable defense against the charge that Emma is a gold digger, it undermines the film's heretofore proud assertion of romantic love between those in the elder generation.

Ronnie is in Canada on a hunting trip and does not read about the trial until it is already underway. When he finds out, he sends a telegram to Emma and rushes back to his plane. A storm is raging over the Northeast, but his determination to help Emma outweighs his concern for his own life. So a second cloud hangs over the trial. Ronnie is in danger. This added poignancy contributes to the melodramatic charge of the courtroom—Emma's life is in danger on the ground, and her favorite child is in peril in the air (figure 24). The courtroom scenes use several crane shots, showing the action from a high angle, as if to remind the viewer that Ronnie is in the sky. A particularly bravura moving crane shot shows the jury filing back in to pronounce Emma not guilty. The camera movement suggests that Ronnie's spirit hovers over the courtroom moments before the district attorney informs Emma that her favorite child's plane has gone down in the storm. Emma physically collapses.

Back at the Smith mansion, Ronnie's casket is set up in the parlor with large candles on either side of the body, transforming the room into a church-like space. The casket is barely visible at the bottom of the frame as Emma says goodbye to her favorite, the great candles flanking her. The shot is eerily reminiscent of the scenes of Ronnie's birth, when the headboard of the mother's bed occupied the same position in the frame where the casket is now located, and the bedposts framed Emma's distraught figure as the candles do in this later shot. Both the unrepresentable trauma of childbirth and the terror

FIGURE 24. Solitude in *Emma* (1932).

of death lay in the abyss before Emma, outside the camera's reach. Ronnie emerged from that space, and he returns to it, while Emma stands vigil. Like the moment on the stairs, this framing suggests a kind of liminal space, where Emma guards the gate between life and death. And it also suggests the space in the theater auditorium, where the audience sits. Looking directly toward the coffin, which is just below the camera, Emma seems to direct her love at the spectator, who is placed in the position of the beloved child.

Mr. Smith and Ronnie thus gone, Emma transfers her affections to a new generation of children, despite the pleas from the now-repentant Smith children that she should stay. The film ends with Emma happily employed in a new household, with a middle-class doctor's growing brood. The scene fades in to a shot of Emma diapering a baby. The doctor's wife thanks Emma for saving her youngest's life when he was born, but she insists that slapping the baby's back to make it breathe is "an old trick." When the young mother asks her if there is any way they can thank her, Emma replies that she would like it if they named the baby Ronnie. The young mother agrees, and immediately points out that little Ronnie has had an accident and soaked the front of Emma's skirt where she's holding him in her lap. Shaking out her skirt with robust good humor, Emma replies, "That's nothing. That's not the first time that's happened to me!" Holding the leaky baby against her cheek, she coos, "Ronnie." She has replaced the object of her desire and brought a new Ronnie into being.

In fact, as Ronnie's accident on her dress demonstrates, she revels even in the excesses of children's physical lives, insisting on no boundaries between her body and their needs. The physical love promised by her ample body, always ambiguously split between the childlike husband and the loverly child, is redirected at the new children in her care. Because the children are surrogates, plentiful, indeed interchangeable, the children in her care become surrogates for the audience. Emma's love for Mr. Smith/Ronnie is transposed onto the viewer.

Christopher Bean

> NEW MAID: "I see, old-fashioned kind, sleep in one bed. All the places I works at, the Mr. and Mrs. has twin beds."
> ABBY: "Land sakes, weren't they married?"

In the play *The Late Christopher Bean*, the character of Abby is described as "a Yankee villager, aged vaguely between young and maturity, of a wistful prettiness, simple and serious."[37] In the Broadway version of the play, Abby was played by Pauline Lord, an actress slightly younger, far thinner, and a bit more vulnerable than Dressler. Lord specialized in playing naïve characters, women whose strength was drawn from a certain trusting and incorruptible innocence (figure 25).[38] The reviewer for *Life* claimed that this was another of Lord's "wrung-out dish-raggy characters."[39] The play is essentially a morality tale, demonstrating the gradual degradation of Dr. Milton Haggett, who slowly convinces himself of the righteousness of exploiting Abby's ignorance to profit from Bean's paintings. For the film version, a less wistful Marie Dressler was cast, a choice that changed the trajectory of the film, making Abby necessarily older, wiser, more knowing and physically imposing. As was conventional for Dressler vehicles, some wry lines and broad slapstick comedy were also added. The resulting film is a comic morality tale, one that pits the doctor not against an aging, fragile naïf, but against a hearty, good-natured woman whose only blind spot is her protective and sentimental memory of her late, secret spouse, the artist Christopher Bean.

While *Emma*'s evaluators tended to miss Dressler's performance of sexuality altogether, *Christopher Bean* hinges even more directly on the character's romantic past. Reviews of the film generally noted outright whether the writer could accept Dressler as the subject or object of desire. The *Los Angeles News* reviewer wrote approvingly, "MGM plugged this picture of [*sic*] Marie Dressler's birthday gift to her public. At that time it created conjecture as to whether or not Marie's pan permitted making understandable the intense love between herself and the painter. Chris Bean could not have put on canvas the mental beauty and devotion that Marie manages to convey.

FIGURE 25. In the Broadway play *The Late Christopher Bean* (1931–32), Pauline Lord played Abby as a fairly slim, naïve, and vulnerable woman.

Her performance refutes previous predictions of miscasting; it is, rather, a triumph for Marie and a tribute to MGM for its recognition of the warm, sincere quality of the grand ol' gal."[40] The writer for the rival *Los Angeles Examiner* disagreed: "It seems to me that Marie Dressler, as good an actress as she is, was scarcely the choice for Abby, the hired girl. Pauline Lord played the role in New York, and making a choice at random, I should think that Marjorie Rambeau would have been an excellent type for the screen. Grand trouper that she is, Marie Dressler does not quite bring the suggestion of romance that the picture should have."[41] The film is a kind of Rorschach test of the public's willingness to view Dressler as a romantic heroine.

Perhaps because of the consternation, MGM made some effort to push audiences toward a more romantic interpretation of the film. On December 17, 1933, the *New York Times* reported that MGM had changed the name of the film, already in release, to *Her Sweetheart*. The studio's reported reason for this unusual gesture was that "the public demanded it."[42] I have found no particular evidence that the public demanded it. It is perhaps more plausible that the name "Christopher Bean" didn't mean anything to the general public and wasn't packing the movie houses with eager fans. But the effect of this new title was to make explicit and oddly bland what in the film is intriguing and half hidden: Marie Dressler is an object of desire.

A brief prologue shows a Boston art auction, in which a Christopher Bean painting brings fifteen thousand dollars. This previously unknown, deceased artist is hailed as a newly discovered genius. A recent issue of "Artist's Life Magazine" contains reprints of Bean's letters, describing his last days as a boarder in the Haggett household of Massachusetts. Two unscrupulous art dealers and one high-minded critic set out to reach the Haggetts and inquire about other Bean canvases. The film then moves to the Haggett household, populated by the good-natured but harried Dr. Haggett (Lionel Barrymore), the sour Mrs. Haggett (Beulah Bondi), and their two grown daughters, vain Ada (Helen Shipman) and kind Susan (Helen Mack). The whole plot takes place on the day their maid, Abby, is packing to leave the household after nineteen years; she is planning to move in with her brother and his children, who need her after the death of their mother. In the course of the day, each of the two crooked art dealers comes to the house posing as an old friend of Bean's, looking to buy any remaining Bean paintings before the Haggetts learn of their true value. While the Haggetts fall all over themselves to provide Bean's paintings to the shysters, Abby is the only one who treats them with suspicion.

After the Boston art auction prologue, the film begins with Dr. Milton Haggett returning from the late-night delivery of a baby. As in *Emma*, the film begins with a birth, and with extensive discussion of human sexuality and fertility. Mrs. Hagett hollers to Abby that she should get Dr. Haggett his breakfast. As in *Prosperity*, our first view of Dressler is of her bending over, with her rear end toward the camera: she is bending over to fetch a puppy from under a fence. As she places the puppy in a basket with its mother and siblings, Abby scolds the mother dog as though she were an unwed human mother: "Don't look at me like that. You brought it on yourself." Walking into the garage, Dr. Haggett asks what Abby has. "Two boys and three girls," Abby replies, still humanizing the litter. Dr. Haggett comments on the diversity of the puppies: "Two terriers, two scotties, and one that looks like a bull. Where's the father?" "Over there," Abby says, as she points toward a fence. Three dogs of various sizes and breeds are lined up at the fence, looking earnestly toward the camera. Dr. Haggett laughs in appreciation of the dogs' wicked ways. This opening portrait of illicit canine sexuality sets the scene for a film that will essentially turn on Abby's secret marriage, the childless and legitimate sexual secret she has harbored for many years.

The conversation quickly turns to human mothers.

> ABBY: My Goodness Dr. Haggett, you look all worn out. Doesn't it beat the old scratch so many women have their babies in the middle of the night? Say, you'd think they was brought by owls, not storks.
> DR. HAGGETT: That's the doctor's life, Abby.
> ABBY: Come to think of it, Mrs. Jordan didn't get married none too soon. You'd think when they have the babies so soon after the wedding, you'd have to brush the rice off of them.

Abby locates childbirth in the middle of the night, associated with mystery, with danger, indeed with "old scratch" himself. She references the sanitized fairy-tale stork, but replaces it with the predatory owl, the night bird. And then she passes judgment on Mrs. Jordan. Counting the months backward, she calls out the young couple's illicit sexuality, but locates the chronological problematic in the woman; it is *Mrs.* Jordan who got married none too soon.

Heading inside, Abby reads a newspaper article describing the fifth wedding of a "Mrs. Jordan-Miller," no noted relationship to the previous mother. Reading the text aloud, Abby relates to the Haggett family that "the bride looked beautiful as usual." This whole opening sequence of the film is a tongue-in-cheek indictment of marriage, in which the dog's promiscuity, the young mother's early delivery, and Mrs. Jordan-Miller's fifth husband stand as examples of excessive sexuality in the country village, where sexuality is a wholesome and natural part of life, but hypocrisy dictates the town's easy scorn for those who do not contain their sexuality within marriage. The only fathers included in this indictment of unbridled sexuality are the three dogs, proudly aligned at the fence. It is the female who bears the responsibility, the shame and anxiety of illicit sexual desire. These opening scenes set up the film's central conceit—that even within marriage, there is something a little secret, a little shameful about sexuality and motherhood. The film acknowledges from the outset that to be married is to admit to sexual conduct. The exchange between Abby and the new maid that opens this section points to Abby's frankness about sexuality, her rejection of the chilliness or the pretense represented by the Hollywood bugaboo of twin beds. In Abby's world, married people sleep together. This is the reason she has told no one about her secret marriage to Christopher Bean.

Abby's romantic past is contrasted with the present-day attachments of the two young ladies of the Haggett household. The Depression has caused their father to cancel the annual family trip to Miami, a sacrifice that devastates Ada, whose romantic hopes are pinned on warmer climates because the local boys don't like her. Her father dismisses her melodramatics, teasing her, "Well, what makes the Florida boys like you so much better—is it because they've seen you in your swimming suit? Why don't you give the boys here a chance. Invite them in, put on your swimming suit, and go sit by the fire." This comment cuts through Ada's fussy class-conscious ideas about courtship and reduces sexual attraction to its physical plane. The bald physicality of sexual attraction is replicated in the way the young girls compete for the affections of a young neighbor, the aspiring artist Warren Creamer. When he stops in to finish the job of hanging wallpaper in the study, he comes with an oddly primordial gift to each daughter—paintings of game animals. To Ada he presents a still life of a dead fish, and to Susan he presents a dead duck. Warren's admission that he learned to paint from Christopher Bean cements the connection between Abby's past and the girls' future.

Bean's masterpiece, a portrait of Abby, has hung in her bedroom for nineteen years, unobserved. This room is glimpsed only though a half-open door leading off the kitchen, the foot of a bed protruding into the screen. This veiled space is a visual reminder of the housekeeper's hidden self—a visibly invisible offscreen space. As the new maid comes to replace Abby, the two women discuss the offscreen room. "Well, I hope it's a soft bed," the new maid whines. "You won't be in it long enough to know the difference," Abby replies. Late in the film, this half-hidden space becomes a source of much desire in the household, when it is discovered that Abby's portrait is in there. When the crooked art dealer Tallant learns about the portrait, he begs Abby to show it to him. "Oh, no, I couldn't take you in my room. Mrs. Haggett's been waiting for me to do something like that for nineteen years." The room is off limits, not only because of empty bourgeois propriety, but because Abby keeps her secret self there. And yet, the Haggetts consciously and secretly violate that space in order to profit from the painting. When they discover its existence, the Haggetts send Ada into the bedroom to steal the painting, but she cannot get it off the wall and causes the foot of the bed to collapse in her clumsy efforts. Abby's secret is inviolable.

Even when Abby willingly brings the painting out into the dining room (because the Haggetts want to hang it over the mantel in a preliminary effort to wheedle it out of her), the family is unable to see the sexual history written into the painting. It reveals a beautiful, younger, softer woman, aglow with love (figure 26). In this scene, the audience sees two Dresslers, the mournful and lined face of her live self juxtaposed with the radiant and softer self in the portrait. It is an image that literalizes the idea of a public self and a sexual self, made visible only through the Haggetts' invasion of Abby's private space. Trying to convince Abby to sell the painting, Mr. Haggett accuses her of vanity, arguing that to keep the picture is "no better than sitting all day in front of the looking glass." But Abby insists, "Oh, it ain't me I see; it's the time when I was young, you know, like it was in the old days. It's the . . . it's the, uh . . . I can't say it." Abby stumbles over her description of what the painting represents, leaving an elliptical "uh" in place of her history and her sexuality. It is unspoken, and to the Haggetts invisible, though the audience can see it hidden in plain sight in the painting.

Precisely because her own secret history is being played out among the young women, Abby takes an active role in enabling the elopement of Susan and Warren, despite the meddling of Mrs. Haggett and older sister Ada. To grease the wheels of romance, Abby insists they should hang Warren's paintings in the office, and she asks Susan to climb the ladder while Warren holds it. Proudly noting Susan's eye for decor, she tells Warren, "Susie's so artistic. She's going to make a great wife to some artist." But the jealous Ada, recognizing that Warren Creamer is the only game in town, pulls Susan off the ladder, insisting that she will hang the pictures herself. Trying to sound

FIGURE 26. Dressler, Beulah Bondi, and Lionel Barrymore in *Christopher Bean* (1933): Abby's secret is out in the open, but the Haggetts still cannot see it.

seductive, she asks for help: "Now, Warren, you stand close and steady me." Mischievous Abby grabs the older girl's ankle herself, pretending to be Warren. Ada declares theatrically, "Thanks, Warren, now I feel safe." Abby quietly sends the young lovers out of the study while she continues her ruse with Ada, which quickly devolves into a kind of queer farce. The older daughter pounds a nail inexpertly into the wall and falls backward, landing her hind end on Dressler's face. Wordlessly, Abby uses both hands to push the younger woman's buttocks upward. Awkwardly, they struggle for several seconds of physical comedy, Dressler wrestling with Ada's recalcitrant rear. Throughout, Ada is aglow with sexual pleasure, teasing, "Why Warren Creamer, you're just terrible, ha, ha, ha." Steadying the girl, Abby lets go, looks down at her own hand with disgust, puts the hand jauntily back on her hip, and settles in for sacrificial duty. This fabulously suggestive interaction places Abby in the position of being an invisible, subversive, and reluctant suitor. Even their relative positions—Ada on the ladder, and Abby standing below her—suggest that the scene is a travesty of the idealized Romeo and Juliet arrangement.

And the ways in which Ada is incapable of recognizing Abby in this scene also suggest the ways that her family will fail to recognize—until the very last moment—Abby's romantic history with Christopher Bean. The film is making a point of her invisibility—by making her sexuality, her bodily presence, plainly visible to the audience—in the form of comedy. And her farce is successful in realigning the romantic adventures of the young women. While Abby distracts Ada, Warren secretly proposes to Susan in the next room.

A reflection of her own secret marriage, the elopement of these two young people becomes Abby's personal project. When these crafty young people hide in the back of the old family jalopy that Abby drives to the train station to buy her ticket, they give the older woman such a start that they provoke the film's second indulgence in physical comedy, a wacky driving sequence. It is an important element of this moment that Abby sees the young people in her rear-view mirror; they are like a vision of herself in her past. When she looks in the mirror and sees the young couple reflected back at her, Abby is so startled she turns around to yell at them and loses control of the car. Accidentally putting her foot all the way through the floorboard, Abby desperately tries to steer the now-brakeless car to a stop, veering right and left to avoid obstacles along the country road. A comic spectacle of physical danger follows the revelation of the young people's plan to elope; the film links Dressler's slapstick panic to the notion of sexuality. She crashes the car, and all three get out to help push. When Susan then turns to kiss Warren, Abby is so satisfied with the spectacle that she leans against the car as she watches them, causing it to roll down the hill, out of control. Like the veering and crashing, this accident was set in motion by the sexual charge of the young couple, and Abby's desire to look at them. Her gaze creates a kind of catastrophic energy, in that she sees in them a reflection of her own erotic past. The old car is utterly destroyed by the force of this recognition.

When she returns to the Haggett home with the battered car ("Guess you and me is quittin' the job on the same day."), Abby finds that the Haggetts have been visited several times by imposters posing as friends of Christopher Bean. Cornering Abby out by the laundry line, the con man Tallant poses as Bean's best friend, Bert Davis (he has read Bean's old letters to Davis). Though Abby is suspicious at first, turning her back on the man as she pulls stockings off the laundry line, she finds that he knows many intimate details of Abby's relationship to Bean, including the way she brought him coffee, knitted him a sweater, and wore a gingham dress. But he does not know that they were married. As in many other scenes of this film, Dressler channels the character's discomfort into manic hand motions—bunching up her apron, straightening her hair, smoothing down her skirt, and fondling the laundry—to provide a suggestion of the sexuality that is always buried in discussions of Abby's history with Bean. The obsequious Tallant thanks Abby for her kindness, and for "giving him [Bean] things that other women denied him; you gave him all the little things," at which point Abby cuts him off with a suspicious, "What do you know about me?" Though Tallant is ignorant of the marriage, the dialogue certainly suggests that what "other women denied" Bean was more intimate than coffee or sweaters. Warming to the imposter, Abby fiddles with a stocking, sensually pulling it over her hand like an opera glove as she fondly remembers her late spouse, and finally reaching out to shake Tallant's hand, stocking still on.

The Haggetts, in their greed for Abby's portrait, speak to her as though they own her body, because she is their servant. A desperate Dr. Haggett hollers at Abby, "This is my house, and everything in it is mine, and you're my hired help." He even claims the painting should be payback for the time she spent posing for it: "It's time I paid for. Wasted, sitting for Chris Bean to paint it when you ought've been working." But Abby refuses his logic of ownership. When the Haggetts find the seventeen other paintings she has rolled up and hidden in her trunk, she finally must reveal her marriage, and she does so by reaching into her dress, and pulling out a wedding ring hung on a gold chain. Abby's sexual self, the only aspect of herself that is free from the class system, is revealed in a series of secret spaces: the portrait hung in the privacy of her bedroom; the rest of Bean's paintings stashed in her trunk. Finally, Abby reveals that the space beneath her dress, her body, holds its own secrets that are outside the ownership of the class system. She declares her liberation from the ownership of the class system by insisting on the legitimacy of her marriage: "I am Mrs. Christopher Bean, just the same as Mrs. Haggett is Mrs. Haggett."

Though the play ends with the revelation of Abby's secret marriage, the film includes a honeymoon epilogue that completes the sexual and maternal logic of the narrative, the elements that connect the film to the rest of Dressler's history. An establishing shot frames a night train speeding toward the camera—as in *Emma*, the journey by rail suggests a honeymoon, an impression that is strengthened by the presence of Susie and Warren on the same train, though sleeping in separate berths because they are not yet married. Inside, Abby wears a big nightgown, frilly hat, and dark robe, bustling among the sleeping berths with a hot water bottle in one arm, and the bundle of paintings under the other. When the porter tries to take the paintings from her, she replies that she will sleep with them. The art dealer Rosen appears and offers Abby twenty thousand for Bean's painting of a covered bridge. She sends him away, but as she settles into her bed, she mumbles to herself about how many people she could help with that money. It could provide for her brother's children, send Susie and Warren to Niagara Falls, and even help the Haggetts get to Florida. As in *Emma*, the iconography of a honeymoon is all in place: the train ride, Niagara Falls, a bed. And since Rosen is played by Jean Hersholt, she even has a strange echo of her previous husband on the train. But as Abby lies in her cramped upper berth, she is accompanied not by a lover, but by the bundle of Bean's canvases, and the portrait of herself wedged in at an angle over her body. Smiling down at the reclining Abby from an intimate distance, the portrait looks like an uncanny mirror over the bed.

This final scene shows a strangely ambivalent honeymoon scene, for there is something very sensual, and delightfully queer, about Dressler's going to bed with herself, settling in for the honeymoon she never had. However, the train is not headed to Niagara Falls, but to Chicago. There is not a lover waiting for her at the station, but her brother's children. Her erotic energies, so vividly on display in this scene, are again being channeled toward the next generation. She is even contemplating the sale of one of her paintings, one piece of her heart, to benefit those around her. The film ends in a way that suggests that MGM, facing the Depression, could not end the film with Abby simply absconding with her treasures, as did the play. Although Abby counters the Haggetts' claim that they somehow own her, Marie Dressler could make no such stand against her audience. A Dressler film always ended with a sacrifice made for the children; as usual, the needy children stood as a metaphor for the film audience: they are somewhere out in the dark night, motherless and sad, waiting for Dressler to come take care of them.

Conclusion

> I'm not against skinny little no-bosomy girls who diet down to their bones, but in my day a man wanted an armful to love. Give him his choice between a featherbed or a corn crib, and you know darned well which he'd choose.
>
> —Marie Dressler

Marie Dressler's magnetic screen presence was always erotic, and always queer.[43] At the end of *Tillie's Punctured Romance*, Tillie embraces Mabel, rather than Charlie. Dressler's films often sought these alternatives to heterosexual closure, finding endings that avoided, trickster-like, the question of sexuality in a long series of "punctured romances." While Dressler's sensuality was continually on display, her sexuality was both visible and elusive, whether it was manifested through her affectionately combative relationship to Wallace Beery, or her affectionately combative relationship to Polly Moran. Like Laurel and Hardy, Hope and Crosby, Martin and Lewis, or Lucy and Ethel, there is something clearly homoerotic in the physical chemistry of the classic comedy "team." Focusing their considerable energies mainly on each other, the two ladies touch, fight, fall, drink, argue, scheme, and keep house together. But those films made comedy out of the differences between the two women, moving them farther and farther apart as the series progressed, until Moran had taken on all the negative qualities of lesbian stereotypes, including a preening hatred of men, while Dressler was drawn deeply into the patriarchal fold. So of all these candidates for queer readings, I find the two "late marriage" films discussed in this chapter to be far richer, subtler explorations of the star's queerness because they insist on Dressler's sexuality even while they marvel at it.

Andrea Weiss argues that films containing "poignant lesbian moments," like Greta Garbo's showing affection for her serving girl in *Queen Christina* (MGM, 1933), or Marlene Dietrich's flirtation with a woman in *Morocco* (Paramount, 1930), were inevitably "constricted by the demands of heterosexual narrative closure."[44] For Dressler, films that contained poignant romantic moments of any kind were inevitably "constricted" by a return to Dressler's inevitable role of caring for the younger generation. But these films are still extraordinary for two important reasons. First, they eroticized that relationship with the younger generation, thereby making visible the ways that Dressler's lush physicality had always already been sexual. And second, they provided audiences with a kind of roadmap for how to *see* the invisible sexuality of marginalized figures. That same roadmap pointed the way to Dressler's own lived bisexuality, and the queerness of her star persona.

Conclusion

Dinner at Eight: The Unclosed Body

> Her forte is being funny, and she's good at it—so good she can dictate to directors, buy herself diamond bracelets—and let herself get fat. Which is at least one more right than any other screen star can exercise.
>
> —Eleanor Pringle, *San Francisco Chronicle*

Dressler's unique stardom presented an ideological challenge to the generic logic of Hollywood filmmaking that went beyond the right to dictate to directors (career control), buy diamond bracelets (economic control), and get fat (bodily control—or pleasurable uncontrol). Her films also afforded the actress a certain ideological flexibility, bending generic boundaries to accommodate her performances of excess. But Richard Dyer cautions against too much enthusiasm for so-called subversive stars, asking if "these represent real challenges to the *status quo* and the dominant ideology or are simply 'holidays' from it."[1] Most of Marie Dressler's films opened up the possibility of female agency, physical freedom, and political power, but then pulled back from those issues to achieve generic closure. I have saved the 1933 ensemble comedy *Dinner at Eight* for last, because it shows what Dressler's films might have looked like if they had not labored to contain the unruly potential of the star's body by resolving the narrative with her self-sacrifice for the next generation.

Scripted by Frances Marion, Herman Mankiewicz, and Donald Ogden Stewart from the play by George S. Kaufman and Edna Ferber, *Dinner at Eight* casts Dressler as the great Carlotta Vance, an aging diva. Carlotta's brilliance and fame permit her to be uncommonly frank, in a social milieu where no one seems to speak the truth. The hostess in the film's dinner party values the cachet that the venerable actress will bring to her gathering, but she also dreads the sudden truths that emerge from Carlotta's conversation, and her unorthodox physical decorum. The old diva is famous and socially prominent, but she brings her little dog to dinner, and takes her shoes off in the Manhattan socialite's parlor. The stage play cast tall, slender Constance Collier as Carlotta, and as happened whenever Dressler was given a romantic role, her casting in the film caused some grumbling about her appearance. *Newsweek* nitpicked: "that grand old trouper, Marie Dressler, unlike Constance Collier, simply cannot give the idea that she was once sought after for her beauty."[2] And the director George Cukor conceded, "The role in DINNER AT EIGHT was really written with someone like Maxine Elliot in mind, a great beauty, a leading lady; nevertheless, Marie was able to give the impression that she was a somebody. She had that quality, in spite of her looks; in the way she carried herself, the way she wore the clothes. She wasn't at all like her friend, Polly Moran, who really was rough and ready."[3] But it is the fact that this film casts Dressler, "in spite of her looks," that makes the character of Carlotta interesting, not just a slightly cruel portrait of desiccated vanity.

Instead, Dressler's performance as Carlotta suggests the comforts of wealth and retirement—the good food, easy rest, expansive clothing, devoted little dogs, and complete freedom of action. She is kind, but not self-sacrificing. She is sage, but not maternal. And perhaps most important, she is utterly ludicrous, but she frankly intimidates nearly everyone she meets. This character, then, captures the ambivalence of Dressler's appeal; she represented a combination of vulgarity and nobility that usually chafed at the restrictions of the sentimental narratives she was given to play. An utterly unsentimental comedy, *Dinner at Eight* leaves this tension nicely unresolved.

Dinner at Eight

> The story is too complicated to explain and why should I? With that cast, you'd see the picture anyhow.
>
> —Harry Evans, *Life*

Dinner at Eight was a prestige picture closely modeled on MGM's groundbreaking *Grand Hotel* (1932), a glossy ensemble melodrama that cast not one or two, but five of the studio's top stars: Greta Garbo, John and Lionel Barrymore, Joan Crawford, and Wallace Beery.[4] *Grand Hotel* won the Best Picture Oscar and was the biggest financial success of the year for the most profitable studio in town.[5] Both *Dinner at Eight* and *Grand Hotel* are based on successful Broadway plays. Both combine light, sophisticated comedy with a couple of poignant, ironic subplots. Both used the same craftsmen to create a "sophisticated, high-sheen milieu" for the film: Adrian on costumes, Cedric Gibbons on sets, and William Daniels on cinematography.[6] But *Dinner at Eight* upped the ante on stars, listing eight names in equal font:

Marie Dressler, Jean Harlow, Wallace Beery, John and Lionel Barrymore, Lee Tracy, Edmund Lowe, and Billie Burke. The smaller stars Madge Evans, Jean Hersholt, Karen Morley, and Phillips Holmes play smaller parts, and even the bits are played by important character actors like May Robson and Louise Closser Hale. The multitudinous stars, then, are a kind of luxury item in this film—the ultimate proof of quality in a film that already offers the audience the promise of excess: visual opulence, literate writing, many narratives, and the cultural capital of a Broadway hit. Audiences responded enthusiastically, and the picture grossed more than three million dollars.[7]

Dinner at Eight follows the intricately entangled lives of twelve people invited to a dinner party hosted by Millicent Jordan (Billie Burke), the socialite wife of shipping tycoon Oliver Jordan (Lionel Barrymore). The subplots are too intricate to examine in detail here, but a short summary of Dressler's few scenes gives a representative impression of the film. Marie Dressler's Carlotta Vance weaves her way through these stories in a series of ostentatiously outrageous costumes: she is a great shapeless mass of furs and hats and jewelry and lace (figure 27). Now living in Europe, Carlotta has returned to New York for a few weeks to divest herself of some assets and repair her financial health.

Carlotta has four scenes in the film. In the first, she visits Oliver in his office, talks about old times, and asks if he would like to buy back the stock she owns in his company. Oliver reveals that he cannot afford to buy the stock, and his company is in danger of a takeover. In her second scene, Carlotta returns to her hotel and accidentally witnesses the Jordans' nineteen-year-old daughter, Paula (Evans), leaving the hotel room of her secret lover, the aging matinee idol Larry Renault (John Barrymore). Tsk-tsking to herself, Carlotta does not interfere, although Paula is engaged to a polite young man, Ernest DeGraff (Holmes). In the third scene, Carlotta stops by the Jordans' house the afternoon of the dinner party to tell Oliver that she has sold her stock to a man named Baldridge, information that sends him into a panic. He phones his account manager and learns that this Baldridge now owns the majority of his company. Jordan forgives Carlotta, and she goes home to change for the party. Jordan collapses, and his wife learns that his heart is failing. In the final scene, Carlotta arrives at the party and seeks out Paula in the study to tell her quietly that her lover Renault killed himself that afternoon. She convinces the younger woman to keep her past concealed and go through with her planned marriage to Ernest. The two women return to the party, where Jordan happily learns that he will retain ownership of his company. The final scene shows all the characters going in to dinner.

FIGURE 27. Dressler with Lionel Barrymore in *Dinner at Eight* (1933). Her costume is lush and excessive, just like her performance.

Carlotta Vance was a throwback to Dressler's queen roles, the first regal character the actress had played since *One Romantic Night*, in 1930. But unlike those earlier roles, Dressler played Carlotta with great warmth, investing her narcissism and irresponsibility with the playful impression that the actress cultivated her excesses as a shield against criticism. Roberta Raider argues that Dressler's performance in *Dinner at Eight* "presented humorous contrasts in the character, moving from the great lady to the girl from Quincy, Illinois. Her movement was very graceful and elegant, but the glint in her eyes revealed to the audience that this was practiced gesture and she reveled in its grace."[8] It is, in fact, a testament to Dressler's skill that the rash inconsistencies in her performance as Carlotta lend the character a magnetic complexity, rather than outright incoherence. Carlotta's accent, vocabulary, and tone of voice, for instance, fluctuate wildly in the film: a broad "A" or supercilious "Oh, my dear" in one line will give way to a slang-filled growl or wheezing request for a drink in the next. Dressler's performance far exceeds the text in the film, investing the character with three vivid contradictions: she is old but childish, refined but slovenly, and frivolous but wise. By playing up these contradictions, her performance celebrates the artifice of social propriety and undermines the film's pretensions of luxury.

In Carlotta's flirtatious scenes with Jordan, her vocal inflection and body language shift between aged dowager and girlish flirt. The diva speaks continually of her age and makes a great show of her sensitivity to insult. Speaking to Oliver, she insists that although she is broke, she refuses to go back on the stage. "I'll have my double chins in privacy," she declares, patting the underside of her chin affectionately. When he suggests that she move to New York to save money, she insists she is out of step with the metropolitan city, musing dreamily, "I belong to the Delmonico period—ah, table at the window, looking out on Fifth Avenue, boxes with flowers in, pink lampshades, string orchestra, and I don't know . . . yes, yes, willow plumes, Inverness capes, dry champagne, and snow on the ground." Lowering the tone of voice to break the romantic lilt of her reminiscence, Carlotta adds wryly, "Say, they don't even have snow anymore." Just at the end of this trip down memory lane, Jordan's secretary enters to remind her boss that he must take a call. Jordan exits the room, and the secretary, an awkward, middle-aged woman, lights a cigarette for Carlotta and declares herself a fan. The star accepts the adulation with bored good humor, saying, "Oh, how sweet," as she pulls a speck of tobacco distractedly from her mouth. But when the younger woman notes that she remembers Carlotta's performance "as plainly as if it was yesterday, even though I was only a little girl at the time," Carlotta goes instantly hard, locking the secretary in her gaze, flicking her cigarette with venomous disdain, and replying, "We must have a nice talk about the Civil War sometime, just you and I." When an Oklahoma businessman, Dan Packard (Beery), enters the office and recognizes her, Carlotta cuts him short with a glib, "Yep, saw me when he was a boy. Nursey held him up so he could get a good look." When she meets Paula's boyfriend Ernest, she warns him, "Don't tell me that your grandfather saw me when he was a boy." Being sensitive about her age, the diva is often the first to mention it, as well as the youth of those around her.

Remembering the old days, Carlotta quantifies things; her life is a collection of memories and possessions, intimately connected. Speaking of Jordan's proposal, she says, "One thing I shall always remember: the day you were twenty-one. You asked me to marry you, Oliver." Noting that she was "thirty-something," Carlotta confesses that his sincerity made her cry. She remembers how much she paid for her Jordan stock, $61,240, with a precision that shocks Oliver. And when she tries to express to Millicent how tired she is, she again places it in mathematical terms: "What a city. I left my hotel at eleven this morning a young and lovely girl, and now look at me. I took on ten years trying to get from the Versailles to Times Square." When she learns that Paula's fiancé is named DeGraff, she muses, "DeGraff, DeGraff . . . I think I knew his father." Looking over each ring on her fingers, she finally settles on a big diamond brooch pinned prominently at her cleavage. Fingering it, she confirms, "I did." Every diamond on her person signifies a memory, a conquest. "If there's one thing I know, it's men," she tells Paula, "I ought to; it's been my life's work."

But for all that she carries around this catalog of her past, Carlotta often takes on the mannerisms of a child. When she confesses to Jordan, "I haven't got a sou," Carlotta pushes one finger demurely against her face, but she does so with such force that she distorts the shape of her slack mouth into a kind of false half-smile. This odd gesture suggests a studied and ironic naïveté. When she sits down to introduce the issue of selling her Jordan stock, Carlotta sits on the arm of the chair, resting her feet on the seat cushion like a child. She compounds this impression by shifting toward Oliver so her feet dangle freely from the front of the chair. Dressler kicks her legs girlishly a few times as she says, "Oliver, you wouldn't want to buy it back yourself, would you?" Later, in his apartment, she informs him that she has sold the stock, and inquires, with a studied naïveté, "Oliver, sweet, you won't be cross with Carlotta, will you?" Twisting her handkerchief in her lap, she awaits his answer with agitation. Carlotta's attempts to be ingratiating are accompanied by physical motions that are more suited to Shirley Temple than Marie Dressler.

When Carlotta visits Millicent a few hours before the party, the contrast deepens a bit. Without Oliver to flirt with, Carlotta plays gracious guest to Millicent, but she is unable to contain her bodily excess. The scene presents a stark contrast between the unruly physicality of the weary diva and the disapproving composure of the thin, well-groomed society wife, ignoring the social faux pas of her distinguished visitor. Billie Burke's fluttering performance in the film is a model of hysterical control, her hands rarely falling below her waist, so the eye stays on the top half of her body, never the "lower bodily stratum." Entering the house in a whirl of furs and jewelry, Carlotta greets Millicent with an empty, "I was never so glad to see anyone in all my life," before begging for a drink and finding a chair to sit in—her labored breathing suggesting the weariness of her ample flesh. Once seated, Carlotta carries on the semblance of polite conversation with Millicent, while busily seeing to her own physical comfort. She kicks off her shoes, asking perfunctorily, "Oh, Millicent, you don't mind if I take off my shoes, do you?" when the deed is already done. Surrounded by her hostess's pristine parlor, Carlotta proceeds to rub her sore feet through the reinforced toes of her stockings, making little vocalizations of relief as she does so. And although she asks for a whiskey and soda, when the maid brings the drinks, Carlotta doesn't allow her to add any soda to the whiskey and downs a big glass of straight liquor with one gulp. She speaks the controlled language of gentility, but her unruly body betrays her physical appetites for comfort and pleasure.

At the party, Carlotta enacts a contrast between foolish social butterfly and wise elder. She glides in, carrying her Pekingese dog, and apologizes insincerely to Millicent for having brought the animal to the party. She blurts out the fact that the guests of honor, Lord and Lady Ferncliff, have gone to Florida on a fishing trip, a blunder that exposes Millicent's lie that the Ferncliffs had missed the party due to ill health. "Isn't Bunny a swine?" she asks of the mortified Millicent, amid embarrassed glances from the other guests. Passing the reluctant party guest Ed (Grant Mitchell), who would rather be at the new Greta Garbo picture, Carlotta exclaims, "Oh, my dear. You poor little man, you look so lonely. Here," handing the dog over to the startled man, "Tarzan will keep you company." Dogless, Carlotta continues into the library to greet Paula and Ernest. She teases the young man, "Oh, I can tell an Ernest twenty feet off," and flirtingly sends him out the door so she can speak to Paula alone.

But after Ernest is dispatched safely, Carlotta turns very serious and reveals to Paula that she knows about her affair. The intensity of the following conversation is in stark contrast to Carlotta's frivolous entrance and suggests that her slightly batty behavior at the party is a very practiced cover. When Carlotta gives Paula the news that Larry is dead, Paula starts to walk out of the room to go to her dead lover. But Carlotta grabs the younger woman's shoulders and stands behind her, the two women framed in a quiet medium shot for the most emotional moments of the scene. Dressler's lack of fidgeting contrasts with her performance in the previous scenes and lends her an unexpected air of gravitas. Positioned in front of the diva, Paula blocks Carlotta's excessive costume of furs and jewelry and lace. All the focus is on Dressler's stricken face. Paula strokes her hands together and stares into the middle distance as she laments, "My poor Larry." Carlotta, still standing behind her, gives her a speech that is meant to comfort the younger woman but turns on the usual topic of age: "I realize that I'm an old woman, and young people have a right to do what they want. . . . That's the unfortunate thing about death, it's so terribly final. Even the young can't do anything about it." The women don't look at each other, but each stares into a kind of private abyss beyond the camera. Finally, Paula breaks down in tears and turns around to embrace Carlotta. When she recovers, Carlotta helps pull the girl together, pats her arm comfortingly, and counsels her to keep her love for Larry a secret. Carlotta takes her own compact and powders Paula's nose, giving the visual impression that she is recreating the younger woman in her image, before forcing Paula to take the powder puff and finish the job. Taking Paula's now-limp arm, Carlotta physically leads her back to the party. This scene shows Carlotta schooling Paula in the ways femininity is a kind of deception—through makeup, pleasantries, and the erasure of one's past.

But Carlotta does not follow the advice she gives Paula. Not only does she reveal her past to anyone who will listen, but she quantifies it, revels in it, even wallows in it. She wears the evidence of her history on her chest, like so many medals. The woman at the party who most resembles a young Carlotta Vance is not the naïve Paula, but the vulgar Kitty Packard (Jean Harlow)—the Oklahoma businessman's untutored and uninhibited young wife. While Kitty lacks Carlotta's shrewd wit, she shares the older woman's talent for dealing with men, her fearless candor, and her essential kindness (it is Kitty who prevents Packard's takeover of Jordan's shipping business). Carlotta's last scene is not the maudlin episode with Paula, but a wickedly funny exchange with Kitty, which turns unintentionally on the question of women's "professions." This scene also pairs interestingly with Paula's scene because it shows Carlotta in a very ironic maternal relationship with the younger woman. Neither scene appears in the original play, and both emphasize Dressler's wit and authority.

Dressler's final exchange with Jean Harlow is the scene for which she is best, and justly, remembered. The two women walk in to dinner together, Carlotta's eyes trained on Kitty's diamond bracelets. Dressler holds her own arm close to the younger woman's, and turns her wrist over several times, to catch the light, and to show that she is comparing the size of her own bracelets to the young trophy wife's. Dressler keeps the viewer's eye with this motion as Harlow starts to speak. Kitty starts the conversation with a comment that comes completely out of the blue, obviously a bit of small talk she has been saving up to impress the swells at the Jordan's party: "I was reading a book the other day." It is impossible to capture in words the precision of the double take with which Dressler greets this remark: she stops in mid-stride and nearly loses her balance, tipping slightly backward with shock. Reaching outward delicately with her arms, like a ballet dancer recovering from a stumble, Carlotta pulls herself upright and turns to Kitty. With her hands now clasped eagerly together and her face betraying the expectation that she is about to be profoundly amused, she eggs Kitty on, "Reading a book?" Kitty does not disappoint. She answers, "Yeah, all about civilization or something. A nutty kind of a book—Do you know that the guy says that machinery is going to take the place of every profession?" Looking Kitty up and down with her expert eye, Carlotta takes the younger woman by the arm and casually tosses off the funniest line in the film, as she walks Harlow into the dining room with the comforting dismissal: "Oh, my dear, that's something you never need worry about."

There is something admiring in this comment, and Kitty reacts with pleasure to the older woman's remark. Maria DiBattista argues, "The famous quip has all the zing of an unanswerable putdown, but it also comes as a compliment from a fellow professional."[9] Carlotta's comfort has been built on artifice; she is an old woman who acts like a little girl, with refined manners and slovenly behaviors, who brings both frivolity and gravity to the party. *Dinner at Eight* embraces this contradiction, and Carlotta is the most dynamic character in the film. Although her energies are channeled into a vaguely maternal role relative to Paula and Kitty, there is nothing of the sentimental motherhood of her earlier films. The ending does not suggest that the vain old woman is contained, punished, or must subordinate her happiness for a young adult. Rather, she encourages the young people to follow her vivid lead.

Happy Endings

> She's one trouper I'd never try to steal a scene from. It would be like trying to carry Italy against Mussolini. She knows all the tricks and she knows all the answers and she's the best loved personage in Hollywood.
>
> —Jean Harlow on Marie Dressler

Patricia White argues, "The subversiveness of the best character stars, such as [Eve] Arden and [Thelma] Ritter, can be neutralized by their being enthusiastically adopted as cuddly curmudgeons."[10] But while Dressler was clearly the cherished star of the picture, her performance was not neutralized by the narrative context. Jean Harlow's comparison of Dressler to Mussolini in the epigraph above suggests the extent to which her status as beloved mascot of the film colony was accompanied by a certain expansive authority. She was an intimidating figure, whose unruliness was never fully contained by her stardom—here she was stealing scenes in the second-to-last film she ever made.

In fact, Dressler's performance in *Dinner at Eight* prompted the most attention from the Production Code enforcers that one of her films had achieved in years, surely a sign of her disruptiveness. Nearly all the suggested eliminations offered by the Studio Relations Committee (a forerunner of the more powerful Production Code Administration) focused on the character Carlotta. The SRC's James Wingate warned Irving Thalberg, "The expression, 'Son of a . . . ' used in Carlotta's line is usually eliminated by the censors and in this instance it seems to us likely to prove particularly offensive because it is spoken by a woman and, therefore, ought to be omitted."[11] Similarly problematic was a scene where one of Carlotta's small dogs makes a mess on the hotel carpet. Picking up the offending pup, Carlotta scolds, "Now, aren't you ashamed? For fifteen minutes I walked you around the block so you . . . and then you come right in to . . ." But gazing into the animal's eyes, she softens, "Ah, ha, muzzy's sorry. She doesn't give a darn for the old man's carpet. No. Gandhi, I'm awfully sorry, Gandhi." Wingate, upon first viewing of the film, recommended the line be cut after the first "aren't you ashamed" but the scene was evidently left intact, for he later reported to the Association of Motion Picture Producers that British Columbia had cut the whole incident out of the release print.[12]

These little dogs named after world figures caused some additional trouble. Both the original play and the screenplay list the Pekingese dog Carlotta brings to Millicent's party as "Benito" (as in Mussolini). In the release print, Dressler's mouth moves in a way that suggests the word "Benito," but in the soundtrack she is heard saying "Tarzan." The shift in the soundtrack is not seamless, and even a casual viewer can catch the fact that the wrong word is being spoken. It remains in the film as a visible, incomplete erasure of Carlotta's devilish humor. The line "son of a . . ." also remains in the final film, with Dressler scowling as her voice trails off, never filling in the absent word. But the line acknowledges the space reserved for what cannot be said aloud. That space comes to signify Carlotta's rich history, her irreverence, and her bodily excess.

An ensemble picture that follows five story arcs, rather than one, the film is full of such loose ends. The dinner party never actually happens—the characters disappear into a room outside the camera's range, and the doors of the dining room close ominously, as "The End" appears in script lettering over the closed doors. This is less an ending than a suggestion that the audience is not invited to view the rest of the story. The lack of a true conclusion prevents the film from imposing on Dressler some kind of definite role, a conversion or enclosure. Unlike the films discussed in chapter 3, Dressler here is not a mother. She mothers young women when she wishes, but she is not tied down to the role. Unlike the films discussed in chapter 4, Dressler here is not a sacrificial savior. She puts her own financial needs above Oliver's, and nearly ruins his business. And unlike the films discussed in chapter 5, Dressler here is not a wife. She has a longstanding flirtation with Oliver that lets her enter and exit his life with perfect freedom and great style. It is taken for granted that she is desirable, and also that she has chosen not to marry. The shedding of these three categories takes the Dressler character out of the binding "roles" of narrative and creates greater space for her unruly body. Dressler's unruly performance, then, takes a dominant position, never subsumed by the narrative compulsion to move forward, solve problems, change, or step aside to make room for the romantic leads. *Dinner at Eight* ends not with a heterosexual clinch, but with a moment of feminine solidarity, and a slightly naughty joke. It is a nicely punctured romance, and a terrific capstone to Dressler's outrageous career.

Notes

CHAPTER 1: *TILLIE'S PUNCTURED ROMANCE*

The epigraph that opens this chapter is from "A Great Big Girl Like Me," lyrics by Edgar Smith, sung by Marie Dressler in the Broadway show *Higgledy-Piggledy*, 1904.

1. In 1986, Douglas Gomery challenged historians on using the cliché "The Tiffany of Studios" to describe MGM in the 1930s: "Marie Dressler pushes us to reconsider the 'Tiffany' image, for she surely represented MGM to the movie-going public of America in the Depression." Gomery, *The Hollywood Studio System* (New York: St. Martin's, 1986), 64. Since that time, history textbooks have made a point of noting the popularity of Dressler's films. Few critical studies have discussed their importance.
2. Matthew Kennedy, *Marie Dressler: A Biography; With a Listing of Major Stage Performances, a Filmography and a Discography* (Jefferson, N.C.: McFarland, 1999), 9, 29.
3. Lyrics by Edgar Smith, 1909.
4. See "Marie Dressler Not Wife of J. H. Dalton Who Is Buried Here," *Evening Leader* (Corning, N.Y.), December 3, 1921, 12; and "Dalton Sought to Wed Marie Dressler," *New York Times*, December 2, 1921, 8.
5. For a thorough account of this film's centrality to censorship debates of the late silent era, see Frank R. Walsh, *Sin and Censorship: The Catholic Church and the Motion Picture Industry* (New Haven: Yale University Press, 1996).
6. *Time*, August 7, 1933.
7. Jack Jamison, "Hollywood's Cruelest Story," *Modern Screen*, July 1932, 28.
8. Josephine Jarvis, "Queen Marie of Hollywood," *Photoplay*, January 1932, 33.
9. "Marie Dressler Rallies from Coma," *New York Times*, July 1, 1934, 23; "Dressler's End Near," *Los Angeles Examiner*, June 29, 1934, 1.
10. Buster Keaton and Charles Samuels, *My Wonderful World of Slapstick* (Cambridge: De Capo, 1982, 1960), 201. Keaton finished the remark, ". . . (until Lucille Ball appeared)."
11. The epigraph for this section comes from Will Rogers, foreword to Marie Dressler's *My Own Story as Told to Mildred Harrington* (Boston: Little, Brown, 1934), vii.
12. Francisco Alberoni, "The Powerless Elite: Theory and Sociological Research on the Phenomenon of the Stars," in *Sociology of Mass Communications*, ed. Denis McQuail (London: Penguin, 1972), 75–98.
13. See Richard Dyer, *Stars* (London: BFI, 1998), 20.
14. Ibid., 152.

15. Ibid., 154.

16. This list is suggestive, rather than exhaustive. These are a few of the more prominent women directors and screenwriters working in America in the silent era. Around the world, there were hundreds more.

17. Janet Staiger, "Authorship Approaches," in *Authorship in Film*, ed. David A. Gerstner and Janet Staiger (New York: Routledge, 2003), 30.

18. Jane Gaines, "Of Cabbages and Authors," in *A Feminist Reader in Early Cinema*, ed. Jennifer M. Bean and Diane Negra (Durham: Duke University Press, 2002), 111.

19. Cari Beauchamp, *Without Lying Down: Frances Marion and the Powerful Women of Early Hollywood* (New York: Scribner, 1997), 199.

20. Samuel Marx, *A Gaudy Spree: The Literary Life of Hollywood in the 1930's When the West Was Fun* (New York: F. Watts, 1987), 31.

21. Beauchamp, *Without Lying Down*, 356.

22. Ibid., 12.

23. The epigraph for this section comes from George Hill, *New York Post*, quoted in Kennedy, *Marie Dressler*, 4.

24. "Marie Dressler Is Her Own Stage Manager," *Star Weekly*, December 5, 1914, quoted in Roberta Ann Raider, "A Descriptive Study of the Acting of Marie Dressler" (Ph.D. diss., University of Michigan, 1970), 86.

25. Dressler, *My Own Story*, 152.

26. Amy Leslie, "Real Fun at Illinois," *Chicago News*, April 1905, quoted in Raider, "Descriptive Study," 98.

27. Archie Bell, "Scene from 'A Mix-Up,'" *Cleveland Leader*, November 8, 1914, quoted in Raider, "Descriptive Study," 85–86.

28. "Marie Dressler Entertains," *New York Times*, February 26, 1913, 8.

29. Raider, "Descriptive Study," 176.

30. Marie Dressler, *The Life Story of an Ugly Duckling* (New York: R. M. McBride, 1924), 64–65.

31. Review, *New York Dramatic Mirror*, February 26, 1913, quoted in Raider, "Descriptive Study," 177.

32. Bo Berglund, program notes for *Tillie's Punctured Romance*, Twenty-third Annual Silent Film Festival, Pordenone, Italy, October 9–16, 2004.

33. "Marie Dressler Strong for the Impromptu," *Moving Picture World*, December 29, 1917.

34. The epigraph for this section comes from "The Stage and Its Players," *New York Times*, March 4, 1906, X3.

35. Linda Williams, "Melodrama Revised," in *Refiguring American Film Genres*, ed. Nick Browne (Berkeley: University of California Press, 1998), 42.

36. Ben Singer, *Melodrama and Modernity: Early Sensational Cinema and Its Contexts* (New York: Columbia University Press, 2001), 44–49.

37. Ibid., 46.

38. Charles Condon, "A Six-Reel Keystone Comedy," *Motography* November 14,

1914, 657. The running times for these two epics are approximate and based on the running times of the most recent restoration of each film. The hand-cranked projection speed of silent films make precise running times impossible to pinpoint.

39. George Blaisdell, "Tillie's Punctured Romance," *Moving Picture World*, November 14, 1914, 914.

40. Ibid.

41. Jennifer M. Bean, "Technologies of Early Stardom and the Extraordinary Body," in Bean and Negra, *Feminist Reader*, 406.

42. "Tillie's Punctured Romance," *New York Daily Mail*, November 1, 1914, 36.

43. The epigraph for this section is from Jeanine Basinger, *A Woman's View: How Hollywood Spoke to Women, 1930–1960* (Hanover, N.H.: University Press of New England, 1993), 19.

44. Steve Neale has demonstrated that trade magazines of the 1950s and 1960s rarely used the term "melodrama" to describe sentimental or "women's" films, reserving the term for war pictures, gangster films, and other more direct descendents of the "blood-and-thunder" school. Steve Neale, "Melo Talk: On the Meaning and the Use of the Term 'Melodrama' in the American Trade Press," *Velvet Light Trap*, Fall 1993, 66–89. Ben Singer has found a similar pattern in publications of the 1910s (*Melodrama and Modernity*, 37). While these historical perspectives are invaluable and compelling, I do not think they undermine the school of criticism that has always seen sensational and sentimental forms of melodrama as closely linked (the resemblance between adventure serials and soap operas is just one obvious indication of how much the two forms have in common). Singer argues that sentimental melodrama generally includes only two of the characteristics on his list (pathos and emotional intensification) (57). I am challenging this claim by using the entire five-category list as the basis for my definition of sentimental melodramas of the 1930s. By limiting my examples to the earliest sound melodramas, I hope to achieve the kind of historical specificity that both Neale and Singer call for, while retaining the useful critical term of "melodrama" as something closer to a "mode" of representation, rather than a "genre" of films that would be defined by the trade discourse of the time.

45. Williams, "Melodrama Revised," 58.

46. Singer, *Melodrama and Modernity*, 54.

47. Williams, "Melodrama Revised," 61.

CHAPTER 2: BREAKING BOUNDARIES

The epigraph that opens this chapter is from Matthew Kennedy, *Marie Dressler*, 3.

1. Although I am certain that it was produced around 1930, I don't know anything else about the origins of this publicity photo, which I confess I found on the auction Web site eBay. The only text on the back of the image says "Marie Dressler, left, Anna Christie." It seems to be a composite from two separate publicity stills, although the image from *One Romantic Night*, on the left, has been textured to resemble a painting. Both films were made in 1930, although the latter was a United Artists release, so it is hard to see why MGM would have chosen to promote this image.

2. Kathleen Rowe, *The Unruly Woman: Gender and the Genres of Laughter* (Austin: University of Texas Press, 1995), 1–29. The epigraph for this section is from Marjorie Rosen, *Popcorn Venus: Women, Movies, and the American Dream* (New York: Coward, McCann, and Geoghegan, 1973), 91.

3. Christopher Beach, *Class, Language, and American Film Comedy* (New York: Cambridge University Press, 2002), 13.

4. Henry Jenkins, *What Made Pistachio Nuts? Early Sound Comedy and the Vaudeville Aesthetic* (New York: Columbia University Press, 1992), 245–76.

5. Peter Stearns, *Fat History: Bodies and Beauty in the Modern West* (New York: New York University Press, 1997), 4.

6. Dressler, *My Own Story*, 59.

7. Raider, "Descriptive Study," 59.

8. "At the Playhouse," *Theatre Magazine*, June 1910, quoted in Raider, "Descriptive Study," 81.

9. Rebecca Bell-Metereau, *Hollywood Androgyny*, 2nd ed. (New York: Columbia University Press, 1993), 70.

10. E. J. Mannix to Col. Jason S. Joy, memo, July 7, 1927, *The Callahans and the Murphys*, Margaret Herrick Library Special Collections, Academy of Motion Picture Arts and Sciences, Los Angeles, Calif. (hereafter, AMPAS). The epigraph for this section comes from a press release from the National Catholic Welfare Conference News Service, AMPAS.

11. Dressler, *My Own Story*, 238.

12. Diane Negra, *Off-White Hollywood: American Culture and Ethnic Female Stardom* (London: Routledge, 2001), 26.

13. Ibid., 31–32.

14. Scenario (2nd version), March 16, 1927, *The Callahans and the Murphys* file, Metro-Goldwyn-Mayer Collection, University of Southern California (hereafter, MGM Collection, USC).

15. Frances Marion, *Off with Their Heads: A Serio-comic Tale of Hollywood* (New York: Macmillan, 1972), 157.

16. Unless otherwise noted, all of the following examples come from the second version of Frances Marion's scenario, March 16, 1927, *The Callahans and the Murphys* file, MGM Collection, USC.

17. Eddie Moran, "Suggestions for Gags at Picnic," April 15, 1927, *The Callahans and the Murphys* file, MGM Collection, USC.

18. Beauchamp, *Without Lying Down*, 205; Walsh, *Sin and Censorship*, 40.

19. *Tidings*, July 15, 1927, quoted in Walsh, *Sin and Censorship*, 38.

20. R. E. Sherwood, "The Silent Drama," *Life*, August 4, 1927, 26.

21. William Orr to Will Hays, memo, August 23, 1927, *The Callahans and the Murphys*, Margaret Herrick Library Special Collections, AMPAS.

22. W. D. Kelly to Eddie Mannix, telegram, July 22, 1927, *The Callahans and the Murphys*, Margaret Herrick Library Special Collections, AMPAS.

23. "Irish Film Causes another Disturbance," *New York Times*, August 26, 1927, 5.

24. "Condemn Two Irish Films," *New York Times*, September 14, 1927, 26.
25. *Irish World*, August 13, 1927, quoted in Walsh, *Sin and Censorship*, 42–43.
26. *Irish World*, August 13, 1927, quoted in Raider, "Descriptive Study," 195.
27. Catherine M. Eagan, "Still 'Black' and 'Proud': Irish America and the Racial Politics of Hibernophilia," in *The Irish in Us: Irishness, Performativity, and Popular Culture*, ed. Diane Negra (Durham: Duke University Press, 2006), 24.
28. Digital reproductions of these songs are available through the Web site of the Cylinder Preservation and Digitization Project, Department of Special Collections, Donald C. Davidson Library, University of California, Santa Barbara: http://www.cylinders.library.ucsb.edu (accessed July 18, 2008).
29. Marion, *Off with Their Heads*, 158.
30. Garson Kanin, *Hollywood* (New York: Viking, 1974), 41. The epigraph for this section comes from Hedda Hopper, *From under My Hat* (Garden City: Doubleday, 1952), 89.
31. "A Chat with Marie Dressler," *New York Times*, June 22, 1930, X2.
32. Jenkins, *What Made Pistachio Nuts?* 245–76.
33. Jarvis, "Queen Marie of Hollywood," 32.
34. Elizabeth Barton, "Be Yourself, Marie Dressler's Secret of Success," *Boston Herald*, November 1932, quoted in Raider, "Descriptive Study," 200.
35. Polly Moran, "Marie Dressler," *Screenland*, undated clipping, 111, Wisconsin Theatre Collection, quoted in Raider, "Descriptive Study," 27.
36. William J. Mann, *Wisecracker: The Life and Times of William Haines, Hollywood's First Openly Gay Star* (New York: Penguin, 1998), 67.
37. Mordaunt Hall, "The Prince or the Tutor," *New York Times*, May 31, 1930, 36.
38. Creighton Peet, "The Girl Said No," *Outlook and Independent*, April 16, 1930, 632.
39. "A Party on Long Island," *New York Times*, July 12, 1930.
40. "Let Us Be Gay," *Variety*, July 16, 1930, 15.
41. "Let Us be Gay," *Outlook and Independent*, July 30, 1930, 510.
42. Mordaunt Hall, "Rudy Vallee's First Talker," *New York Times*, November 27, 1929, 33.
43. Kennedy, *Marie Dressler*, 163.
44. Mann, *Wisecracker*, 169.
45. Alma Whitaker, "Comedienne Dons Robes of Royalty," *Los Angeles Times*, February 2, 1930, 13. The epigraph for this section comes from a fan profile in Josephine Jarvis, "Queen Marie of Hollywood," 32.
46. Joanna Rapf, "Queen of the Movies: Marie Dressler and 'Politics,'" *Quarterly Review of Film and Video* 19 (Winter 2002): 313.
47. Dressler, *My Own Story*, 152.
48. Harry Evans, "Movies," *Life*, March 21, 1930, 20.
49. "Anna Christie," *Variety*, March 19, 1930, 35.
50. James R. Quirk, "Long Shots and Close-Ups," *Photoplay*, April 1930, 27.
51. The epigraph for this section comes from Creighton Peet, "The Movies," *Outlook and Independent*, February 26, 1930, 351.

CHAPTER 3: *POLITICS* AND *PROSPERITY*

The epigraph that opens this chapter is from a 1932 fan letter that was quoted in Dressler, *My Own Story*, 275.

1. Mordaunt Hall, "Boisterous Fun," *New York Times*, June 22, 1930, 637.
2. Jarvis, "Queen Marie of Hollywood," 33.
3. Quoted in Adela Rogers St. Johns, "Marie Dressler's Own Story," *Photoplay*, October 1932, 102.
4. Quoted in Adela Rogers St. Johns, "Youth Hasn't Changed," *Photoplay*, November 1932, 122.
5. Ibid.
6. "Cal York's Gossip of Hollywood," *Photoplay*, December 1931, 86.
7. Jamison, "Hollywood's Cruelest Story," 28–29.
8. Davis W. Houck, *FDR and Fear Itself: The First Inaugural Address* (College Station: Texas A&M University Press, 2002), 6.
9. Amy Kaplan, "Manifest Domesticity," *American Literature* 70, no. 3 (September 1998): 582.
10. Giuliana Muscio, *Hollywood's New Deal* (Philadelphia: Temple University Press, 1997), 20–21.
11. Mack Sennett, "The Best Motion Picture Interview Ever Written," interview by Theodore Dreiser (August 1928), reprinted in *Spellbound in Darkness: A History of Silent Film*, ed. George C. Pratt (Greenwich, Conn.: New York Graphic Society, 1973), 186. The epigraph for this section comes from this interview.
12. Molly Haskell, "Women and the Silent Comedians," in *Movie Comedy*, ed. Stuart Byron and Elizabeth Weiss (New York: Penguin, 1977), 36.
13. Joanna Rapf, "Comedy Theory from a Feminist Perspective: A Look at Jerry Lewis," *Journal of Popular Culture* 27, no. 1 (Summer 1993): 193.
14. Lucy Fischer quotes Cavell in her essay "'Sometimes I Feel Like a Motherless Child': Comedy and Matricide," in *Comedy/Cinema/Theory*, ed. Andrew Horton (Berkeley: University of California Press, 1991), 64. A similar point is made in Alan Dale, *Comedy Is a Man in Trouble* (Minneapolis: University of Minnesota Press, 2000), 92–131.
15. The exception may be May Robson in Capra's *Lady for a Day* (Columbia, 1933). Capra initially wanted Dressler for the role, but he could not get the idea past Harry Cohn. Frank Capra, *The Name above the Title: An Autobiography* (New York: Macmillan, 1973; Vintage Books, 1985), 148–49.
16. Lyrics by Clyde Hager, music by Walter Goodwin.
17. Lyrics by Joe Goodwin, music by Gus Edwards.
18. Anita Loos, *Gentlemen Prefer Blondes* and *But Gentlemen Marry Brunettes* (1925 and 1928; rpt., New York: Penguin, 1998), 131.
19. Thomas Elsaesser, "Tales of Sound and Fury: Observations on the Family Melodrama," in *Home Is Where the Heart Is: Studies in Melodrama and the Women's Film*, ed. Christine Gledhill (London: BFI, 1987), 47.

20. E. Ann Kaplan, *Motherhood and Representation: The Mother in Popular Culture and Melodrama* (London: Routledge, 1992), 173.

21. Tom Mahoney, story outline, "Self-Protection," March 9, 1931, 7, *Politics* file, MGM Collection, USC.

22. Rapf, "Queen of the Movies," 309–22.

23. Nick Roddick, *A New Deal in Entertainment: Warner Brothers in the 1930's* (London: BFI, 1983), 66.

24. Rheta Childe Dorr, *What Eighty Million Women Want* (1919; rpt., New York, 1971), 327, quoted in Paula Baker, "The Domestication of Politics: Women and American Political Society 1780–1920," *American Historical Review* 89, no. 3 (June 1984): 632.

25. Nancy S. Dye, "Introduction," *Gender, Class, Race and Reform in the Progressive Era*, ed. Noralee Frankel and Nancy S. Dye (Lexington: University Press of Kentucky, 1991), 4.

26. Aristophanes, *Lysistrata*, trans. Sarah Ruden (Indianapolis: Hackett, 2003), 34.

27. Kennedy, *Marie Dressler*, 189.

28. Ibid., 189.

29. *Boston Herald*, January 20, 1932, quoted in Raider, "Descriptive Study," 224.

30. Kennedy, *Marie Dressler*, 99.

31. *New York Daily News*, January 14, 1934, quoted in Raider, "Descriptive Study," 149.

32. Dressler, *My Own Story*, 180.

33. Davis W. Houck and Amos Kiewe, *FDR's Body Politics: The Rhetoric of Disability* (College Station: Texas A & M University Press, 2003), 89–90.

34. Franklin Delano Roosevelt, acceptance speech, Democratic National Convention, July 1932, quoted in Halford R. Ryan, *Franklin D. Roosevelt's Rhetorical Presidency* (New York: Greenwood, 1988), 42.

35. Houck and Kiewe, *FDR's Body Politics*, 95.

36. Ibid., 77.

CHAPTER 4: *MIN AND BILL* AND *TUGBOAT ANNIE*

The epigraph that opens this chapter is from a poem by Joel Keith, sent to Marie Dressler by a fan. Dressler, *My Own Story*, 276.

1. For the fan's comment, see Dressler, *My Own Story*, 276. The account of Dressler's funeral is from Kennedy, *Marie Dressler*, 219.

2. See Jackie Stacey, *Star Gazing: Hollywood Cinema and Female Spectatorship* (London: Routledge, 1994), 142–45.

3. Rapf, "Queen of the Movies," 321.

4. Erika Doss, "Toward an Iconography of American Labor: Work, Workers, and the Work Ethic in American Art, 1930–1945," *Design Issues* 13, no. 1 (Spring 1997): 53–66 (quote, 53).

5. Ibid., 62.

6. Barbara Melosh, "Manly Work: Public Art and Masculinity in Depression Amer-

ica," in *Gender and American History since 1890*, ed. Melosh (London: Routledge, 1993), 173.

7. "A Modest Actress," *New York Times*, October 8, 1933, X4.

8. *Los Angeles Record*, November 11, 1930.

9. Sadly, Beery was also a villainous character off screen. The autobiography of his first wife, Gloria Swanson, contains a harrowing account of how he raped her on their wedding night and beat her throughout their marriage. *The Fixers*, a history of how MGM executives helped shield stars from prosecution and scandal throughout the 1930s and 1940s, claims that Beery actually murdered Ted Healy in a fistfight, and was quickly shipped off to Europe to cover his crime. These unsavory details were unreported during Beery's lifetime, when he was generally described as a lovable mug. See Gloria Swanson, *Swanson on Swanson* (New York: Random House, 1980); E. J. Fleming, *The Fixers: Eddie Mannix, Howard J. Strickling, and the MGM Publicity Machine* (Jefferson, N.C.: McFarland, 2004).

10. Quoted in Alma Whitaker, "Marie Dressler Madly in Love with Beery," *Los Angeles Times*, August 13, 1933, sec. 2, 1.

11. Unknown source, clipped advertisement for *Flesh*, Jean Hersholt Scrapbook 10, AMPAS.

12. Joanna Rapf challenges Marion's version of this story, based on *Min and Bill* production documents, and argues that Harry Rapf knew about the deception. Introduction, *Min and Bill*, invited talk at the Coburg Vintage Film Festival, October 27, 2006.

13. Marion, *Off with Their Heads*, 206.

14. Marx, *Gaudy Spree*, 31.

15. Frances Marion and Marion Jackson, *Min and Bill* complete treatment, May 15, 1930, MGM Collection, USC.

16. Olive Higgins Prouty's novel *Stella Dallas* was published in 1923, and the first movie version of the story was released in 1925, starring Belle Bennett and Ronald Coleman. I discuss the 1937 version simply because it is the best known and most heavily studied iteration of the story.

17. William J. Hynes, "Inconclusive Conclusions: Tricksters—Metaplayers and Revealers," in *Mythical Trickster Figures: Contours, Contexts, and Criticisms*, ed. William J. Hynes and William G. Doty (Tuscaloosa: University of Alabama Press, 1993), 210.

18. See Marilyn Jurich, *Scheherezade's Sisters: Trickster Heroines and Their Stories in World Literature* (Westport, Conn.: Greenwood, 1998), xiii–xviii; Lori Landay, *Madcaps, Screwballs, and Con Women: The Female Trickster in American Culture* (Philadelphia: University of Pennsylvania Press, 1998), 2.

19. Kathleen Rowe's analysis of Hollywood's romantic comedy heroine as "unruly virgin" offers a similar examination of how a heroine experiences liminality as freedom. No longer a child, not yet a wife, the virgin heroine occupies a precious in-between space in which she can negotiate for the terms of her future. Rowe, *Unruly Woman*, 133.

20. Hynes, "Inconclusive Conclusions," 210.

21. Besides motherhood, the other main form of Hollywood melodrama that

resembles a trickster tale is the "passing" narrative, such as that in *Show Boat* (Universal, 1929) or *Imitation of Life* (Universal, 1934), which depict young black women disguising themselves as white in order to avoid the stigma of racism. Lori Landay argues that these melodramas are not true trickster tales. Because "the mixed-race heroines are never invested with the spirit of the adventuress, but are essentially sentimental, melodramatic characters, the genre of passing narratives casts liminality, masquerade, and deception as wrong, dangerous, and unacceptable." Landay, *Madcaps, Screwballs, and Con Women*, 20. These movies tend to emphasize the terrible consequences of deception, in many cases precisely because passing is a rejection of the mother, a denial of the racial stain she imparts on the child. Tales of maternal tricksters, on the other hand, tend to cast the mother's deception as an act of heroism. She may or may not suffer for her choices, and her choice may even separate her from the child, but her child always benefits.

22. Kennedy, *Marie Dressler*, 167.

23. Landay, *Madcaps, Screwballs, and Con Women*, 10.

24. The epigraph for this section comes from Mordaunt Hall, "A Clever Film Fantasy," *New York Times*, November 30, 1930, 5.

25. "Min and Bill," *Variety*, November 26, 1930, 18.

26. Creighton Peet, "The Movies," *Outlook and Independent*, December 3, 1930, 552.

27. "Min and Bill," *Time*, December 8, 1930, 42.

28. Mordaunt Hall, "A Waterfront Shrew," *New York Times*, November 24, 1930.

29. Marion, *Off with Their Heads*, 209.

30. Bruno Bettelheim, *The Uses of Enchantment: The Meaning and Importance of Fairy Tales* (New York: Knopf, 1976), 69.

31. The first epigraph that opens this section is from B. A. Botkin, *The American People: Stories, Legends, Tales, Traditions, and Songs* (1946; rpt., New Brunswick, N.J.: Transaction, 1998), 5.

32. Norman Reilly Raine, *Tugboat Annie* (New York: Dell, 1934), 33.

33. Botkin, *American People*, 4.

34. Clemence Dane, "American Fairy Tale," *North American Review* 242, no. 1 (Autumn 1936): 143.

35. Through most of the 1930s, novels were a stronger source for serial movie heroines, notably Torchy Blane (the scrappy reporter), who hit the screens in 1936, and Nancy Drew (the teenage detective), who made her movie debut in 1938. Neither as outrageous nor as stylized as the comic heroes, these characters did ordinary occupations with wit and genius, but were not heroes in the sense I am using here.

36. During World War II, Tugboat Annie did use her ship and her wits to help with the war effort.

37. Peter Brooks, *The Melodramatic Imagination: Balzac, Henry James, Melodrama, and the Mode of Excess* (New Haven: Yale University Press, 1976), 15–16.

38. Botkin, *American People*, 107.

39. Judith Yarnall, *Transformations of Circe: The History of an Enchantress* (Urbana: University of Illinois Press, 1994), 20.

40. Kennedy, *Marie Dressler*, 210.

41. Tania Modleski, "Time and Desire in the Woman's Film," *Cinema Journal* 23, no. 3 (Spring 1984): 23.

42. Dressler's remarks that form the epigraph for this section come from a 1933 interview, quoted in Kennedy, *Marie Dressler*, 193.

CHAPTER 5: *EMMA* AND *CHRISTOPHER BEAN*

The epigraph that opens this chapter is from Marie Dressler, *My Own Story*, 17.

1. Amy Leslie, *Chicago Record*, January 4, 1910, quoted in Kennedy, *Marie Dressler*, 61.

2. Dressler, *My Own Story*, 15.

3. Ibid., 82.

4. Ibid., 210.

5. Photo caption, *Photoplay*, September 1931, 20.

6. Barrett C. Kiesling, "When Hollywood Cried Real Tears," *Photoplay*, February 1931, 43.

7. St. Johns, "Marie Dressler's Own Story," 29.

8. "Questions and Answers," *Photoplay*, February 1931.

9. Llewellyn Miller, "Marie Dressler in Absurd, Funny and Dramatic Picture" (review of *Emma*), *Los Angeles Record*, January 16, 1932, Jean Hersholt Scrapbook 10, AMPAS.

10. Mollie Merrick, "Hollywood in Person," *Los Angeles Times*, June 7, 1931, sec. 3, 25.

11. Eleanor Packer, "She Was the Noblest Lady of Them All," *Photoplay*, October 1934, 102.

12. Patricia White, *Uninvited: Classical Hollywood Cinema and Lesbian Representability* (Bloomington: Indiana University Press, 1999), 111.

13. Rowe, *Unruly Woman*, 110.

14. Kennedy, *Marie Dressler*, 78.

15. Ibid., 94.

16. Quoted in Marion, *Off with Their Heads*, 155.

17. Dressler, *My Own Story*, 137.

18. Quoted in Packer, "She Was the Noblest Lady of Them All," 4.

19. Judith Mayne, *Framed: Lesbians, Feminists, and Media Culture* (Minneapolis: University of Minnesota Press, 2000), xviii.

20. Betty Lee, *Marie Dressler: The Unlikeliest Star* (Lexington: University Press of Kentucky, 1997), 186.

21. Ibid., 187.

22. Photo caption, *Screen Book Magazine*, April 1932, Jean Hersholt Scrapbook 9, AMPAS.

23. Lee, *Marie Dressler*, 276.

24. "Candid Biography of Marie Dressler," *New York Times*, August 27, 1934, 13.

25. Kennedy, *Marie Dressler*, 144.

26. Dressler, *Life Story*, 25.

27. Israel Zangwill, *Merely Mary Ann* (1904; rpt., London: William Heinemann, 1913), http://www.gutenberg.org/etext/20078 (accessed April 16, 2007).

28. "Min and Bill," *Time*, December 8, 1930, 42.

29. White, *Uninvited*, 140.

30. Ibid., 193.

31. *Los Angeles Evening Herald-Express*, January 25, 1932, Jean Hersholt Scrapbook 10, AMPAS.

32. *New York Liberty Magazine*, February 6, 1932, Jean Hersholt Scrapbook 10, AMPAS.

33. Elsie Finn, "Marie Dressler Stars Again with Sympathetic Character in 'Emma' on Boyd Screen," *Philadelphia Record*, February 4, 1932, Jean Hersholt Scrapbook 10, AMPAS.

34. *Portland Oregon Journal*, January 13, 1932, Jean Hersholt Scrapbook 9, AMPAS.

35. Lee, *Marie Dressler*, 194.

36. Claire Ellen Van Ens, "The Poetics of Excess: Images of Large Women on Stage and Screen" (Ph.D. diss., University of Texas at Austin, 1999), 112.

37. Sidney Howard, *The Late Christopher Bean* (New York: Samuel French, 1932), 10.

38. Lord also played the title role in the 1921 Broadway production of *Anna Christie*, so Anna's dig at Marthy, "You're me in twenty years," is strangely echoed in the careers of these two actresses.

39. Don Herold, "The Theatre," *Life*, January 1933, 32.

40. Charles Vanda, "Chris Bean Film Is Triumph for Marie Dressler," *Los Angeles News*, December 1, 1933, Jean Hersholt Scrapbook 10, AMPAS.

41. Marquis Busby, "Christopher Bean Charms and Amuses," *Los Angeles Examiner*, December 1, 1933, Jean Hersholt Scrapbook 10, AMPAS.

42. "Activities in Hollywood's Studios," *New York Times*, December 17, 1933, X7.

43. The epigraph for this section comes from a Dressler quotation given in Marion, *Off with Their Heads*, 233.

44. Andrea Weiss, "A Queer Feeling When I Look at You: Hollywood Stars and Lesbian Spectatorship in the 1930's," in *Stardom: Industry of Desire*, ed. Christine Gledhill (London: Routledge, 1991), 293.

CONCLUSION: *DINNER AT EIGHT*

The epigraph that opens this conclusion is from Eleanor Pringle, "Feminine Clowns," *San Francisco Chronicle*, April 24, 1932, 7.

1. Dyer, *Stars*, 52.

2. "'Dinner at Eight' Is Firmament of Movie Stars," *Newsweek*, September 2, 1933, 30.

3. George Cukor, biographical notes, circa 1972, George Cukor Papers, Margaret Herrick Library Special Collections, AMPAS.

4. The epigraph for this section is from Harry Evans, "The Movies," *Life*, October 1933, 42.

5. Thomas Schatz, *The Genius of the System: Hollywood Filmmaking in the Studio Era* (New York: Henry Holt, 1996), 119.

6. Ibid., 164.

7. Tino Balio, *Grand Design: Hollywood as a Modern Business Enterprise* (Berkeley: University of California Press, 1993), 187.

8. Raider, "Descriptive Study," 255.

9. Maria DiBattista, *Fast-Talking Dames* (New Haven: Yale University Press, 2001), 96–97.

10. White, *Uninvited*, 187. The epigraph for this section is from an article that quoted Jean Harlow, "World's Fair Tires Jean," *Kansas City Star*, June 21, 1933.

11. James Wingate to Irving Thalberg, memo, March 15, 1933, *Dinner at Eight*, Margaret Herrick Library Special Collections, AMPAS.

12. James Wingate to Association of Motion Picture Producers, memo, deletions for territory of British Columbia, December 12, 1933, *Dinner at Eight*, Margaret Herrick Library Special Collections, AMPAS.

Filmography

Dressler's Feature Films

Tillie's Punctured Romance (Keystone, 1914)
Tillie's Tomato Surprise (Lubin, 1915)
Tillie Wakes Up (Peerless/World, 1917)
The Callahans and the Murphys (MGM, 1927)
The Joy Girl (Fox, 1927)
Breakfast at Sunrise (First National, 1927)
Bringing Up Father (MGM, 1928)
The Patsy (MGM, 1928)
The Divine Lady (First National, 1929)
Hollywood Revue of 1929 (MGM)
The Vagabond Lover (RKO, 1929)
Chasing Rainbows (MGM, 1930)
Anna Christie (MGM, 1930)
The Girl Said No (MGM, 1930)
One Romantic Night (United Artists, 1930)
Caught Short (MGM, 1930)
Let Us Be Gay (MGM, 1930)
Min and Bill (MGM, 1930)
Reducing (MGM, 1931)
Politics (MGM, 1931)
Emma (MGM, 1932)
Prosperity (MGM, 1932)
Tugboat Annie (MGM, 1933)
Dinner at Eight (MGM, 1933)
Christopher Bean (MGM, 1933)

Index

VICTORIA STURTEVANT is an associate professor of film and video studies at the University of Oklahoma. A specialist in the areas of race, class, and gender in American film, she has published scholarly work on Hattie McDaniel, William Haines, and Lupe Velez, in addition to Marie Dressler. She is currently at work on her next book, a treatment of social class in American film comedy.

The University of Illinois Press
is a founding member of the
Association of American University Presses.

University of Illinois Press
1325 South Oak Street
Champaign, IL 61820-6903
www.press.uillinois.edu